THE AID EFFECT

Anthropology, Culture and Society

Series Editors:
Professor Thomas Hylland Eriksen, University of Oslo
Dr Jon P. Mitchell, University of Sussex

RECENT TITLES

THE AID EFFECT

Giving and Governing in
International Development

Edited by
DAVID MOSSE AND DAVID LEWIS

Pluto Press
LONDON • ANN ARBOR, MI

First published 2005
by PLUTO PRESS
345 Archway Road, London N6 5AA
and 839 Greene Street,
Ann Arbor, MI 48106

www.plutobooks.com

British Library Cataloguing in Publication Data
A catalogue record for this book is available from
the British Library

ISBN 0 7453 2387 1 hardback
ISBN 0 7453 2386 3 paperback

Library of Congress Cataloging in Publication Data applied for
ƒ

10   9   8   7   6   5   4   3   2   1

Designed and produced for Pluto Press by
Chase Publishing Services Ltd, Fortescue, Sidmouth EX10 9QG, England
Typeset from disk by Stanford DTP Services, Northampton, England
Printed and bound in the European Union by
Antony Rowe Ltd, Chippenham and Eastbourne, England

CONTENTS

ACKNOWLEDGEMENTS

The chapters of this book (with the exception of Chapter 1) made their first appearance as contributions to a conference held at the School of Oriental and African Studies (SOAS) in London between 26 and 28 September 2003 on the theme of 'Order and Disjuncture: The Organisation of Aid and Development'. This was jointly organised by SOAS and the London School of Economics by the two editors under the auspices of EIDOS (the European Inter-University Development Opportunities Study Group) founded to bring together anthropologists studying development from across the continent. We would like to thank EIDOS co-members who provoked the organisation of this event, especially Rüdiger Korf, Philip Quarles van Ufford, Monique Nuijten, Oscar Salemink and Heiko Schrader. The volume editors are grateful to all the participants in the conference, both paper givers and discussants, for a highly stimulating and intellectually productive event (for details see Benedetta Rossi, 'Order and Disjuncture: Theoretical Shifts in the Anthropology of Aid and Development' *Current Anthropology*, 45 (4) August–October 2004, 556–560), and to those who offered behind the scenes and 'on the day' administrative support, as well as website and CD preparation. We would like to extend special thanks to Benedetta Rossi, and also to Charlotte Wilcox, Kazu Ahmed, Becky Stringer, Mora Mclagan, Azzura Malgieri, Maria, Duncan Franklin, Robert Whiteing and David Martin. Further outputs from this conference which will appear under our joint editorship are *Brokers and translators in international development* (Kumarian Press Bloomfield, CT), and a special issue of the journal *Oxford Development Studies* (Vol. 34, No.1 March 2006) on the theme of 'Encountering order and disjuncture: contemporary anthropological perspectives on the organisation of development'.

We would like to thank the authors of the book's chapters for their insightful contributions, their efforts in revising earlier drafts, building on parallel and complementary perspectives and so making this such a coherent and distinctive volume. We would also like to thank Sophie Richmond for her copy-editing labours, and Anne Beech, Robert Webb and the team at Pluto Press for their support of this project.

David Mosse and David Lewis
July 2005

1 GLOBAL GOVERNANCE AND THE ETHNOGRAPHY OF INTERNATIONAL AID

David Mosse

Today international development policy is characterised by the convergence of ideas of neoliberal reform, democratisation and poverty reduction within a framework of 'global governance'. What insights into the social processes and effects of this new consensus on aid and global governance can anthropology give? This is a good moment to ask such a question. In recent years there has been a gradual expansion of the scope of ethnography from its classical concern with 'the local' and 'the other', or the impact of global processes on local places, to more sophisticated conceptions of local–global relations. Some of these examine the way in which global capitalism has to negotiate its presence in specific settings; some explore the 'production of locality' in the context of global processes (Appadurai 1997); and yet others focus on the production of globalisation in terms of the relationships and institutions through which 'the global' is articulated (Burawoy 2001).

The aid effect is a contribution to this ethnographic trajectory. Its chapters demonstrate the fruitfulness of an ethnographic approach to aid, policy reform and global governance. Together they provide powerful commentary on hidden processes, multiple perspectives or regional interests behind official policy discourses. The book raises important questions concerning the systematic social effects of aid relationships, the nature of sovereignty and the state, and the workings of power inequalities and biases built through the standardisations and efficiencies of a neoliberal framework. At the same time, a 'global aid architecture' presents new challenges to the anthropology of development. How are relationships (international, state–citizen) reconfigured in the contemporary transnational aid domain? Are boundaries between nation-states, donors and self-governing international financial institutions (such as the IMF and the World Bank) blurred by the new technical demands of managing aid flows? Does the 'moral resurrection of aid' with its emphasis on ownership, participation and good governance in fact conceal an era of greater intervention by international agencies in the internal affairs of developing countries?

The contributors here do not regard 'governance' in its global form as simply a matter of 'super-state' dominance and hegemony. Rather they turn research attention to understanding how legitimacy is won for international policies, how programmes enrol participants with the rhetoric of freedom, partnership, ownership or participation; how order or control is achieved through internalised disciplines of power (Rose and Miller 1992); how (as in the past) states govern through community control (Li 2002); and how the representational practices through which state power operates (e.g. spatial metaphors of vertical encompassment which put the state 'above', people 'below') are extended, but also disrupted, within the transnational sphere (Ferguson and Gupta 2002). Since the work of 'governance' is dispersed to private sector service providers, enterprises, communities, NGOs (non-governmental organisations), donors (and a host of competing, rival or parasitic transnational lobbying and financing networks, 2002: 994), it is, as Tania Li noted,[1] 'an empirical question whether these are coordinated by state bureaucracy', or located within the framework of the nation-state at all. Attention has then to be directed to transnational systems. Focusing on those of international aid, ethnographers in this volume ask what might be the instruments (technical, procedural, legal, statistical) of an aid regime of 'rule' through mutual complicity? What (or on whom) does the order of an internationalised policy regime impose, exclude, suppress or depoliticise? Alternatively, how does it liberate, include and make accountable? In answer, the chapters of the book trace the paper trails, the protocols and practices, the rules and routines, the idioms and identities through which people become subjects of, as well as subject to, global development. Drawing attention to these dispersed procedures and instruments of governance, often autonomous from the state and national politics, some authors draw on the notion of 'governmentality' (of a transnational kind, cf. Ferguson and Gupta 2002), although, as will be clear, overall the book challenges this Foucauldian concept as an explanation for the workings of the international aid system.[2]

This introductory chapter begins with an explanation of the new framework of international aid, its commitments and modalities. I then set out the neoliberal and institutionalist underpinnings of this framework, and examine concerns raised in the recent literature about the implications of policy convergence. Third, I ask what approach has anthropology taken, or might it take, to researching global governance. In this context I reflect, fourth, on the significance and limitations of the Foucauldian notion of 'governmentality' for an ethnographic approach to global processes. Finally, I examine some alternative conceptualisations that allow simultaneously for the contingencies and specifics of power and the reproduction of universal policy frames.

THE NEW AID FRAMEWORK: GLOBALISATION, GLOBAL GOVERNANCE AND AID

Much of this book focuses on what has sometimes been characterised as a 'new architecture of aid'. To what does this refer? First, it refers to the focus of aid on policy reform rather than conventional investment projects; reform which is 'neoliberal' in the sense of promoting economic liberalisation, privatisation and market mechanisms as the instruments of growth and efficiency. Instead of funding individual projects donors collaborate (in principle) to make concessional finance available (in the short term through budgetary support) to assist governments to develop their own overall strategies for economic growth and poverty reduction (through Comprehensive Development Frameworks, sector-wide approaches [SWAPs], and the like) or finance the cost of fiscal, governance or pro-poor reforms that would make these strategies sustainable in the long run (such as privatising loss-making public sector operations, cutting civil service, decentralisation and anti-corruption measures). In some cases loans and grants are now made to states on the basis of demonstrable commitment and past performance on the reform agenda – that is aid 'selectivity' rather than 'conditionality' – and outcomes known through state-level poverty monitoring.[3] This change in aid, Eyben (with León, this volume) suggests, can be regarded as a shift from 'gift' to 'contract'.

Second, in the new architecture, aid is framed by an international commitment to poverty reduction. In particular many donor agencies have pinned their goals to internationally agreed development targets.[4] Among other things, this means that austere 1980s structural adjustment lending is replaced by debt-relief initiatives linked to pro-poor policy reform as part of new aid packages resulting from Poverty Reduction Strategy Papers (PRSPs). A policy drive for poverty reduction and empowerment is thus joined onto and, under the rubric of 'making globalisation work for the poor' (DFID [Department for International Development] 2000), helps to re-legitimise continuing donor emphasis on policies of trade liberalisation, macro-economic stability and fiscal discipline overseen by the IMF, while mobilising new aid resources.[5] Third, reform agendas go beyond economic and financial management to 'governance' more generally, including aid packages for public sector management, the support of civil society, and the promotion of consultative and participatory mechanisms for development planning. The failings of ruling regimes (including corruption within them) are no longer censored as internal matters but have become central to the concerns of external donors; although at the same time (as noted) aid relationships are reframed in the language of partnership and local ownership. These approaches to aid have brought about new levels of convergence in the agendas of major donors underpinned by greater interdependence through country-level coalitions (although important differences of approach remain – between British, Scandanavian, US or Japanese aid, bilateral and multilateral – which deserve separate comparative study).[6]

This new aid framework has two key theoretical underpinnings: neoliberalism and institutionalism. Following the collapse of communism, international aid became underpinned conceptually by a neoliberalist confidence in market exchange, the doctrine of comparative advantage and the framing of development goals not in terms of national economic development (through the administered economy) but rather in terms of establishing the conditions for successful participation in (production for) world markets. As international markets replaced independent states as the real agents of change, the role of government was to secure the conditions for market integration, including the rule of law, secure private property, anti-corruption measures, accountable and effective government, 'economic freedom' (liberalisation, deregulation, privatisation, controlled inflation, the removal of protectionism), as well as investment in education, health and communications (Burawoy 2003; Robinson 2002: 1052–53, 6). And the instruments of aid – stabilisation and structural adjustment programmes engineered and imposed by the international financial institutions (IFIs – the IMF and the World Bank) – were oriented towards assisting an internal restructuring of national economies to harmonise with the 'new legal and regulatory superstructure for the global economy' so as to allow the free movement of capital. And the 'enterprise models' applied ensured that various state functions were increasingly taken over by the market (Ferguson and Gupta 2002: 989).

Now, growing evidence of 'market imperfections', economic instability and the financial crises of the 1990s challenged the neoliberal vision, but did not derail the project. Instead, a second complementary body of theory was deployed to explain and *manage* market imperfections – the new institutional economics (NIE) (Soederberg 2004a: 284). Grounded in neoclassical models of rational choice, the NIE is concerned with institutional constraints on individual behaviour, which account for the fact that information is not perfect and that transactions have costs (Robinson 2002: 1058). Policy prescriptions can thus focus on institutions conceptualised as sets of rules structuring incentives and modelled mathematically, reshaping social behaviour so as to increase efficiency and enhance the economic behaviour of individuals (2002: 1058–59). Recent work extends institutional analysis to the relations of international aid itself, so that 'partnership' and 'local ownership' become strategies to restructure incentives and overcome the 'moral hazard' or 'principal agent' problems inherent in aid processes (Ostrom et al. 2002). In parallel, the idea of 'path dependency' allows that structures of incentives are shaped by the historical interactions of institutions (e.g. Putnam 1993; Robinson 2002: 1059). These ideas, and especially the importance of getting institutions and incentives right, underpin a re-accommodation of the role of both the state (in the rubric of 'good governance') and self-organising society (community or social capital) as complementary mechanisms for development in a 'post-Washington consensus', although the market retains its inherent powers of organisation, rational allocation, benefit optimisation and non-territorial transnational regulation (Duffield 2002: 1055; cf. Fine 1999).

The conceptual tools of the 'new institutional economics' allow a new managerialism in international development, no longer confined to project cycles, and driven by a combination of poverty target orientation and policy-based objectives.[7] Indeed, as its ends have narrowed to the achievement of quantified targets on poverty or ill-health, the *means* of international aid have expanded from the management of economic growth and technology transfer to the reorganisation of state and society needed to deliver on targets (Mosse 2005a: 3–4, 237–38; Quarles van Ufford et al. 2003).

Globalisation and universal knowledge for global governance

So, international aid policy frameworks continue to endorse globalisation as a process of economic and political freedom (democracy) and poverty reduction, despite the fact that free trade seems more clearly linked to growing inequality than gains in income or welfare for the poor (Storm and Rao 2004: 571), and that the experience of sharp increase in relative deprivation and distributional conflict is only intensified by reduced state protection (Chua 2003; Storm and Rao 2004: 573–74). Despite long being questioned (Storm and Rao 2004: 571, citing Marx), the notion that there is a close positive relationship between freedom for capital and freedom for the poor carries more conviction than ever; while this view of development as a matter of free markets and democracy persistently ignores the highly interventionist course of much actual employment, welfare and poverty alleviation (Fine 2004: 586).

Those who hold the free-market faith while proposing that its failings can be addressed by further building democratic institutions for global governance (e.g. Griffin 2003) in fact face considerable academic scepticism. The view that imperfect (monopolistic, oligopolistic) markets can be dealt with by a new global architecture of law and institutions is challenged as simultaneously instrumentalist and utopian (see *Development and Change* 2004). Indeed critics of 'global governance' question the selective representation of 'globalisation' itself. It is a deeply problematic descriptive and analytical category having, Fine suggests, at least three critical omissions. The first is the complexity and diversity of 'globalisation', which has no singular logic. Despite this, not only economic but also social policy is internationalised through donor knowledge systems that emphasise the universal over the contextual, that is knowledge which is deductive and oriented to general predictive models or 'universal principles', and which ignores national frameworks (or construes their specifics as obstacles to be overcome) and constantly organises attention away from the contingencies of practice and the plurality of perspectives (Mosse 2004).[8]

The second omission is the continuing importance (and economic role) of the state, especially the pursuit of US partisan interests (cf. Frank 2004: 608). Globalisation is by no means synonymous with neoliberalism, and the concept conceals the realities of power in the current international order.[9] Correspondingly, 'global governance' inevitably involves the exercise of power over both markets and institutions (trade, knowledge, environment), which then allows economic globalisation to concentrate power and centralise decision-making (Frank 2004: 609; Storm and Rao 2004: 574). In short, 'globalisation' is a policy idea that denies the political economy of capitalism as a 'system of power and conflict' (Fine 2004: 586, 588).

The third omission is the role of speculation-driven and *ungovernable* international financial markets, which provoked the financial crises of the 1990s and which weaken the potential for independent macro-economic policy anywhere (Fine 2004: 587). As Castells points out, neither international institutions, nor the US, nor corporations run the world, 'they don't even run the economy because they are dependent on an uncontrollable system, which is the global financial markets' (in Kreisler 2001; Fine 2004: 583, 590).[10]

An ethnographic literature on 'globalisation' contributes to the exploration of a further set of three critical observations. The first is that internationalised policy is not a product of some global democratic process, but is produced by transnational epistemic communities and translated into the prescriptions of donors led by the US-influenced World Bank and the IMF. Unlike the UN, voting rights in these institutions are not one-member-one-vote. The Bank's Director of Social Development has himself expressed concern about

an international institution without democratic governance trying
to 'design the global social policy'.[11] Knowledge production for
global governance, as Randeria points out, erases the boundaries of
national and international. Development regimes produce 'scattered
sovereignties' as governments implement IFI norms, comply with
credit conditionalities, execute project 'proto-law' or supranational
legal regimes in such areas as patent law, tax law, industrial licensing,
trade liberalisation and other forms of 'legal globalisation',[12] which
take place 'outside the arena of legislative deliberation and democratic
decision making' (2003: 29, 42). Among the many other forms of
transnational knowledge imposed in different national contexts, the
categories, classifications and lexicons of World Bank environmental
discourse are examined by Goldman to show how '[w]hat counts
as biodiversity in Laos is defined by actors other than the people
who live there' (2001: 207). Internationalised policy prescription,
such studies suggest, derives from the independent power of *global*
networks of expertise autonomous from government, made possible
(as well as necessary) by micro-electronic based technologies and
the information, communication and social networks (and labile
markets) they allow (Castells 1996; Kreisler 2001).[13] At the same time
the 'networks of practice' through which the regulations of aid are
executed locally involve a growing role for equally unaccountable
non-state private actors and contractors evading global democratic
processes (Duffield 2002: 1063).

Second (and in consequence), the 'universal' principles, the
singular common-sense models, the agreed international standards
of governance, and the financial guidelines and benchmarks are all
oriented towards the interests of selected players. Specifically, 'free'-
market based solutions are institutionally underpinned and socially
engineered so as to ensure that emerging markets will develop in
a legal, political and economic environment embedded in Anglo-
American behavioural norms and suited to Western investors, while
subjugating regional forms of capitalism (Soederberg 2003: 17–18,
23). A case in point is Susanne Soederberg's (2003) analysis of the
IMF's international standards to regulate market behaviour (and
manage financial liberalisation),[14] and specifically the standards
of 'corporate governance'. On the one hand, she shows that *one
particular* social form of 'corporate governance' – of Anglo-American
origin – and its notion of 'moral hazard', is enforced to the exclusion
of other variants, despite the empirically weak relationship between
governance systems and market performance (not to mention the
recent high-profile cases of US corporate corruption such as Enron).
And it is this view of corporate governance that was buttressed by a
particular interpretation of the East Asian financial crisis (1997–98)
that undermined the legitimacy of alternative business cultures

(whether pyramidal, bank-focused or state influenced) as 'crony capitalism'.[15] On the other hand, she argues that the market-centric focus on 'shareholder value' involved in the chosen model serves the interests of US institutional investors – pension funds, insurance companies, bank trusts, mutual funds – increasingly looking to higher-risk, higher-profit foreign investment (2003). Of course there are many other areas such as water policy, trade or property rights, in which global policy can also be viewed as built upon selected national or corporate interests.

Third, the ethnography of new global aid frameworks suggests that they involve an unprecedented level of intervention and social engineering in developing countries. Soederberg's work on standards points to the disciplining of emerging markets through intrusive regimes of surveillance that monitor practices in public and private sectors against 'universal principles' while constructing a reality around free capital mobility (2003). Anders and Gould in this volume are among those who argue that the shift from the external controls of conditionality under structural adjustment programmes (SAPs) to the internal discipline of PRSPs and 'good governance' (from hard to soft conditionality) has brought increased powers of surveillance and control over sovereign states, and more invasive monitoring of liberalisation by IFIs. In Chapter 2 Anders examines such techniques of control through his analysis of loan arrangements between IFIs and the government of Malawi. First, he shows how the legal character of loan documents works to turn the external conditions of IFIs into modes of self-discipline through the language of 'local ownership', while absolving donors of the need to consider the political implications of their own interventions.

Second, he shows how the 'technical' assistance that accompanies aid packages does the political work of building compliance with external demands into the fabric of national administrative orders; and does so by instituting systems, standards and procedures – target-setting, monitoring, auditing, data collection and a characteristic 'normativity of numbers' – that deeply entrench donor interests and perspectives. Such an argument is endorsed from work on PRSPs by Craig and Porter, who conclude that the ranked goals of global economic integration, good governance, poverty reduction and safety nets amount to a convergence:

optimising economic, juridical and social governance in order to create ideal conditions for international finance and investment ... with a *disciplined* inclusion of the poor, [which] represents an attempt to generate a level of global to local integration, discipline and technical management of marginal economies, governance and populations unprecedented since colonial times. (2003: 54–55, emphasis in original, cf. Ferguson and Gupta 2002: 992)

And, as Gould shows, the ordering power of international aid is rarely explicit (as aim or outcome), but effects compliance with its formal demands through the self-governing disciplines of 'capacity-building' (see Chapter 3).

Intrusive aid: development, security and local ownership

It seems from the above that to the critical anthropological eye all aid is a 'relation of government: a set of technologies having the power to reorganise the relationship between people and things to achieve desired aims' (Duffield 2002: 1050, citing Dean 1999).[16] But the greater intrusion of aid is especially evident (and now explicit) in relation to states that are weak, 'failing', poorly integrated into, or excluded from, global markets, where poverty is constructed as a dangerous threat to security, remedied through the assertive promotion of neoliberal prescriptions.[17] Indeed, Soederberg suggests that the stronger the implicit connection between poverty and the environment of terrorism, the greater the shift in donor attention from a state's external actions to its *domestic* behaviour (2004b: 292). This is nowhere clearer than in the new 'pre-emptive development' in US foreign aid illustrated by Bush's Millennium Challenge Account, established in parallel to USAID with grant finance conditional upon measured performance on the trio of 'ruling justly', 'investing in people' and 'economic freedom' – a self-consciously *American* internationalism, resting on some version of Benjamin Franklin's sentiment that 'America's cause is the cause of all mankind' (Soederberg 2004b: 279). Here, unilateralism, more stringent conditions, internal intervention, a shift from loans to performance-based grants (offering closer surveillance and monitoring that allows value-based judgements by carefully selected assessors) are all part of the US reinvention of aid, fuelled by, but in place well before, the terror attacks of '9/11' (2004b: 292–93). Such initiatives illustrate how, as Duffield puts it, 'the security concerns of metropolitan states have merged with the social concerns of aid agencies'; how 'aid and politics have been reunited' (2002: 1067). He notes that 'the link between development and security is now a declaratory position within mainstream aid policy' (2002: 1067), focusing on places where exclusion from globalisation coincides with the collapse of state structures, 'social regression', the destruction of the social fabric, criminality, violence and war (2002: 1067).

Here an idiom of 'borderland barbarianism', on the one hand sustains distancing dichotomies of 'us' and 'them', justifying interventions to reform and reconstruct state and society and demonstrating a radicalised development and 'the will to govern' (Duffield 2002: 1052–54);[18] while, on the other, it expresses the inadequate reach of capitalism and provokes projects for the capitalist incorporation of a 'non-integrating gap' (Soederberg 2004a, 2004b). In 'zones of insecurity', Duffield suggests, the arrangements of aid set up as part of short-term conflict resolution or social reconstruction become instruments of increasingly permanent international governance, often through 'expanding public–private networks of aid practice' (2002: 1062). In confrontation with violence and the new wars, he argues, development has been rediscovered 'as a *second chance* to make modernity work' (2004: 1064, original emphasis).

It is in the context of this greater intrusion of aid that the progressive policy emphasis on partnership, putting aid-recipient countries in the driving seat, and the local ownership of development strategies appears most paradoxical. As the chapters of this book demonstrate, the emphasis on 'partnership' and 'local ownership' can be regarded as *instrumental* (improving aid efficiency), as *political* (shoring up flagging support/legitimacy for aid) or as *governmental* (a Trojan horse, enabling deeper international penetration into national development choices, Crawford 2003: 142). Of course, these need not be alternatives. For instance, Dahl notes (referring to Swedish aid) that 'partnership' is a complex and clever signifier that conveys the radical idea of solidarity or equality while also meeting a neoliberal demand for contract, responsibility and self-interest that fits with a new business environment without losing old supporters (2001: 13). Some anthropologists emphasise the way policy rhetoric on 'ownership' or 'partnership' conceals the actual working of aid, 'dispossessing' its agents of their own rationales and true instrumentalities (Abdelrahman and Apthorpe 2002; cf. Mosse 2005a: 233–34), or hiding persistent donor–recipient inequalities. In this vein, Crawford (2003) examines the way in which an external neoliberal donor agenda (of the World Bank and United Nations Development Programme [UNDP]) became built into the 'Partnership for Governance Reform' programme in Indonesia through closed decision-making bodies that excluded dissent by limiting parliamentary, civil society and trade union representation, while emphasising those reforms (political stability, anti-corruption, police reform) that would safeguard foreign investment and growth based on free-market capitalism rather than locally negotiated national interests.

Others, such as Anders and Gould (this volume), regard 'ownership' or 'partnership' as integral to techniques of aid as a mode of transnational governmentality (see below).

In Chapter 4, van Gastel and Nuijten further unpack the complexity of polysemic aid policy ideas through their historical analysis of the meanings of 'ownership' and 'partnership' in the Dutch Ministry of Development Cooperation. They reveal, first, how over time very different principles and modalities of aid have been advanced under the rubric of 'local ownership'; and, second, how the different meanings of 'ownership' itself – national self-determination, ownership by the people and protection of their rights vis-à-vis the state, national ownership of externally engineered reform – are themselves produced both as strategic responses by key political actors (Dutch ministers) and as pragmatic adaptations in different country contexts. So, in one case the theme of 'ownership' accompanies the centring control of aid in the bureaucracy, in another the promotion of civil society as a countervailing power; in one a shift to budgetary support, in another the maintenance of networks and 'established contacts' around projects.

Now, the above are not to be taken as arguments against globalised aid or the need for supra-national institutions, as if anthropologists have some *in principle* hostility to an agenda of global governance and the attendant modernising of institutions (as one World Bank economist put it to me). On the contrary, these are needed more than ever. Rather, ethnography points to the need to recognise contradiction and the potential for hidden bias and unilateralism in the new 'global' order. When it comes to suggesting alternatives, there is a characteristic diversity of institutional options. These range from the selective curbing of trade liberalisation in recognition of the inherent disadvantages faced by poor nations and people ('developing country exceptionalism') or reinstating policy autonomy for nation-states ('development-enhancing protectionism') (Storm and Rao 2004: 570, 573), or in some way embedding global markets in society (2004: 579); to strengthening 'forms of action that are not channelled though global governance' by supporting civil society networks as forms of 'informal governance' (Boyce 2004: 594), or 'non-anarchical global civic activism' (Nuesiri 2004: 603) on human rights or justice which allow 'local' actors to 'jump scale' (Ferguson and Gupta 2002: 996, citing John Rugge). However, the primary aim of this volume is neither to critique nor to amend global aid, but to better understand its social processes; to show through cases such as those already cited how anthropology (or ethnographic sociology or political science) can contribute to the study of 'globalised aid'. But before introducing further ethnographic work we have to ask how such research can be framed and undertaken?

ANTHROPOLOGY OF INTERNATIONAL AID AND GLOBAL GOVERNANCE

One anthropological approach, so far, has been to focus on the local effects of macro-processes of free-market democracy and neoliberal development. Anthropologists have joined political economists in examining the selective integration of social groups into global markets, the consequences of reduced social protection, the casualisation and de-unionisation of labour, or environmental exploitation and impoverishment, especially in countries such as the post-Soviet states that have experienced rapid transition to market economies (Dudwick et al. 2002).

Here they contribute to broader analyses of the processes that result in metropolitan 'concentration zones' of global production/ trading (investment, trade, finance, production and technology), 'feeder zones' (of labour or raw materials) and 'marginalised zones' (Robinson 2002: 1064–67; cf. Duffield 2002: 1054), but help show that ultimately the logic of concentration and exclusion is *social* rather than geographical, and operates as powerfully within as across regions (Castells 1996; Robinson 2002); something that is evident in the patterns of stratification, inclusion/exclusion that have brought ethnic hatred and violence to many parts of the world (Chua 2003). In other words, ethnographers contribute to arguments about the 'social irrationality' of neoliberal logic (Robinson 2002: 1057, 1062), even as their colleagues explore new social orders and attendant cultural dynamics manifest in consumption, media, migration and 'modernity at large' (Appadurai 1997).

A second approach has been to treat international development policy as an ethnographic object in itself (Shore and Wright 1997), to ask how global orders of policy are produced and how, in turn, they produce their objects (localities, regions, countries of the Third World) and 'what new kinds of subjectivity and identity are being created in the modern world' (Shore and Wright 1997: 3; cf. Grillo 1997). Critical writing influenced by Foucault and Said (e.g. Escobar 1995; Ferguson 1994; Sachs 1992) is now well known for its challenge to 'development' as cultural imperialism, as a discursive formation whose instruments of objectification and control prove as powerful (and as concealing of power) as their orientalist colonial antecedents (Ludden 1992). Its institutionalised practice renders planning a process of rational design unshaped by politics, 'transforming potentially explosive political questions about rights, entitlements, how one should live and who should decide, into technical questions of efficiency and sustainability' (Li 2002: 2). It removes the agency of donors from sight (Mitchell 2002: 230), constructs development problems as *internally* generated by the conditions of region, economy or nature acted upon by 'expertise and intelligence that stands completely apart from the country and the people it describes' (2002: 210), while having the hidden 'instrument effect' of maintaining or extending bureaucratic power (Ferguson 1994).

This critical analysis of discourse has also tracked progressive, participatory, indigenous or community-based development alternatives to reveal 'the collapse of social emancipation into social regulation' (Escobar 2004: 213; cf. Cook and Kothari 2001; Mosse 2005a).

However, the idea of development as a knowledge/power regime (a discourse) of political or cultural domination seems to unravel on closer inspection. It relies on claims about all-powerful development institutions which are poorly substantiated (Watts 2001: 286); it assumes an implausible institutional homogeneity (Grillo 1997), a capacity for donor coordination (around new aid frameworks) which is scarcely credible (Mallarangeng and van Tuijl 2004: 930), and a discursive stability which is contradicted by the fact of prolific policy change needed to preserve legitimacy (Gardner and Lewis 2000; Goldman 2001). A third approach, then, acknowledges that international development does not (for the most part) operate through the negative power of compulsion or domination, but through a positive (or productive) power that wins legitimacy and empowers action while putting in place arrangements and 'regimes of truth' that structure the 'possible field of action' so that individuals constitute themselves, their desires, aspirations and interests 'in terms of the norms through which they are governed' as 'free' economic and social agents – as governable subjects (Foucault 1982: 221, in Watts 2003: 12; Shore and Wright 1997: 9). This – Foucault's (1991) notion of 'governmentality' (the 'conduct of conduct') – provides a way in which authors in this volume reconcile the power effects of converging aid policy frameworks and global 'harmonisation' with the liberal principles of partnership/ownership, democracy, social accountability or rights-based development. By examining the new aid framework as a 'liberal art of government' through internalised disciplines, where 'local' (national, regional, community) actors come to assume responsibility for externally engineered policies and in which 'rule' is through complicity and the hegemony of trust and mutual interest, contributors such as Anders and Gould (the latter taking a Tanzanian case) extend Foucault's concept of 'governmentality' to a transnational plane (cf. Ferguson and Gupta 2002).

The neoliberal and institutionalist framing of international aid policy falls easily into this perspective on development. For one thing, aid is not now about alliances between states, but about 'how to modulate and change the behaviour of the populations within them' (Robinson 2002: 1064). For another, the institutionalist view of market and society (or state and international relations for that matter, Ostrom et al. 2002) as respectively a self-regulating mechanism and a set of self-organising networks maintained by a given structure of incentives, implies a notion of governance without sovereign authority and allows change through the design of institutions with rules that can restructure incentives and so 'responsibilise' the social space of community (Li 2002; Rose 1999; Watts 2003: 12). The fact that, from this perspective, international development involves power that does not require a state, bureaucratic or territorial framework makes it hard to conceive of 'non-state spaces' (Scott 1998) or 'post-development' sites of resistance outside power (Li 2002: 3; Watts 2003: 8–9).

But if the idea of 'governmentality' provides a productive line of thought, it is also a problematic one. It can be at once too precise about the effects, and too vague about the location, of ordering power – exactly which relations are governmentalised? The world does not appear to 'correspond to the well-oiled machine of disciplinary and biopower' (Watts 2003: 26). Not only is it hard to sustain the idea of a 'perfect synthesis' of neoliberalism 'with actual power structures and state policy apparatuses in much of the world' (Robinson 2002: 1056), but also this is a world comprised of 'network societies', a complex array of formal and informal, state and non-state agencies, and ungovernable global financial markets that exceed the control of even the most powerful transnational actors (Castells 1996); a world in which actor networks that include non-human natural or physical elements 'overflow' human intention and technology (Mitchell 2002: 299), and where there is a multiplication of manifestly ungovernable spaces or 'economies of violence' (Watts 2003). At the same time, governmentality locates power too vaguely in 'the West' or 'the state' so that it is entirely abstracted from particular institutions and structures in which political and economic action takes place (Cooper and Packard 1997: 3). This conceals the contingent networks of practice, the diversity of actors, brokers, perspectives and interests behind universal policy models, and overlooks the fact that, as Li puts it, 'the actual accomplishment of rule owes as much to the understandings and practices worked out in the contingent and compromised space of cultural intimacy as it does to the imposition of development schemes and related forms of disciplinary power' (1999: 295). In short, Gould points out, as a framework for anthropological analysis of aid, governmentality is empirically weak and suspiciously functionalist (Chapter 3 this volume). It needs to be deepened through accounts of the actual relations of aid (from within) that attend to power as embedded in organisational and personal relationships and trust (Eyben with León, Gould, this volume) as well as overt political-national ambitions.

The social production of policy order: text, context or network

In anthropology, overstatement of the capacity of international development to objectify and control third world people, and the mistaken idea that donors rule through representations, arises in part from the fact that, at first, critics of development gave so much importance to donor policy texts as representations of discourse: their history-suppressing genre of technical optimism (Apthorpe 1996, 1997; Gasper, 1996), their aesthetics (Stirrat 2000), the scientific knowledge they assert and the politics they conceal (Booth 1994; Chambers 1997; Sachs 1992), their construction of places, problems and substitutable expertise (Ferguson 1994; Mitchell 2002), or the way they label the subjects of development (Wood 1985). Recent work challenges the implicit 'discursive determinism' (Moore 2000: 657). As I have argued elsewhere:

> precisely because such a large proportion of the time and expertise of development personnel is organised with reference to writing and negotiating texts, they cannot be read at face value without reference to the arguments, interests and divergent points of view that they encode and to which they allude ... [donor] design texts have to be interpreted backwards to reveal the social relations that produced them, the future contests they anticipate and the wider 'discourse coalitions' (Fairhead and Leach 2002: 9) they are intended to call forth. In short, a sociology of the document is needed to 'dispel the discursive hold of the text'. (Apthorpe [1996]: 16). (Mosse 2005a: 15)

Several studies have now begun to examine how the organising policy ideas and 'universal codes and principles' for poverty reduction or managed liberalisation are produced and legitimised *socially* (Soederberg 2003: 14; cf. Crawford 2003). In doing so anthropologists focus not only on texts but also on the practices of closed epistemic communities, policy networks, the managed agenda-setting consultations and consultant experts (including themselves), and the consensus formation involved in manufacturing transferable expert knowledge (Mosse 2005a: 132–56). Here policy ideas (especially ambiguous ones like good governance, ownership or civil society) take social form, being important less for *what* they say than for *who* they bring together; how they enrol, unite or divide (2005a). By looking at the power and professional life of experts across disciplinary, institutional and global/local divides, within and between epistemic and advocacy networks, research examines *how* universal models are produced in socially specific contexts (Grammig 2002; Mosse 2005a; Stubbs 2004; Wood 1998).[19]

Goldman (2001), for example, uses textual and ethnographic methods in his study of how World Bank environmental knowledge is produced and then 'localised' through particular institutional processes (incentives, the organisation of time, political demands and aid flows that fund research and training institutions). Similarly my own reflections on the production of 'social development' knowledge in the World Bank (Mosse 2004) shows how widely applicable policy ideas such as 'empowerment' or 'social capital' have to be understood in the context of the particular position and relationships that a group of institutionally marginal anthropologists has to maintain in the Washington DC headquarters (cf. Bebbington et al. 2004).

Wedel's (2000, 2004) ethnography of aid in post-Soviet countries goes further, drawing attention to the social systems through which donor *and* recipient actors operate. She examines the 'flex organisations', the role of ambiguity, the boundary crossing (state–private, bureaucracy–market) 'transidentities', and multiplex relationships that – through overlapping positions on state, company or NGO boards – equivocate, mediate and otherwise work the spheres of public and private, bureaucracy and market, legal and illegal in making development. 'The same pool of people made up of actors from both the U.S. and Russian sides', she notes, 'not only ran the Russian economy and directed international aid, but were also connected to each other by so-called "foundations" and business activities' (2004: 166–67). The same individuals (representing different organisations and interests) negotiated policy, allocated contracts or licensed businesses (2004: 166–67). These processes which disperse accountability and maximise deniability (2004: 168), bring to the fore the importance of social networks, relationships and key brokers (such as nationally recruited donor advisers on, *inter alia*, governance) in negotiating international aid. This will be taken up in Eyben and León's account of the overlapping networks of Bolivian elites and donor staff, and the importance of personality where 'the process of relationship building [is] more significant for effective aid than the transfer of resources'(Chapter 5, this volume).

The 'constructed communities of interest' that anthropologists of development study are not only forged from shared class, kin or social backgrounds, but also from values and policy. Global policy shapes, as well is shaped by, coalitions of interest, identities and relationships between and within organisations. For instance, Cornwall and Pratt (2004), studying the self-representations of home and overseas-based Swedish aid (SIDA) staff, emphasise the significance of policy discourse (in their case that of 'participation') *both* in the expression of individual values, beliefs, feelings, disillusionments, professional styles and strategies, *and* in the negotiation of organisational relationships. Bureaucratic fiefdoms, internal solidarities and divisions (and their regrouping at times of restructuring, staff turnover or policy change) are all formed with reference to the interpretation of policy; for example neoliberal versus rights-based interpretations of 'participation', or 'empowerment' as 'freedom of choice' versus 'collective bargaining'. And these divisions reappear in operational strategies as the tensions between spending budgets, following procedures or empowering partners (cf. Mosse 2005a: 104). Such ethnography reveals an unstable donor world in which the nature of the target, the 'field', the role of expertise or consultants, and even what it means to be a donor is constantly in question.

By showing how systems of relationships that are *internal* to organisations or epistemic communities become externalised as global policy or country development strategies, ethnography refigures scale. International development policy is framed by personal histories, individual passions and bureaucratic strategies (see Chapters 4 and 5, this volume, by van Gastel and Nuijten, and Eyben with León). 'Globalisation from the middle' is the apt phrase that Jai Sen gives to the 'revolving doors' and 'clandestine global management' that give inordinate influence to a relatively small border- and agency-crossing class of like-minded individuals with shared ideas and values, childhoods, education, lifestyle, social and professional circuits, who occupy official positions within government and IFIs, with limited public accountability (Sen 2002, via Jeremy Gould; cf. Henry et al. 2004: 847, 850; Schwegler 2003: 5; Soederberg 2003). It is *within* these communities that aid transactions, international partnerships or technologies of monitoring and surveillance between donors and nations are negotiated.[20] And it is because aid partnerships are so 'starkly individualising' (Gould, Chapter 3, this volume) and neoliberalism such an 'intensely interpersonal process' (Schwegler 2003) that 'globalisation' can be subject to detailed ethnographic study (which the Foucauldian notion of governmentality does not demand) in which the objective is not to place 'aid policy' in its context, but to show how development's actor-networks *make* their context (Latour 1996: 133). As Latour points out, from an ethnographic point of view politics, economics or social 'context' are rigid abstractions that explain nothing (1996: 133). 'To get rid of one's own responsibility', Latour argues:

> ... the big explanations are useful, but as soon as one stops trying to blame someone else, these big explanations have to be replaced by little networks ... a matter of 8 people all interviewable. Adding to the filaments of the network. The few elected officials recruited by the project are not 'Politics', the economists who calculate ... are not 'Economics'. The impression of a context diverts from mediating individuals ... (1996: 134)

In this sense, aid workers themselves (donor advisers, bureaucrats, consultants) are right to challenge the crude categories of analysis of some of their academic critics, and a few have begun to do so. When Mallarangeng and Van Tuijl respond (as practitioners) to Crawford's critique of the 'Partnership for Governance Reform' in Indonesia, they rightly question an analysis that situates the programme 'in a one-dimensional North–South, donor–recipient dichotomy' and point out that processes of opinion-forming and decision-making are 'located in complex and transnational settings, characterised by shifting alliances' (2004: 927–28).

Without question, new challenges are presented to anthropologists of development by the 'real time contextual study of ideas and institutions' (Olivier de Sardan 2005) of elites and administrators, policy advisers, consultants or aid agency staff; possessors of universal principles and expert knowledge and inhabitants of diplomatic and business districts in capital cities. Gould (Chapter 3, this volume) reflects on the need for multi-level, multi-context and team-based comparative research. Gaining access and engaging those with the 'power to exclude themselves from the realm of the discussible' (Cooper and Packard 1997: 5) is one well known problem of 'studying-up'. Some contributors to this book overcome this by writing as insiders, not only researching in, 'but as part of donor policy making bodies, consultant design teams, project meetings ... and the writing of texts' (Mosse 2005a: 11). Moreover, in two joint authored chapters ethnographic analysis itself arises from the cross-institutional relationships and friendships of aid networks. Field and home no longer divide (Gupta and Ferguson 1997), and personal connections and affinities that tie researchers to their fields of studies have become central rather than concealed (Marcus 1998: 16). Here the anthropological challenge is to break free from, or at least become sensitised to, the discursive hold of even one's most cherished policy discourse and one's own expertise, to try to understand perceptions and actions from another perspective. But when ethnography focuses on the professional communities of which we are members, objectifying and subjecting our employers, patrons, colleagues or clients to critical analysis, new questions are asked of (or objections made to) the production of ethnographic knowledge, the relations of power and systems of values which shape our representations.[21]

These concomitants of 'studying up' are uncomfortable challenges to ethnographers. But they are also aids to research. As Latour reminds us, ethnography cannot remain the *classical sociology* that:

> ... knows more than the 'actors'; [it] sees right through them to the social structure or the destiny of which they are patients ... Its judgements are beyond the fray; they are scientific; an abyss separates them from the interested interpretations of the patients obliged to perform the reality that the sociologists analyse ... (1996: 199–200)

Ethnographic objectivity depends *not* upon a detached state of mind or suppression of subjectivity (the objectivity of the judge), but rather on creating a situation in which actors influence researcher perceptions to the maximum degree through their capacity to object, to raise their concerns to insert their own questions and interpretations, in their own terms (Latour 2000). The real danger is that people 'lose their recalcitrance by *complying*' (2000). The objections of our informants, then, add to our understanding; indeed by 'drawing their fire' ethnography enrols aid professionals who would not otherwise articulate analytic perspectives as engaged interlocutors and co-researchers. But given that aid officials also have a professional commitment to the protection of singular authorised accounts, to convergence, unity and consensus, and to a managerial outlook and a positivist epistemology, which are at odds with ethnographic perspectives, these research encounters are potential sources of dispute (Mosse 2005b).

In sum, this section has argued that the new international aid framework can be understood *ethnographically*. By describing the interplay of ideas and relationships the ethnographies of aid in this book reconnect power to agency, rejecting the idea of a micro-physics of power occurring entirely beyond the intelligence of actors (Ferguson 1994) – a world of duped perpetrators and victims of development. Instead, they examine the social life of documents drafted by known actors around tables in specific institutions. Sometimes these professionals are *us*. Several of the anthropologists who write in this book are not only observers, they are also participants in global policy processes, with biographical access to motives, emotions and personal power, able to speak from within, in the first person, beyond the coarse calculation of interests.

Eyben and León (Chapter 4) provide such a reflexive analysis of aid relationships as participant ethnographers. Their account revolves around a dilemma that arises within the new aid framework. Donor finance contributes to national development and poverty reduction frameworks which aid-recipient governments are supposed to develop in dialogue with civil society (as well as with the donor). But what if they fail to do so? What if the poor for whom the development strategies are designed are excluded from the political process (by incomplete electoral rolls in this particular case)? How do donors pursue their agenda of social and political inclusion, good government and democracy while retaining the impression that national governments are in control? Eyben and León's is a nuanced insider account of how such a dilemma was worked out by DFID staff and NGO partners in Bolivia; how the donor had constantly to break the very rules of the game that they had established, by supporting civil society activists without appearing to do so. The case reveals the complex social networks through which donors operate in order to sustain but also conceal the contradictions of aid. It shows how aid depends upon conspiracies of vagueness, enabling fictions and alliances which are forever fragile and subject to disruption as the ambiguous concepts that bring the players together are subject to divergent interpretations. Like van Gastel and Nuijten (in Chapter 5),

Eyben shows the importance of shifting relationships *between* donor agencies – alternatively complementary, competitive or cooperative – to the harmonisation of aid frameworks, but also how the national government interlocutors strategise to resist donor power and to limit the ability of donors to 'gang up' in advancing shared agendas.

Eyben argues that at the heart of the dilemma of aid is the notion of *the gift*. Always inadequately clothed in new policy garb (the rubric of cooperation, partnership or ownership), the logic of the gift constantly recalls the inequalities, power and patronage that new aid policy seeks to erase. The relationships of the gift are simultaneously denied and reasserted. Aid legitimacy demands that gifts appear either as 'contracts' (in neoliberal economic speak, e.g. PRSPs) or as 'entitlements' (in rights-based speak). But contracts are never binding; they are turned back into gifts conveying moral values (solidarity with the poor, personal commitment) and relationships (perhaps the exercise of patronage) that involve a mixture of power, acquiescence and anger. In Chapter 3, Gould comes to a similar conclusion when he points out that aid partnership is a moralising process expressed through an ideology of 'capacity' (a will to modernise) which is both personal and has an 'ordering power' which creates its own hierarchy of authority and expertise, even while allowing the acquisition of skills (e.g. at donor workshops) which can be used subversively.

Clearly, then, international policy regimes do not simply arrive, but are produced by intermediary actors, frontline workers (middle managers, bureaucrats, clinicians, technicians, NGO staff, health workers or engineers) who translate abstract global policy into their own ambitions, interests and values. These actors are both objects and agents of global policy, charged with bringing about the new normative/legal and administrative orders, imposing definitions which categorise people, making them into proper consumers, clients, users or patients. Other ethnographies of aid in this book locate these sites and social processes that produce the 'global'.

The tyranny of globalised categories within a development order is vividly explored in Ian Harper's (Chapter 6) study of an 'internationally sanctioned system of disease control', namely tuberculosis in Nepal. Harper gives an account of the social processes associated with tightening definitions, the use of protocols, standards and administrative frames to impose order and allow centralisation. At the centre of the analysis are the dehumanising effects produced by the imperative to maintain the order of categories when this overrides the experience of patients and the clinical practice of doctors. Internationalised order produces an administrative abstraction – 'statistico-TB' – aggregated at higher and higher levels and subject to sophisticated and predictive mathematical modelling. The conceptual and political orders that are created and reinforced around the bacillus, and that produce a population-level problem, do not emerge out of disorder, but out of other orders, subjective experiences and multiple medical and diagnostic histories. 'Statistico-TB' is a virtual reality with material effects. Its centralisation, surveillance systems and link to a globalised 'war' against TB impose themselves locally. Ethnographic study allows us to trace these effects through the operations of the abstract order in the daily practices and dilemmas of those whose responsibility it is to apply the rules; to 'perform TB'.

Aet Annist (Chapter 7) provides another case of the production of order out of contingency by frontliners who are both agents and objects of international policy. She shows how Estonian workers in an NGO subcontractor are scrupulous in their application of rules and regimes established by their Western funding agency (DFID), for instance in the processing of local community project applications for funding. Partly this expresses a desire to be included in the international development community, and to anticipate and contend with outsider objectifications of them as corrupt, nepotistic ex-Soviets. But the point is that in practice 'rule following' (the application of policy) is nothing of the sort. Rather, it is an after-the-event rationalisation of decisions on funding that are based on relationships of trust, identity and social knowledge. Annist's ethnography shows how 'local developers' contribute to the production and stabilisation of the rational order of policy without being guided by its logic; how they carefully translate the social reality of identity and relationships into the formality of rules, scores and professional judgement so as to conceal their own practice. Once again, the virtual reality of rules and regulations nonetheless has real social effects. The structural position in which fund flows place NGO workers fosters a paternalistic or parental orientation to community group applicants, whom they seek to discipline into 'proper' aid beneficiaries and clients. The effect is to undermine the objectives of the programme (to build managerial capacity in communities) and to marginalise and exclude certain groups of people. In short, following procedure undermines programme goals.

If Annist reveals the way in which people come to see the world and themselves in outsiders' terms, and how global policy frames shape these workers' own subjectivities, Karen Coelho (Chapter 8) records the way in which neoliberal orders are resisted. At the centre of Coelho's ethnography of privatisation of municipal water supply in Chennai (Madras) are the 'frontline' junior engineers who put public sector reform and 'corporatisation' into practice. First, like Harper and Annist, she reveals the social processes of global policy through an examination of the depot engineers' discretionary use of rules and procedures (e.g. of complaint) and the social classifications that they deploy, and through which a particular normative public – a citizenry of private paying consumers – is constructed. Second, Coelho, argues that this is an order in terms of which the poor are newly distanced and objectified as non-paying, non-deserving and difficult customers. When they act collectively to make demands they, and their rights-based claims, are judged as unruly, a disorderly nuisance from uncivilised slum dwellers. In this way, frontline engineers not only control access to amenities, but also make themselves arbiters of appropriate citizenship, while a managerialist discourse conceals the bestowal of identities that are strongly informed by social constructions of class-caste transposed into the idiom of being a proper consumer. The social and classificatory practices of the junior engineers again reveal neoliberal reform as kind of 'governmentality'; but one that is also resisted by the poor, who refuse to behave as clients or paying consumers of privatised services, and insist on constituting themselves as a 'political society' demanding rights. Interestingly, Coelho's study reveals ethnographically the sharp contradiction between an externally 'engineered' economic reform agenda, with its implication of autonomy from the political and elected civic bodies (a depoliticised society), on the one hand, and a political reform agenda which demands democratisation and (re-) politicisation, on the other. And this is significant because of the convergence of the two at the representational level in the 'neoliberal' agenda of free market democracy.

Disjunctures and contradictions of aid

These ethnographies of aid reveal the new aid framework as a complex, diverse and contradictory set of policy goals and practices. The principles of 'good governance' imply simultaneously ownership and conditionality (Eyben with León); public sector reform (privatisation/ corporatisation) is at odds with political reform (democratisation), modernity with mass politics (Coelho); and both decentralisation and centralisation (vertical programmes) are concomitants of health sector reform (Harper). Ethnographic study shows how such contradictions are generated, lived and resolved. It focuses on the politics behind policy: the relationships of control disguised as local ownership, the politics of the gift behind the legality of the contract, and points to the interpretive flexibility and productivity of development policy.

These ethnographic studies clearly challenge a rational-instrumental understanding of development as the execution of international policy. For one thing, they show that the practices of development actors are not governed by policy prescription, but generated by very different and diverse administrative, political or social-relational logics which are concealed by rationalising policy.[22] Alternatively put, because the ordering principles of global policy *have* to be translated into the intentions, goals and ambitions of the diverse individual and institutional actors they bring together – whether these are national politicians, international experts, middle managers, bureaucrats, clinicians, technicians or NGO workers and field staff – they *'cannot shape actual practice in the way that they claim'* (Mosse 2005a: 16; cf. Latour 1996). Nonetheless, there is persistent political demand for clarity, integration and coherence in global development policy.[23] This requires and brings into play the many mediators and brokers (experts, advisers, consultants, bureaucrats, NGO workers – among them Harper's TB workers, and Annist's NGO staff) that characterise aid, and who translate global policy into the different institutional languages of state, donor, NGO and other agencies involved, and diverse practices back into global policy (Mosse 2005a: 6, 172). The result is the maintenance of a characteristic (and necessary) disjuncture between rationalising policy and the world of practice.

As van den Berg and Quarles van Ufford argue in Chapter 9, the hegemonic potential of international aid is always limited by this autonomy of practice from policy (and policy from practice). Quarles van Ufford draws on the post-Weber organisational theory of Mintzberg (1979) to argue that 'the scope for control in professional organisations such as development bureaucracies is limited, and even decreases as they become larger' (1988: 26; cf. Heyman 1995). He points out that those at the centre (ministers and policy makers) are in fact rather marginal. Indeed all actors are in intermediate positions. This, he and van den Berg illustrate with reflections on the position of evaluation studies and organisational learning in the Dutch bilateral agency. If we depart from modernist visions and accept that 'disjuncture comes first' – if, that is, we accept that the orderliness of policy formulations emerges from an ocean of contingency (or a conjunction of other orders) – then apparent policy order becomes the problem to explain, and departures from the plan are less surprising. Moreover, once the illusion of manageability, of order and a commanding centre are set aside, development actions can, these authors suggest, once again be framed by the moral logic of 'appropriateness' rather than the instrumental logic of consequences.

The chapters of this book not only describe the production of globalised orders of one kind or another, they also show that these orders are unstable. The pervasiveness of contradiction, contingency and threats from the autonomous field of practice below makes regimes of neoliberal reform fragile, even illusory. The production of 'global' (or 'scientific') orders requires hard work. Neoliberal orders have to be re-made in each place. Systems of classification, rules and identities have to be stabilised and protected against constant eruption of the problematic case, the personal judgement, the unruly crowd, the mess of politics. As I have shown elsewhere, actors in development work hard to sustain representations, to connect local events to global logics, because these are the channels through which power and finance flows and so it is always in their interest to do so (Mosse 2005a). Ultimately, harmonised global development policy is an *interpretive* order that conceals the complex politics and passions of practice, while being powerful enough (that is, in allocating both resources and legitimacy, and providing the frameworks that judge performance) to ensure that diverse events, ambitions and political exigencies *are* translated into a singular global logic which helps sustain the comforting metropolitan illusion that global policy makes history. But even though global policy does not produce the orders it describes (they do not involve *de facto* control), its effects, brought through directing resource flows, are real, especially for those compelled to buy into them, or who are excluded from them.

REFUSING GLOBALISATION ITS *GLOBAL* LOGIC: THE WIDER SIGNIFICANCE OF ETHNOGRAPHY

In various ways, the ethnographic work brought together in this book helps to locate the new ambitions of aid within (trans-) institutional networks. It shows that convergent, harmonised and imposed international aid policy is neither framed nor executed independently from the *different* goals, interests, ambitions, social relationships and passions of the many people and institutions brought together in development's 'long chain of organisation' (Quarles van Ufford 1988). It also shows how the different logics and contingent practice of national politicians, international experts, middle managers, bureaucrats, clinicians or NGO workers (among others) are constantly translated into 'global' policy. Indeed, the particular contribution of an anthropology of 'global processes' is that by 'highlighting the ethnographic worlds of the local, it challenges the postulated omnipotence of the global, whether it be international capital, neoliberal politics, space flows, or mass culture' (Burawoy 1998: 30).[24] To misquote Latour 'we have never been global'.

Ultimately ethnography refuses to concede a *global* logic of globalisation. But it does *not* do so by opposing the global to something else – the local or the indigenous – nor by focusing on non-capitalist residues, grassroots or alternative modernities, all of which characterise much anthropological writing on development. The problem here is not just that these 'opposed-to-global' arguments lurch from 'populist myopia' to 'vain hope' (Watts 2003: 28), but that they concede too much to the universality of capitalist modernity in its own terms. Anthropologists drawn to the postcolonial 'borderlands and spaces of marginality' or 'hybridisation' (2003: 28) leave the grand story intact. The universal themes of modernisation and globalisation are simply replayed (Agrawal 1996), and, moreover, continue to define (and confine) anthropology as a discipline of the non-modern local (see Ferguson 1997). The question is how can anthropologists understand what is going on without affirming ruling policy and reaffirming globalisation as a structure of representation, even in protest. How, for instance, as Mitchell puts it, do we grasp events except in the terms dictated by the logic of free-market capitalism 'as a unique and universal form ... propelled forward by the power of its own interior logic' whether taken as the growth of individual economic freedom or the power of international capital driven by the need to accumulate (2002: 244–45, 271).[25]

Mitchell's work is instructive for the ethnography of globalised development. Through carefully unpicking the complex actions underlying aid and economic change in rural Egypt in the 1970s and 1980s, he shows how transformations that appear to constitute the expansion of capitalism (the successful transition to a rural market economy), or which are taken as demonstration of the efficacy of policy models of market reform (the abolition of price controls, the removal of input or food subsidies, etc.), are in fact shaped and transposed by a quite different logic (or embedded in existing networks) that involves persisting 'non-market' practices, state intervention, government control. They involve 'free agricultural markets' that are actually 'controlled by five or six international grain-trading corporations', and politically driven subsidised American grain exports.[26] Reforms intended and appearing to integrate Egypt into global markets actually depend upon reorganising local protection *against* international markets: it is state intervention not the market that is fundamental (2002: 275, 279). The same thing happens with 'privatisation': 'The IMF's confident report that Egypt ranked fourth in the world in privatisation missed the complexity of arrangements and the multiple forms of ownership, interconnection, and power relationship involved' (2002: 280–81). As in Eastern Europe, donors quantifying privatisation success refused to grasp the inseparability of 'public' and 'private', the many 'phoney privatisations' or 'the 'importance of networks that combined them', even if these involved their own contracted agencies, such as the Harvard–Moscow networks that managed Russian 'privatisation' (Mitchell 2002: 282; Wedel 2000, 2004).

Mitchell shows how, through the fabrication of ideas of 'national economy', free market, 'neoliberal reform', the 'self-regulating market', 'privatisation' or 'globalisation' (i.e. processes that follow a global logic), policy discourse abstracts from and misrepresents the actual 'multilayered political re-adjustment of rents, subsidies, and the control of resources' in particular places, concealing (in his case of Egypt) the hand of the US or government interventions, protection, force and political repression, informal and clandestine and unreported economic activity (2002: 277–89). The point is *not* that this reveals a domain of non-market, non-economic, non-capitalist relations – as secondary, residual 'externalities' constraining market relations – but that *all* economic actions are fundamentally socio-political, dependent, among other things, upon forms of law, government and corporate power as well as non-human elements from which the 'economic' is abstracted (2002: 289–91).

In a parallel way, Duffield (2002) refuses the narrative of the new wars as the product of market exclusion – irrationality erupting at the margins of the global system – and regards these conflicts as arising *from* the extension of markets encouraged by structural adjustment, being expressions of autonomy and resistance by those who de-link themselves from liberal market values. These 'adaptations' include informal trans-border networks, extra-legal shadow economies, and 'non-liberal forms of reinvention and reintegration', wealth creation or social regulation that he calls 'reflexive modernisation' (2002: 1056 ff.).[27] Watts makes a parallel point in relation to Islamism as a challenge to development (and secular nationalism) and the self-representation of modernity (2003: 7–11). Both cases question the inherent and global logic of market capitalism which is built into international aid policy, and which makes the link between development (integration into markets) and security appear inevitable.

At the same time, starting from the politics of US aid policy itself, Soederberg (2004a) suggests that the post-9/11 policy shifts that established the link between security and aid and underpinned US unilateralism had less to do with the nexus of market exclusion, insecurity and economic and political freedom, and more to do with a US economic crisis[28] and the *failing* legitimacy of neoliberal policies associated with declining economic and social conditions both in the US and southern countries that was in place well *before* September 2001. In this analysis, neoliberal reform is not the liberation of market forces, but a political strategy legitimised as the removal of a threat accompanied by the rhetorics of global governance and local ownership; but also with the practical implications, Soederberg argues, of shutting civil society out from aid and extending contracts to private companies (2003: 296).

Now these are not accounts of the failure of contemporary aid policy or its inadequate execution. On the contrary, they are demonstration of the *success* of policy and the logic of global capitalism as a structure of representation, an authorised interpretation of events; and its capacity to displace other logics 'constantly reiterating the language of market capitalism ... producing the impression that we know what capitalism is and that its unfolding determines our history' (Mitchell

2002: 266–67); or that where capitalism ends civilised society ends, and that violence and the new wars mark 'the end of capitalism as a geographically expansive and economically inclusive world system' (Duffield 2002: 1053–54). International economic policy works by establishing its principles as the set of self-evident universals, a common sense abstracted and autonomous from actual relations, having a logic of its own (that of market relations) and subject to policy levers acting on behaviour through institutionalised rules and incentives. Economic reform, Mitchell concludes, is based on a highly robust fabrication, 'the idea that the economy existed as a space that could be surveyed and mapped' (2002: 287) when, like 'free-market capitalism', it actually depends upon complex relations and a 'stitching together' of a range of different practices (2002: 279). And in Chapter 6 Harper shows that exactly the same is true of international medical orders that abstract from diffuse experience and clinical engagement with disease. The political processes of aid, then, work successfully to construe their policies (whether neoliberal reform or the war against TB or terrorism) as structural necessity just as they conceal underlying complexity. Modern development policy is abstracted and separated from the social order it governs (as, for example, the law of property, the economy, capitalism). It substitutes universal rational design for the messiness of contingent practice, and actively maintains the gap between policy and practice that is necessary to preserve policy as a structure of representation and the 'rule of experts' (Mitchell 2002), even while it claims the opposite intention of narrowing the gap between theory and practice (Chapter 9).

But there is one final point, which is that this success of policy is not given, but achieved socially. Mitchell's broader project (and challenge) is to examine the historical processes and new social practices, exclusions or violence that have secured stable configurations, which, as he puts it, bifurcate the modern world into objects and ideas, reality and representation (2002). Now, the social processes that stabilise policy can be examined ethnographically to reveal an uncertain world of negotiations between donor managers, national technocrats and politicians, in which there is a contest for authoritative knowledge and authorship of reform, fought in the context of unfolding political and economic events.

Tara Schwegler (2003) examines such processes in her ethnography of negotiations over pension privatisation in Mexico, showing how 'the seamless narrative' of inevitability around neoliberal policy convergence (in this case of the transition to fully funded pension systems) was *neither* a given, *nor* an IFI imposition. Rather it was the outcome of skilful negotiation between World Bank officials and the Mexican bureaucracy (holding its own counter-narrative), resting upon the contingent factors of elections and currency devaluation. The outcome was not a forgone conclusion. The ethnography clearly shows that *neither* the ideological coherence of neoliberal economics *nor* the homogenising power of IFIs, *nor* even the power of epistemic communities of technocrats (in governments and IFIs) is given. Their apparent ordering capacities and the 'rule of experts' 'are the outcome of domestic political struggles ... not the result of in-built ideological affinity and dominance' (2003). Transnational interpersonal alliances do not easily override fields of power produced by divided institutional accountabilities. Coherence is after the fact, and the authority of World Bank economic knowledge has constantly to be negotiated in national contexts where it is conditional on the politics and diversity which it denies.

Nonetheless, it remains the case that players in the arenas of international development often succeed in establishing unequal terms for the negotiation of aid policy frameworks. Gould's ethnographic work in Tanzania (Chapter 3) shows three means for this: the management of *time*, the jumping of *scale*, and the hegemony of *style* (the way in which individual and institutional actors are regulated or clientelised through the funding-related aesthetics of planning, reporting and public relations, illustrated by Annist in Chapter 7). These allow international donor actors to marginalise elected politicians, smaller actors and the slower processes of civil society while securing compliance without coercion. In this way, the mechanisms of pro-poor partnership can have the effect of securing political alliances without making people better able to get services or reasonable leadership from their governments. This book shows how ethnographic research can explore such contradictions and the social processes – simultaneously local and global – that generate them.

NOTES

1. In a commentary at the AAA Meeting, Chicago, November 2003.
2. Rosalind Eyben (personal communication) underlined this point, recalling a remark made at a conference on power in international relations on 'how "governmentality" does not illuminate why the US invaded Iraq as distinct from not invading Iran' (LSE conference).
3. Selectivity approaches are not without their critics, especially where they encourage the gravitation of aid flows away from weak states with political instability or violence – factors which are themselves major contributors to poverty (cf. Pronk 2001) – or create a 'second-class development world' adding to what are already highly uneven flows of aid dictated by colonial histories or donors favouring the same countries, or the massively distorting effects of post-war aid for reconstruction in Afghanistan and Iraq.
4. International Development Targets were agreed at a series of United Nations conferences in the 1990s. They include a reduction by one-half

in the proportion of people living in extreme poverty by 2015, universal primary education in all countries by 2015, a reduction by two-thirds in infant and under-five mortality rates and by three-fourths in maternal mortality by 2015 (DFID 1997). These were reaffirmed as Millennium Development Goals (MDGs) at the United Nations Millennium Summit in September 2000.

5. Currently, the World Bank is again reframing its Adjustment Lending as 'Development Policy Lending' in what it describes as 'a major overhaul of the Bank's operational policy'.

> The framework unifies policy that applies to a whole range of instruments, including sectoral adjustment loans, structural adjustment loans and poverty reduction support credits. In addition, it deals with core issues of design, fiduciary arrangements, financing options, and dissemination and disclosure. (www.worldbank.org, accessed 3.9.04)

Regarding increased international aid flows, these are to be mobilised through an 'International Finance Facility' that aims to use bond markets to bring forward an extra £50 billion a year for development (reducing the miserly shortfall of most rich countries from the goal of 0.7 Gross National Income for aid).

6. The above trends are not without contradictions. The target- and result-oriented strategies of poverty reduction push back from country-wide to *sector* strategies (putting money into education or health, and projectising aid for accountability), while the pressure to increase aid flows can weaken donor capacity to ensure compliance with policy agendas (Lamb 2004; but see Thomas 2004). Moreover, the convergence of aid policy coincides with growing institutional multiplicity and complexity in official development assistance (ODA), which increases the transaction costs associated with aid transfers (Craig and Porter 2003: 53–54, 66). In the 1960s there were just nine DAC (Development Assistance Committee) members, while in 2004 there were 23 (Roeskau 2004). Having an aid administration is an expression of nationalism, sovereignty, and underpins foreign policy incentives and international negotiations (Roeskau 2004; Saxena 2003). Major aid-recipient countries with growing economies, like India, manage to be significant donors as well as aid-takers. International development constantly creates new agencies, but abolishes none. India, a country that well recognises its power within aid donor–recipient relationships, in June 2003 rationalised the system of aid by permitting only six donors to operate in the country (UK, Japan, USA, Germany, the EC and the Russian Federation).

7. In Chapter 6 Harper examines managerialism in the health field as a move to epidemiologically defined population-oriented disease elimination programmes managed through global information systems.

8. As King and McGrath conclude from their analysis of knowledge systems across four cases – the World Bank, DFID, SIDA and JICA (Japan International Cooperation Agency) – these are characteristics common to large development organisations (2004: 107).

9. One observation is that assertions of US unilateralism (and military power) actually increase as US economic power and dominance declines (Fine 2004: 588; Frank 2004: 608).

10. As Castells put it, 'it's not the U.S. Government but the Federal Reserve Bank [FDR] that has some kind of economic policy, but this economic

policy is highly conditioned and shaped by the interaction with the global financial markets'. 'Alan Greenspan [Chair of the FDR] is an independent economic authority. In principle, after being appointed, he doesn't follow the instructions of the president or the instructions of the Congress.' '[U]ltimately, all these decision-makers in the world economic processes have to interact with the global financial markets; with the other decision-makers in these regulatory policies, too; and with their political institutional environment. It's a meta-network of all these networks' (Kreisler 2001).

11. Online 'Discussion with Steen Jorgensen on Social Dimensions of Development Effectiveness', 11 May 2004 (http: //discuss.worldbank. org/chat/view).
12. For example, the trade-related intellectual property rights (TRIPs) regime of the WTO, and the global harmonisation of patent law (Randeria 2003).
13. The significance of Internet-based globalised information systems, 'gateways' and the like in international aid and 'global governance' (as opportunity, threat or overstated) is a separate subject in its own right (see King and McGrath 2004).
14. The 'Reports on the Observance of Standards and Codes' or ROSCS (Soederberg 2003).
15. For a critical interpretation of the role of the IMF in the East Asian crisis, see Stiglitz (2002).
16. These technologies of aid equally have the capacity to conceal their power behind neoliberal visions of the market or new institutional economic re-modelling of institutions understood as the outcome of rational policy choice (Robinson 2002: 1059).
17. Middle-income countries, on the other hand, being able to secure low-interest credit from other sources, are increasingly intolerant of the procedural demands and surveillance of donors.
18. Harper (ch. 6 this volume) examined disease control as an aspect of this will to govern.
19. Following Stone (2002), Henry et al. (2004) usefully distinguish between 'epistemic communities' build around 'causal beliefs' (i.e. technical cause and effect models) and 'advocacy networks' build around 'principled beliefs'. These intersect and both enrol southern actors and knowledge strategically, just as the latter manipulate the categories of advocacy or science to serve local ends. It becomes clear that networks are agent and/or structure in development, having official and 'system' (self-maintainance) goals (Henry et al. 2004 cf. Gould this volume).
20. Put another way, ethnographic reflection renders 'universal' expertise as specific, local, indigenous and interested – perhaps that of Euro-American monoglot inhabitants of insular, bounded worlds (Argenti-Pillen 2003) – and 'globalisation' as the social process by which this local world, its rules and institutions, its classifications and simplifications become those into which the complex and multicultural lives and aspirations of 'global' villagers – those fluent in many linguistic and symbolic systems – have to be translated (2003: 190).
21. See Mosse (2005a: viii–xiii and 2005b) for a case in point; also Mallarangeng and van Tuijl's (2004) strong response to Crawford's critique of the Partnership for Reform in Indonesia (Crawford 2003, 2004).

22. Duffield makes the point in relation to regions of conflict. '[A]ctual development effects', he writes, 'arise not from the effects of structural adjustment or market deregulation or the activities of aid agencies, but rather [from] the efforts of political entities that base their legitimacy on resisting, adapting and transforming these relations'; although there is 'coherence at the level of assumptions, representations and management tools' (2002: 1059, 1063).

23. Complex realities do not make or sell policy. Arguably both policy and politics are increasingly 'faith-based' rather than 'reality-based' (or evidence-based). George W. Bush wins electoral support, not because his policies correspond to evidence or experience but because people believe that *he believes*, not just in a religious sense, but in a political/policy sense. People vote for coherence and conviction.

24. Burawoy also shows how ethnography subverts descriptive and analytical categories, for instance when his fieldwork reveals that similar social practices lie behind the labels 'socialism' and 'capitalism', and that the 'industrial efficiency of the firm, it seems, is less closely associated with property relations than with organizational attributes ... the hierarchies and markets that shape and guide the production process' (Brown 2003, citing Michael Burawoy and Janos Lukács' *The radiant past*).

25. Mitchell has a second question, namely, how do we explain the social and historical origins of the particular representations that become dominant?

26. Moreover, aid-linked demands for the dismantling of state support in Egypt were accompanied by US state support to the American corporate sector through the allocation of aid-financed contracts (Mitchell 2002: 240). The idea that neoliberal policy models do not work by doing what they say they are doing – and for instance that economic growth in East Asia came from ignoring orthodox paradigms (Stiglitz 1989, in Duffield 2002: 1059) – arises from some recent high-profile criticisms of the IMF (e.g. Stiglitz 2002).

27. Among other non-liberal reactions to the economic and social insecurities associated with marketisation are various religious, cultural-nationalist or ethnic movements (Chua 2003; Storm and Rao 2004: 575)

28. The US experienced a sudden halt to speculatively based expansion in 2000, jobless growth and deteriorating economic and social conditions, a growing budget deficit and the need to attract overseas inflows – in short a failure in precisely the financial discipline that was being imposed on other countries by the IFIs (Soederberg 2004a).

REFERENCES

Abdelrahman, M. and R. Apthorpe (2002) *Contract-financed technical co-operation and local ownership: Egypt Country Study Report* (Stockholm: Swedish International Development Cooperation Agency).

Agrawal, A. (1996) Poststructuralist approaches to development: some critical reflections. *Peace and Change* 21(4): 464–77.

Appadurai, A. (1997) *Modernity at large: cultural dimensions of globalization* (Delhi: Oxford University Press).

Apthorpe, R. (1996) Reading development policy and policy analysis: on framing, naming, numbering and coding. In R. Apthorpe and D. Gasper (eds) *Arguing development policy: frames and discourses* (London and Portland, OR: Frank Cass).

Apthorpe, R. (1997) Writing development policy and policy analysis plain or clear: on language, genre and power. In S. Shore and S. Wright (eds) *Anthropology of policy: critical perspectives on governance and power* (London and New York: Routledge).

Argenti-Pillen, A. (2003) The global flow of knowledge on war trauma: the role of the 'Cinnamon Garden culture' in Sri Lanka. In A. Bicker, J. Pottier and P. Sillitoe (eds) *Negotiating local knowledge: power and identity in development* (London: Pluto Press).

Bebbington, A., S. Guggenheim, E. Olson and M. Woolcock (2004) Exploring social capital debates at the World Bank. *Journal of Development Studies* 40(5): 33–42.

Booth, D. (ed.) (1994) *Rethinking social development: theory, research and practice* (Harlow: Longman Scientific and Technical).

Boyce, J.K. (2004) Democratising global economic governance. *Development and Change* 35(3): 593–99.

Brown, D. (2003) Introduction to Polson Memorial Lecture 'Public sociologies in a global context' by Michael Burawoy, Ithaca, NY, Cornell University, 3 October. <http: //sociology.berkeley.edu/faculty/burawoy/>

Burawoy, M. (1998) The extended case method. *Sociological Theory* 16(1): 4–33.

Burawoy, M. (2001) Manufacturing the global. *Ethnography* 2(2): 147–59.

Burawoy, M. (2003) Public sociologies in a global context. Polson Memorial Lecture, Polson Institute for Global Development, Cornell University, 3 October.

Castells, M. (1996) *The rise of the network society* (Oxford: Blackwell).

Chambers, R. (1997) *Whose reality counts? Putting the first last* (London: Intermediate Technology).

Chua, A. (2003) *World on fire: how exporting free market democracy breeds ethnic hatred and global instability* (London: Arrow Books).

Cook, B. and U. Kothari (eds) (2001) *Participation, the new tyranny?* (London: Zed Books).

Cooper, F. and R. Packard (eds) (1997) *International development and the social sciences: essays in the history and politics of knowledge* (Berkeley: University of California Press).

Cornwall, A. and G. Pratt. (2004) Ideals in practice: enquiring into participation in SIDA. Lessons for Change in Policy and Organisations, No. 12. Brighton: Institute of Development Studies.

Craig, D. and D. Poter (2003) Poverty reduction strategy papers: a new convergence. *World Development* 31(1): 53–69.

Crawford, G. (2003) Partnership or power? Deconstructing the 'Partnership for Governance Reform' in Indonesia. *Third World Quarterly* 24(1): 139–59.

Crawford, G. (2004) 'Partnership for Governance Reform in Indonesia'. Dancing to whose tune? A reply to my critics. *Third World Quarterly* 25(5): 933–41.

Dahl, G. (2001) *Responsibility and partnership in Swedish aid discourse* (Uppsala: The Nordic Africa Institute).

Dean, M. (1999) *Governmentality: power and rule in modern society.* (London: Sage).

Development and Change (2004) Economic globalization and institutions of global governance: comments and debate (1), special collection of responses relating to Griffin 2003. *Development and Change* 35(3): 547–612.

DFID (1997) *Eliminating world poverty: a challenge for the 21st century.* Government White Paper on International Development, Cm 3789 (London: Department for International Development).

DFID (2000) *Eliminating world poverty: making globalisation work for the poor.* Government White Paper on International Development, Cm 5006 (London: Department for International Development).

Dudwick. N., M. Alexandre, E. Gomart and K. Kuehnastn (eds) *When things fall apart: qualitative studies of poverty in the former Soviet Union* (Washington, DC: World Bank).

Duffield, M. (2002) Social reconstruction and the radicalisation of development: aid as a relation of global liberal governance. *Development and Change* 33(5): 1049–71.

Escobar, A. (1995) *Encountering development: the making and unmaking of the Third World* (Princeton, NJ: Princeton University Press).

Escobar, A. (2004) Beyond the Third World: imperial globality, global coloniality and anti-globalisation social movements. *Third World Quarterly* 25(1): 207–230.

Fairhead, J. and M. Leach. (2002) Introduction: changing perspectives on forests: science/policy processes in wider society. *IDS Bulletin* 33(1): 1–12.

Ferguson, J. (1994) *The anti-politics machine: development, de-politicisation and bureaucratic power in Lesotho* (Minneapolis: University of Minnesota Press).

Ferguson, J. (1997) Anthropology and its evil twin: development in the constitution of a discipline. In F. Cooper and R. Packard (eds) *International development and the social sciences: essays in the history and politics of knowledge* (Berkeley: University of California Press).

Ferguson, J. and A. Gupta (2002) Spatializing states: towards an ethnography of neoliberal governmentality. *American Ethnologist* 29(4): 981–1002.

Fine, B. (1999) The development state is dead – long live social capital? *Development and Change* 30(1): 1–19.

Fine, B. (2004) Globalization or panglossianization? A critical response to Keith Griffin. *Development and Change* 35(3): 583–91.

Foucault, M (1982) The subject of power. In H. Dreyfus and P. Rabinow, *Michel Foucault: beyond structuralism and hermeneutics* (Brighton: Harvester).

Foucault, M. (1991) 'Governmentality', in G. Burchell, C. Gordon, and P. Miller (eds) *The Foucault effect: studies in governmentality* (Chicago: University of Chicago Press).

Frank, A. Gunder (2004) Globalizing 'might is right': spaghetti Western law of the West is no solution. *Development and Change* 35(3): 607–12.

Gardner, K. and D. Lewis (2000) Dominant paradigms overturned or 'business as usual'? Development discourse and the White Paper on International Development. *Critique of Anthropology* 20(1): 15–29.

Gasper, D. (1996) Analysing policy arguments. In R. Apthorpe and D. Gasper (eds) *Arguing development policy: frames and discourses* (London: Frank Cass).

Goldman, M. (2001) The birth of a discipline: producing authoritative green knowledge, World Bank style. *Ethnography* 2(2): 191–217.

Grammig, T. (2002) *Technical knowledge and development: observing aid projects and processes* (London: Routledge).

Griffin, K. (2003) Economic globalization and institutions of global governance. *Development and Change* 34(5): 789–808.

Grillo, R.D. (1997) Discourses of development: the view from anthropology. In R.L. Stirrat and R.D. Grillo (eds) *Discourses of development: anthropological perspectives*, pp.1–34 (Oxford and New York: Berg Publishers).

Gupta, A. and J. Ferguson. (1997) Culture, power, place: ethnography at the end of an era. In A. Gupta and J. Ferguson (eds) *Culture, power, place: explorations in critical anthropology* (Durham, NC and London: Duke University Press).

Henry, L., G. Mohan and H. Yanacopulos (2004) Networks as transnational agents of development. *Third World Quarterly* 25(5): 839–55.

Heyman, J. (1995) Putting power in the anthropology of bureaucracy. *Current Anthropology* 36(2): 261–87.

King, K. and S. McGrath (2004) *Knowledge for development? Comparing British, Japanese, Swedish and World Bank aid* (London: Zed).

Kreisler, H. (2001) Identity and change in the network society: conversation with Manuel Castells. Berkeley, 9 May. <http: //globetrotter.berkeley.edu/people/Castells/castells-con4.html> (accessed 27 Aug. 2004).

Lamb, G. (2004) Speaking at ODI meeting on 'Aid effectiveness and volume after Monterrey: does the emperor have clothes?', 4 February 2004 (Meeting reports for the series 'The Future of Aid, 2005–2010: challenges and choices' available via <www.odi.org>).

Latour, B. (1996) *Aramis, or the love of technology*, trans. C. Porter (Cambridge, MA and London: Harvard University Press).

Latour, B. (2000) When things strike back: a possible contribution of science studies. *British Journal of Sociology* 5(1): 105–23.

Li, T. Murray (1999) Compromising power: development, culture and rule in Indonesia. *Cultural Anthropology* 14(3): 295–322.

Li, T. Murray (2002) Government through community and the practice of politics. Paper presented at Agrarian Studies, University of Yale, October.

Ludden, D. (1992) India's development regime. In N.B. Dirks (ed.) *Colonialism and culture* (Ann Arbor: University of Michigan Press).

Mallarangeng, A. and P. van Tuijl (2004) 'Partnership for Governance Reform in Indonesia'. Breaking new ground or dressing-up in the Emperor's new clothes? A response to a critical review. *Third World Quarterly* 25(5): 919–33.

Marcus, G. (1998) *Ethnography through thick and thin* (Princeton, NJ: Princeton: University Press).

Mintzberg, H. (1979) *The structuring of organisations* (Englewood Cliffs, NJ: Prentice Hall).

Mitchell, T. (2002) *Rule of experts: Egypt, techno-politics, modernity* (Berkeley: University of California Press).

Moore, D.S. (2000) The crucible of cultural politics: reworking 'development' in Zimbabwe's eastern highlands. *American Ethnologist* 26(3): 654–89.

Mosse, D. (2004) Social analysis as product development: anthropologists at work in the World Bank. In A.K. Giri, A. van Harskamp and O. Salemink (eds) *The religion of development – the development of religion* (Delft: Eburon).

Mosse, D. (2005a) *Cultivating development: an ethnography of aid policy and practice* (London and Ann Arbor, MI: Pluto Press).

Mosse, D. (2005b) Anti-social anthropology? Objectivity, objection and the ethnography of public policy and professional communities. The Malinowski Memorial Lecture, London School of Economics, 2 June.

Global Governance and the Ethnography of International Aid   35

Nuesiri, E. (2004) Economic globalization and institutions of global governance: a response to Griffin. *Development and Change* 35(3): 601–6.

Olivier de Sardan, J.-P. (2005) Introduction: the three approaches in the anthropology of development. In *Anthropology and development: understanding contemporary social change* trans A. Tidjani Alou (London: Zed Press).

Ostrom, E., C. Gibson, S. Shivkumar and K. Andersson (2002) Aid, incentives and sustainability: an institutional analysis of development cooperation. SIDA Studies in Evaluation 02/01: 1 (Stockholm: Swedish International Development Cooperation Agency).

Pronk, J.P. (2001) Aid as catalyst. *Development and Change* 32(4): 611–29.

Putnam, R. (1993) *Making democracy work: civic traditions in modern Italy* (Princeton, NJ: Princeton University Press).

Quarles van Ufford, P. (1988) The hidden crisis in development: development bureaucracies in between intentions and outcomes. In P. Quarles van Ufford, D. Kruijt and T. Downing (eds) *The hidden crisis in development: development bureaucracies* (Tokyo and Amsterdam: United Nations and Free University Press).

Quarles van Ufford, P., A. Giri and D. Mosse (2003) Interventions in development: towards a new moral understanding of our experiences and an agenda for the future. In P. Quarles van Ufford and A. Giri (eds) *A moral critique of development: in search of global responsibilities*, pp. 3–40 (London and New York: Routledge).

Randeria, S. (2003) Cunning states and unaccountable international institutions: legal plurality, social movements and rights of local communities to common property resources. *European Journal of Sociology – Archives Européennes de Sociologie* 44(1): 27–60.

Robinson, W.I. (2002) Remapping development in the light of globalisation: from a territorial to a social cartography. *Third World Quarterly* 23(6): 1047–71.

Roeskau, M. (2004) Speaking at ODI meeting on 'Multilateralism: the international aid agencies, their owners and competitors: do we still need them all?', 21 January (Meeting reports for the series 'The future of aid, 2005–2010: challenges and choices' available via <www.odi.org>.)

Rose, N. (1999) *Powers of freedom: reframing political thought* (London: Cambridge University Press).

Rose, N. and P. Miller, (1992) Political power beyond the state: problematics of government. *British Journal of Sociology* 43(2) 173–205.

Sachs, Wolfgang (ed.) (1992) *The development dictionary: a guide to knowledge as power* (London: Zed Books).

Saxena, N.C. (2003) The new government policy on bilateral assistance to India. Unpublished paper commissioned by the Embassy of Sweden, New Delhi, posted via <dnrm@panchayats.org>, 8 January 2004.

Schwegler, T. (2003) Narrating economic authority: pension privatization and the discourse of neoliberal policy convergence in Mexico. Paper for the Annual Meeting of the American Anthropological Association, Chicago, 19–23 November.

Scott J.C. (1998) *Seeing like a state: how certain schemes to improve the human condition have failed* (New Haven, CT and London: Yale University Press).

Sen, J. (2002) Civilising globalisation? Globalising civilisation? Some reflections towards civil governance and a conscious, critical globalisation.

Paper presented to the Helsinki Conference, 2002 on Searching for Global Partnerships <http: //www.helsinkiconference.fi/netcomm/news>.

Shore, S. and S. Wright (eds) (1997) *Anthropology of policy: critical perspectives on governance and power* (London and New York: Routledge).

Soederberg, S. (2003) The promotion of 'Anglo-American' corporate governance in the South: who benefits from the new international standard? *Third World Quarterly* 24(1): 7–27.

Soederberg, S. (2004a) American empire and excluded States: Bush's Millennium Challenge Account and the shift to pre-emptive development? *Third World Quarterly* 25(2): 279–302.

Soederberg, S. (2004b) American imperialism and new forms of disciplining the non-integrating gap. In P. Zarembka and S. Soederberg (eds) *Neoliberalism in crisis, accumulation, and Rosa Luxemburg's legacy*. Research in Political Economy, vol. 21 (New York: Elsevier Science).

Stiglitz, J. (2002). *Globalization and its discontents* (London: Penguin Books).

Stirrat, R.L. (2000) Cultures of consultancy. *Critique of Anthropology* 20(1): 31–46.

Stone, D. (2002) Introduction: global knowledge and advocacy networks. *Global Networks* 2(1): 1–11.

Storm, S. and J. Mohan Rao (2004) Market-led globalization and world democracy: can the twain ever meet? *Development and Change* 35(3): 567–581.

Stubbs, P. (2004) Globalisation, memory and consultancy: towards a new ethnography of policy advice and welfare reform. In J. Gould and H. Secher Marcussen (eds) *Ethnographies of aid – exploring development texts and encounters*, pp. 175–97. International Development Studies, Occasional Papers No. 24 (Roskilde: Roskilde University).

Thomas, M.A. (2004) Can the World Bank enforce its own conditions? *Development and Change* 35(3): 485–97.

Watts, M. (2001) Development ethnographies. *Ethnography* 2(2): 283–300.

Watts, M. (2003) Development and governmentality. *Singapore Journal of Tropical Geography* 24(1): 6–34.

Wedel, J. (2000) *Collision and collusion: the strange case of Western aid to Eastern Europe* (New York and Basingstoke: Palgrave Macmillan).

Wedel. J. (2004) 'Studying through' a globalizing world: building method through aidnographies. In J. Gould and H. Secher Marcussen (eds) *Ethnographies of aid – exploring development texts and encounters*, pp. 149–73. International Development Studies, Occasional Papers No. 24 (Roskilde: Roskilde University).

Wood, G.D. (ed.) (1985) *Labelling in development policy: essays in honour of Bernard Schaffer* (London: Sage Publications).

Wood, G.D. (1998) Consultant behaviour: projects as communities: consultants, knowledge and power. *Project Appraisal* 16(1): 54–64.

2 GOOD GOVERNANCE AS TECHNOLOGY: TOWARDS AN ETHNOGRAPHY OF THE BRETTON WOODS INSTITUTIONS

Gerhard Anders

... during the 1980s a new approach was developed, namely conditionality. Aid was provided in return for explicit negotiated commitments to policy reform. The obvious theory underlying this was that aid could be an incentive to policy change. However, an implication of this theory was that governments would be undertaking policy change against what they considered to be their interests, except for the receipt of aid. Policy change was the price which governments would have to pay for aid; or equivalently, policy change would be what donors bought with their aid. (Collier 2000: 9)

Good Governance is the new *shibboleth* of the global development discourse.[1] Without uttering this password it has become virtually impossible to qualify for international foreign aid. Good Governance is concerned with transforming 'dysfunctional' state bureaucracies into efficient and transparent service-providers that are accountable to the public and subject to the rule of law. It is hailed as a new remedy for underdevelopment and poverty by the officials of the Bretton Woods institutions, especially with regard to Africa, where parasitic bureaucrats and their primordial affiliations are seen to frustrate all development efforts (World Bank 1989). The implementation of Good Governance programmes is a condition for the disbursement of loans from the World Bank and the International Monetary Fund (IMF). And yet representatives of both these organisations have consistently pointed out that the resultant reforms are to be 'owned' by the government of the borrowing country. According to their and their lawyers' view, conditionality – the *terminus technicus* for the policy measures financed with a loan – does not contradict country ownership of reform programmes.

The term 'ownership' means that the government of the borrowing country is fully responsible for the policy measures and their implementation.[2] In fact, country ownership is presented as a precondition for the success of policy reforms. Of course, representatives of the World Bank and the IMF concede that ownership cannot be forced on a country. It has to come from an ill-defined 'within' and manifest itself in the political will to implement certain reforms. The lack of ownership is usually identified as one of the main impediments to development programmes. Critical evaluations of the World Bank and the IMF, such as the one quoted above, hold the lack of ownership responsible for the failure of many a development project (Botchwey et al. 1998; Collier 2000). This common observation, however, has not changed the official policy of the international financial institutions (IFIs) that deems ownership of reforms as essential and presents conditionality as the logical consequence of ownership. A recent 'fact sheet' stated that 'conditions reinforce the level of country ownership' (IMF 2002a). Officially, the World Bank and the IMF merely provide support for a programme for which the sovereign government is exclusively responsible.

It would be deceptive to dismiss this claim simply as a clumsy attempt at 'newspeak' that fails to conceal the neo-colonial or neo-imperial agenda of the Bretton Woods institutions and their most powerful member states, most notably the United States. Such an unmasking would remain ignorant of the way power operates in the development discourse and would amount to little more than another conspiracy theory of global capital. Instead, I propose an analysis of the forms of knowledge used to unify ownership and conditionality by means of a set of 'tools' employed to promote Good Governance. The analysis therefore focuses on the mundane bureaucratic practices and the idiom of policy documents that legitimise the neoliberal political agenda of the Bretton Woods institutions to understand how power operates in the formulation of the policy reforms they promote.

GOOD GOVERNANCE AND NEOLIBERAL GOVERNMENTALITY

Such an analysis can benefit from the concept of neoliberal governmentality. This concept owes much to Foucault's idea about the multitude of technologies of control aimed at the 'governance' or steering of the abstract category 'population', based on the rational science of 'statistics' or 'state-craft' that replaced previous more repressive forms of control between the sixteenth and eighteenth centuries (Foucault 1991). The concept of governmentality – the semantic link between forms of control (to govern) and modes of thought (mentality) – has two dimensions: on the one hand, it refers to the rationalisation of power by means of defining specific 'problems' and identifying the 'instruments' to address them; on the other, it refers to processes of subjectification in a comprehensive sense, ranging from the control exercised by state bureaucracies to the various forms of self-control that characterise the modern responsible individual.

Recently the concept has been mainly used to analyse neoliberalism or the expansion of the economic realm to include all aspects of the social domain promoted by the so-called Chicago School. Neoliberal rationality does not distinguish between state and market, or individual and market. Instead, state, society and individual are perceived to function by the same logic as the market and can be understood by using economic models (Barry et al. 1996; Burchell et al. 1991; Lemke 2001; Miller and Rose 1990; O'Malley et al. 1997; Rose and Miller 1992). Governmentality and other Foucauldian notions have also been used in critical studies of the development discourse that succeeded in disengaging the anthropology of development from the practice of development policy (Escobar 1995; Ferguson 1993, 1994, 1998).

The policies of the World Bank and the IMF warrant an analysis in terms of neoliberal governmentality for several reasons. First, they are probably the exemplification of neoliberal dogma in its purest form. Both organisations are dominated by economists of the Chicago School who apply market logics to entities previously perceived to be outside the market, such as state institutions and individuals.[3]

Second, contrary to common perception, the World Bank and the IMF do not exercise control directly and in a repressive manner. Instead, both organisations 'govern at a distance'. To 'govern at a distance' is a phrase coined by Miller and Rose to describe a characteristic feature of neoliberal governmentality: 'indirect mechanisms of rule' such as 'techniques of notation, computation, and calculation; procedures of examination and assessment; the invention of devices such as surveys and presentational forms such as tables; the standardization of systems for training and the inculcation of habits' and other ways to act upon individuals and whole populations (1990: 8).

Third, Bretton Woods neoliberalism exemplifies a central feature of 'governing at a distance', namely the emphasis on self-control or self-regulation. Neoliberalism promotes self-control of the autonomous subject or *homo oeconomicus*, responsible for the management of his or her private affairs, well-being and also the risk of individual failure. This philosophy of self-control applies to individuals, institutions, bureaucracies and even national economies, which all have to be made leaner, more efficient and more service- and performance-oriented. Systems of self-control or auto-monitoring increasingly replace forms of more direct control: in theory an organisation that relies on these techniques functions as a self-regulating organism which no longer requires external direct supervision (Bröckling 2000; Cruikshank 1996; Greco 1993; Lemke 2001; Miller and Rose 1990; Rose 1996; Rose and Miller 1992).

Governmentality is not, as often assumed, a property of the state apparatus. Foucault pointed out that the state constitutes merely the 'effect' or result of the new forms of control that emerged in the early modern period and does not hold a monopoly over the exercise of power (1991). The unit of analysis, therefore, is not the category of state but the technologies of control operating through all kinds of relays of power of which the state constitutes merely one. This allows for a dynamic analysis that traces the shift of governance to the transnational level without reproducing the common fallacy of the 'demise of the state'.

The salience of the policies of the international financial institutions in many so-called developing countries since the 1980s – Structural Adjustment, Poverty Reduction Strategy Papers (PRSPs) and the Heavily Indebted and Poor Country Initiative (HIPC) – necessitates a shift of focus from the state to the transnational dimension of neoliberal governmentality (Ferguson and Gupta 2002). This shift enables us to transcend the conventional conceptualisation of two distinct and unified actors, the nation-state and the international organisation, which are related to one another in a certain way, that dominates legal studies and political science. The perspective adopted in this analysis reveals the extent to which the distinction between the international organisation with its limited mandate and the sovereign nation-state is a fiction that provides a legitimisation for neoliberal policies, rather than an explanation of the predicaments of development.

Here I offer a case study to disaggregate the technologies of ownership and conditionality that are used to implant Good Governance, another technology, in recipient countries in Africa and elsewhere, by analysing a set of loan documents signed between the IFIs and the government of Malawi, a country where policies are largely donor-driven. The case concerns loan documents on civil service reform signed between 1994 and 2002, the Institutional Development Programmes I and II (1994, 1996), three Fiscal Restructuring Programmes (1996, 1998, 2000) and the Poverty Reduction Strategy Paper submitted by the government of Malawi in spring 2002.

Ownership and conditionality are tools employed to promote other tools, such as efficient and transparent systems of management and auditing, expenditure planning and measures to improve performance. The beneficial effects of the policy prescriptions, however, depend on country ownership. Hence, ownership and Good Governance constitute each other. In this sense, ownership and conditionality provide slots into which to insert Good Governance, just as a country has to be constructed as 'underdeveloped' to create possibilities to insert the products offered by development agencies in order to bring development (Ferguson 1994; Finnemore 1997).

Malawi is a country where the introduction of the new ideas about governance and state reforms appeared straightforward since the political leaders did not challenge the vision of the Bretton Woods institutions – at least not officially. Since the country's transition to parliamentary democracy in 1994, the government has been particularly receptive to ideas about governance and management of the state bureaucracy, and has implemented a range of programmes to reorganise the civil service, to privatise government functions and state-owned enterprises, and to deregulate the market. However, the national economy has not responded positively to institutional and economic reforms, and has in fact plummeted since the market liberalisation in 1994.

Although the empirical material is limited to the loan documents signed by the government of Malawi, I intend to make a general point. One of the characteristic features of the products of both organisations is their universal applicability. Although the local circumstances might vary considerably, the tools to promote Good Governance are the same everywhere that national governments apply for loans from the World Bank or the IMF.

The loan documents provide excellent material to analyse neoliberal governmentality and the way it operates through the legal construction of ownership and conditionality. The legal dimension has remained conspicuously absent from studies of governmentality and neoliberal rationality. So far, these have mainly addressed statistics, accounting systems, auditing, various techniques of standardisation, ethical codes and forms of neoliberal subjectivity (Bröckling 2000; Cruikshank 1996; Greco 1993; Miller and Rose 1990; Porter 1995; Power 1997; Rose 1996; Shore and Wright 1997; Strathern 2000). The bias against the legal dimension is by no means warranted. The increasing 'juridification' of the transnational arena necessitates research into the legal dimension of neoliberal governmentality. Originally the term 'juridification' was coined to denote the bureaucratisation and over-regulation of the modern welfare state, and the intervention of the state in previously unregulated areas of social life.[4] Juridification is an ambivalent process: the inflationary growth of official regulation does not result in an expansion of the rights of the individual or increased accountability of public institutions, but is rather associated with a growing alienation and powerlessness of the individual confronted with the explosion of legal regulation (Voigt 1980, 1983). Habermas speaks in this context of the 'colonisation of the life-world' (1981: 522).

Here I use the term to refer to the rapid growth of technical agreements, memoranda of understanding, accounting and auditing standards, regulations of purchase and benchmarks, which results in an ever-increasing density of regulation at the transnational level. This development, however, does not entail better accountability mechanisms. In my opinion, it is apt to speak of a growing de-juridification with regard to this increase in regulation. It is a salient detail of the loan documents that they do not constitute legally binding agreements and are of a merely technical nature, specifying the modalities of reforms aimed at transforming an inefficient bureaucratic apparatus according to the official policy of the World Bank and the IMF. It is ironic (and bears testimony to the ubiquity of legal regulation at the transnational level) that the representatives of both organisations resort to legal language to ensure that their dealings with Third World governments have no legally binding and contractual connotations.

My argument in this chapter will be developed in two steps. The first part is subdivided into two sections and presents a brief outline of the emergence of the concept of governance and its status as a technical instrument to transform the 'dysfunctional' state in the late 1980s and the early 1990s. The second part deals with the construction of ownership and conditionality by means of the loan documents. It is subdivided into three sections. The first addresses the resolution of the tension between ownership and conditionality by the way the loan documents are codified in two separate documents. The second distinguishes different types of conditionality and the difference between 'hard' and 'soft' conditions. Economic data and the collection of specified sets of data play a prominent role in conditionality. These numbers are used as norms or standards in the conditions of the loans. Hence, I speak of the 'normativity of numbers' to describe this use of numbers. The third section reads the loan documents against the grain and undermines the image constructed by the way the content is divided between documents and how they are sequenced. Such a reading reveals the extent to which staff and consultants of the Bretton Woods institutions are involved in drafting documents 'owned' by the government of Malawi.

PART I: THE EMERGENCE OF A CONCEPT

Good Governance emerged as the central concept in development assistance in the 1990s. With the end of the Cold War, the relationships between the West and African nation-states were reconfigured. During the Cold War anti-communism provided the most important criterion for Western support, and the massive extent of support given to autocrats like Seseke Mobuto proves that concerns for human rights and democracy were not very high on the agenda of donor countries. After the collapse of the Soviet Union, the attitude of Western governments changed drastically and in the early 1990s adherence to human rights and democratic values became the benchmark for Western support in sub-Saharan Africa.

Some authors argue that the growing concern for democracy and Good Governance has to be interpreted exclusively in terms of attempts by Western governments, freed from the rigid dualism of the Cold War, to control and discipline African governments (Abrahamsen 2000). Although there is some truth in this assessment one ought not to underestimate home-grown popular protest and social movements in many African countries, which exploited the new donor-country agenda and contributed to democratisation of many African countries when the 'wind of change' blew through sub-Saharan Africa between 1990 and 1994.

The 1990s concept of Good Governance heralded an era of much bolder interference in the domestic affairs of governments of developing countries. Until the late 1980s, the state was considered to be the prime actor in developing the national economy and society. State institutions were to be part of the solution rather than a cause of underdevelopment. In the late 1980s and the early 1990s the tone of World Bank documents changed. A radical overhaul of state institutions according to the neoliberal dogma was now demanded to create favourable conditions for economic development. Good Governance was promoted as the tool or instrument, which would contribute to 'sustainable economic and social development' (World Bank 1992: 5) and 'macroeconomic stability, external viability, and orderly economic growth' (IMF 1997: 1; see also World Bank 1989, 1994).

Governance and development

The booklet *Governance and development*, published in 1992, was the World Bank's first general statement of the new development agenda. It defined governance as 'the manner in which power is exercised in the management of a country's economic and social resources for development' (1992: 3). According to the World Bank, the key dimensions of governance are 'public sector management, accountability, the legal framework for development, and information and transparency' (1992: 6). Although this was the first publication to be exclusively devoted to issues of Good Governance, the World Bank had addressed the problem of state bureaucracies in developing countries earlier. In 1989 a World Bank report on sub-Saharan Africa mentioned 'deteriorating governance' as one of the main causes of the crisis in Africa. It held the expansion of state services and the dominant role of the state in the economy after independence responsible for elusive economic growth:

At independence Africa inherited simple but functioning administrations. They were managed largely by expatriates and were not geared to the development role assigned to them by African leaders. The responsibilities of the state were enormously expanded. But at the same time the rapid promotion of inexperienced staff and the gradual politicisation of the whole administrative apparatus led to declining efficiency. A combination of administrative bottlenecks, unauthorized 'fees' and 'commissions', and inefficient services imposed costs on businesses that have progressively undermined their international competitiveness. The gradual breakdown of the judicial systems in many countries left foreign investors doubtful that contracts could be enforced ... Authoritarian governments hostile to grassroots and nongovernmental organizations have alienated much of the public. As a result economic activity has shifted increasingly to the informal sector. Too frequently ordinary people see government as the source of, not the solution to, their problems. (World Bank 1989: 30)

In line with this neoliberal critique of the interventionist state, World Bank experts designed instruments to transform inefficient African state institutions. It was only logical to push back the state in order to give room for the private sector. From an unfavourable assessment of the postcolonial state followed the plan to change government institutions in order to create the envisaged 'enabling environment' by 'defining and protecting property rights, providing effective legal, judicial and regulatory systems, improving the efficiency of the civil service' as the *World development report* of 1991 stated (World Bank 1991).

Governance and development identified four key aspects of the World Bank's policy on governance: improvement of public sector management, accountability, the legal framework, and information and transparency. The first included public expenditure management, civil service reform and privatisation of state-owned enterprises. The second emphasised the need to hold public officials and political leaders accountable for their actions. Accountability entailed:

... making comprehensive and timely information available, classifying expenditures in a manner consistent with budget and programs, doing appropriate analyses for decision making, comparing budget and actual results, improving the organization and responsibility for accounting in the finance ministry, increasing the legal requirements for financial reporting.

Third, the booklet emphasised the need to create a legal framework for development by promoting the rule of law. As with Good Governance in general, the rule of law is a necessary prerequisite for economic growth 'to create a sufficiently stable setting for economic actors' by 'uniform application of rules, the limitation of the discretionary power of officials and an independent judicial system' (1992: 30–39). All depended on better information and transparency, that is 'transparent budgets and public expenditure programmes, the preparation of environmental assessments and improving domestic and external procurement mechanisms' (1992: 39–47, 49, 50).

The instrumentalist vision

In 1990, the General Counsel of the World Bank, Ibrahim Shihata, issued a memorandum on governance, placing Good Governance firmly within the scope of the mandate of the World Bank. According to Shihata, the Bank should refrain from any political intervention into the affairs of a country and should not be influenced by the politics of other countries. Good governance should only be of concern to the World Bank as long as it was instrumental in promoting 'sustainable economic growth and social development', the World Bank's mandate as it is laid down in the Articles of Agreement (Shihata 1990).[5] The same limitation applies to the operations of the IMF; the IMF's Articles of Agreement explicitly prohibit political interference.

In subsequent years, World Bank staff and researchers developed a whole range of instruments to operationalise the concept of Good Governance, including the 'governance approach' (Dia 1993) that provided an analytical framework for civil service reform in Africa. This approach recognised the failure of prior attempts to reform the civil service in Africa as being due to the 'patrimonial character' of the state in sub-Saharan Africa, where 'recruitment based on subjective and ascriptive criteria; public employment managed as a welfare system; pay levels that are unrelated to productivity; loyalty of officials to the person of the ruler rather than to the state; and formalism of administrative rules and procedures' (1993: ix) were the norm. The 'governance approach' proposed a model of three ideal types of African state based on their 'patrimonial profile': countries with a high patrimonial character, countries with a medium profile and countries with a low patrimonial profile (Dia 1993).

The patrimonial character of a state determined the necessary instruments to modernise the state bureaucracy. Highly patrimonial countries would be in need of a 'comprehensive approach' with 'the aim ... to effect the structural and functional changes needed to correct the patrimonial distortions affecting the institutional environment, incentives framework and the performance of core government functions' (Dia 1993: 2). An 'enclave approach' would be suitable for countries 'with a low patrimonial profile'. In these countries the aim would be 'to build or reinforce the organizational, managerial and technical capacity to improve the performance and productivity of existing institutions' (1993: 3). A 'hybrid approach' mixed elements of the two former ideal types by combining comprehensive public sector reform and isolating a few government core functions that would function as 'motors of development' and applied to countries 'with an average patrimonial profile'.

A variant of the 'governance approach' was applied in Malawi. Key functions such as revenue collection, customs and pre-shipment inspection were removed from the civil service and became the domain of new autonomous government agencies and private companies. In March 2000 the Malawi Revenue Authority (MRA) was established to replace the departments of customs and excise and income tax. The new agency operated on a commercial cost-recovery basis with its own board of directors and conditions of service. Pre-shipment inspection was awarded to a private company, the Société Générale de Surveillance (SGS). These measures aiming to create enclaves were supplemented with a civil service reform programme, the outsourcing of non-core functions such as gardening, security services and carpentry workshops, and the privatisation of state-owned companies.

The 'governance approach' embodied the World Bank's vision of the state, which should not participate in the economy as producer and would be limited to certain core functions the effective management of which would create the necessary room for private initiative to contribute to economic growth. I think it is highly significant that the crude typology of the 'patrimonial state' was presented as scientifically established fact from which the necessary instruments or tools to repair the 'dysfunctional bureaucracy' followed more or less automatically. This construction of factors and causal links should not be regarded as neutral and scientific but as a highly significant representation legitimising 'technical assistance' provided by the World Bank and other donor agencies.

While the World Bank was the forerunner in putting Good Governance high on the agenda in the development debate, promotion of the concept was by no means restricted to the World Bank. In 1997 the IMF adopted its *Guidelines Regarding Governance Issues*. Like the World Bank, the IMF explicitly limits its role to economic aspects of governance. The IMF Managing Director, Camdessus, stated in an address to the United Nations Economic and Social Council that:

... good governance is important for countries at all stages of development ... Our approach is to concentrate on those aspects of good governance that are most closely related to our surveillance over macroeconomic policies – namely, the transparency of government accounts, the effectiveness of public resource management, and the stability and transparency of the economic and regulatory environment for private sector activity. (IMF 1997)

Of course, Camdessus did not omit to point out that 'the responsibility for governance issues lies first and foremost with the national authorities' (IMF 1997: 2). The following section traces the construction of the union between ownership and conditionality in more detail by analysing the loan documents on civil service reform. These exemplify the need to represent all interventions in economic terms and to respect the country's economic and political sovereignty by referring to country ownership. Policy prescriptions are presented as technical instruments based on objective scientific methods of data collection and data-processing that constitute no threat to the sovereignty of the borrowing member states.

PART II: 'CONDITIONS REINFORCE COUNTRY OWNERSHIP': THE LEGAL STATUS OF THE LOAN DOCUMENTS

Tools such as the 'governance approach' require slots in order to be inserted into the national polity. To this end another set of tools or instruments has been developed: conditionality. The former constitute the content of the latter, which provides the legitimate form. Under the current state of international politics, the World Bank/IMF policy prescriptions are only acceptable and legitimate when they are presented as technical advice from specialised agencies with a limited mandate in relation to a sovereign state. World Bank and IMF experts represent conditionality as the logical consequence of ownership. This argument rests on two pillars: first, the legal status of the loan documents and, second, the apparent technical and scientific nature of the reform package offered. I will address the legal status of the loan documents before turning to the representation of the policy prescriptions as technical instruments based on scientific methods.

The loans of the World Bank are referred to as 'credit agreements' and those of the IMF as 'loan agreements' or 'loan arrangements'. Credit agreements and loan agreements are split into two separate parts: a letter to the World Bank or the IMF signed by the representatives of the government, usually the Minister of Finance or the president of the reserve bank, and the credit agreement or the loan agreement. If this letter is addressed to the World Bank it is referred to as the Letter of Development Policy; if to the IMF, as the Letter of Intent. The letter is a document in which the government seeking financial assistance describes a set of policy measures it intends to finance with the requested loan. These policy measures are the conditions of the credit or loan respectively. The conditions of a particular loan are thus not stipulated by the World Bank or the IMF but by the representatives of the borrowing government.

After the World Bank or the IMF decides to honour the request of the government, a credit agreement (World Bank) or loan arrangement (IMF) is signed. The agreement includes clauses on the undertakings of the borrowing government and the World Bank/IMF, the terms of the loan and the repayment obligations of the borrower. In addition the borrowing government 'declares its commitment to the objectives of the Project ... and, to this end shall carry out ... the project with due diligence and efficiency'. However, the agreement does not include a description of the project or programme to be financed with the credit or loan. Instead, the government intention to implement a specific programme and the exact description of the programme is embodied in the Letter of Policy or the Letter of Intent. In other words, it is the government, not the World Bank or the IMF, that sets the conditions of the loan in the letter, which is a government document. The World Bank and the IMF then declare their intention to disburse the money as long as the government honours its intention declared in the letter.

I will proceed by dissecting the loan documents to show how ownership and conditionality is constructed. First, I will discuss in some detail the ambiguous legal status of the various loan documents. Second, I will present the various types of 'soft' and 'hard' conditions, putting special emphasis on the normativity of numbers. Third, I will argue that the participation of World Bank missions and consultants in the drafting process and its preparation undermines the official representation created by the way the documents are separated and how they are sequenced.

Ownership and conditionality

On 3 May 1994, Mr Chimango, then Malawi's Minister of Finance, sent a 'Letter of Policy on Civil Service Reform and Institutional Strengthening' to Mr Jaycox, then the World Bank's Vice-President for Africa, 'describing, inter alia, a program of actions, objectives and policies designed to achieve civil service reform and institutional strengthening and declaring the Borrower's [i.e. the government of Malawi] commitment to the execution of the program'. The minister expressed the government's commitment 'to implementing civil service reforms and institutional strengthening in the public service'. The letter listed a whole range of measures for the civil service reform programme. The government promised to create the necessary 'legislative framework' in the form of a Public Service Act and underlined, *inter alia*, the need for improvement of personnel management and payroll management, reliable data on staff numbers, the retrenchment of redundant staff, expenditure control and the privatisation of government functions.

In response to this Letter of Policy the President of the International Development Association (IDA)[6] sent a memorandum to the executive directors of the World Bank[7] in which he recommends the approval of the proposed credit in May 1994. This memorandum was based on a so-called Staff Appraisal Report. This report contained an assessment of the situation, identified problems to be tackled and described the planned project – the Second Institutional Development Project – including measures to be taken, projected cost and implementation. The executive directors heeded the advice of the IDA president, as they usually do; the President, in turn, according to common practice, followed the advice of the visiting mission that wrote the Staff Appraisal Report.

Because of the way the loan documents are split into the letter and the credit agreement, the conditions of the World Bank credit for civil service reform are included in the Letter of Policy from the government of Malawi. What might be considered a mere formality has far-reaching consequences with regard to the construction of ownership and conditionality. According to the World Bank:

> ... conditionality links the Bank's financial support to implementation of a program of reforms critical for the country's economic and social development ... commitment to reform is essential, and conditions usually reinforce the level of country ownership needed to ensure the implementation of reforms supported under adjustment loans. (World Bank 2003)

The position of the IMF is similar: 'When a country borrows from the IMF, its government makes commitments on economic and financial policies – a requirement known as conditionality' (IMF 2002a).

From the perspective of the representatives of the Bretton Woods institutions the split into Letter of Policy or Intent, on the one hand, and credit or loan agreement, on the other hand, guarantees country ownership of the reforms since the conditions of the loan are set by the government. The World Bank and the IMF deal differently with the ramifications arising from ownership and state sovereignty, although the result is similar. According to the World Bank lawyers, the credit agreement signed with a member state is an agreement governed by public international law that includes the conditions at the request of the government applying for a loan. According to the IMF lawyers, the loan agreement does not constitute an agreement at all. Instead they insist on speaking of an arrangement.

Credit agreements signed between the World Bank and borrowing member states[8] are considered to be agreements between two parties governed by public international law (Broches 1959; Delaume 1982; Head 1996). The credit agreement includes a provision that gives the World Bank the right to suspend disbursement if the programme described in the Letter of Policy is not carried out 'with due diligence and efficiency'. Hence, the lending institution is entitled to suspend disbursement of the credit if the borrowing government fails to implement the conditions of the Letter of Policy. It is crucial to remember that the credit agreement merely refers to the conditions set by the government itself in the letter. Since the conditions are spelled out in a government document it is logical to present ownership as a consequence of 'conditionality' from the perspective of World Bank policy.

In referring to 'arrangements' rather than agreements, the IMF has gone even further than the World Bank in avoiding any contractual implications. Gold[9] has argued, in one of the few discussions of the legal character of the IMF's stand-by arrangements, that the term 'agreement' does not imply any 'intention to contract' by the IMF (1980). Gold states: 'the adoption and performance of a program are the responsibility of a member' (1980: 36). He makes a clear distinction between the Letter of Intent and the arrangement:

The two stand-by documents, the letter of intent and the stand-by arrangement, do not constitute an international agreement under which the member undertakes obligations to observe its objectives and policies. (Gold 1980: 43)[10]

His argument referred to stand-by agreements, the regular form of IMF balance-of-payment support in the 1970s. In the 1980s the IMF developed the Structural Adjustment Facility (SAF) and later the Enhanced Structural Adjustment Facility (ESAF) as the regular form of 'arrangement'. In 1999 and 2000 all SAFs and ESAFs were phased out and replaced by the Poverty Reduction and Growth Strategy and the HIPC initiative. In spite of these fundamental changes in the way the IMF operated, Gold's arguments were never substantially changed and continue to define the legal character of all 'arrangements' of the IMF with borrowing countries.[11]

Gold is surprisingly frank about the IMF's motives in avoiding any contractual implication. He argues that the non-obligatory character of the IMF's arrangements has advantages for both parties, the IMF and the government. He observes that:

To bind governments by agreement to observe their objectives and policies, so that departures from them would be breaches of obligation, could exacerbate political tensions and increase the difficulties of negotiation [with the IMF]. (Gold 1980: 37)

Non-binding arrangements are more flexible, more discreet and do not require parliamentary ratification. With an 'arrangement' the involved parties avoid the violation of political and economic national sovereignty on the one hand, and, on the other, legal and democratic accountability for the policy reforms that 'may impose hardship for a time on the populace as a whole or on sections of it' and 'can provoke domestic political controversy and become a cause of friction even within a government', as Gold openly admits (1980: 37).

Performance criteria and structural benchmarks

Since the 1980s, when the concept of conditionality was introduced, the World Bank and the IMF have developed a whole range of different types of conditions tailored to the perceived needs of the borrowing governments. Both organisations have harmonised their policies to avoid overlaps and conflicts between their respective conditions.[12] To avoid these conflicts both organisations in principle use the same types of conditions that complement each other in their 'arrangements' with borrowing countries (IMF/World Bank 2001). They have developed four types of conditionality, each with specific functions and objectives:

Prior actions are measures that a country agrees to take before the IMF's Executive Board approves a loan and before the initial disbursement takes place ...

Performance criteria (PCs) are specific conditions that have to be met for the agreed amount of credit to be disbursed. There are two types of PCs: quantitative and structural.

Quantitative PCs typically refer to macroeconomic policy variables ...

In arrangements where structural reforms are an essential part of the economic program, *structural PCs* are also used. These vary widely across programs but could, for example, include specific measures to restructure key sectors ...

Initially, conditions may be set as *indicative targets* when there is substantial uncertainty about economic trends beyond the first months of the program. As uncertainty is reduced, these targets will normally be established as PCs, with appropriate modifications as necessary.

Structural benchmarks are similar to structural PCs, except that individual benchmarks are less critical for meeting the program's objectives. Thus, benchmarks may help the Board assess a country's progress on structural reforms, but failure to achieve them would not necessarily interrupt IMF funding.

Another important monitoring tool is the *program review*, which serves as an opportunity for a broad-based assessment ... Reviews are used to discuss policies and introduce changes to the program that may be necessary in light of new developments. (IMF 2002a)

Prior action and performance criteria are the conventional type of conditionality, structural performance criteria and benchmarks have been developed as specific conditionality for Structural Adjustment Programmes. Prior actions and performance criteria are 'hard' conditions, in the sense that they are a condition for disbursement of the credit. Structural benchmarks, on the other hand, are considered to be 'soft', since they would only affect disbursement under exceptional circumstances, such as massive failure to implement a whole range of structural benchmarks without providing the lending institution with a satisfactory explanation. According to the World Bank and the IMF, structural benchmarks merely serve as points of reference for monitoring the government's progress in implementing the reform programme and to assess a country's progress (IMF 2001: 3–20).

Recent reports and policy papers of the World Bank and the IMF present 'hard' conditionality in the form of performance criteria as being too inflexible and not consistent with the principle of country ownership. Of course, the World Bank and the IMF did not give up performance criteria and other 'hard' conditions completely, but, by emphasising the flexibility of 'soft' structural benchmarks, both organisations have tried to avoid the impression that they punish governments for failing to implement certain policies. 'Soft' conditionality was presented as a response to the needs of the borrowing governments by giving them more leeway in adapting to changed circumstances (IMF 2001, IMF/World Bank 2001).

However, the invention of 'soft' conditionality has not resulted in a decrease of conditionality. On the contrary, with the growing importance of 'soft' conditions, such as structural benchmarks and other 'monitoring tools', a considerable increase of conditions can be observed. The Poverty Reduction Strategy Paper, for example, contains a complex mixture of 'hard' conditionality with regard to economic targets and 'soft' conditionality with regard to issues that had not been addressed in the Structural Adjustment Programmes of the 1980s and 1990s, such as corruption (Government of Malawi 2002).

The fight against corruption figures prominently in the latest generation of policy documents.[13] This new element in the policies of the Bretton Woods institutions does not imply a departure from or softening up of the rigorous instrumentalism that characterises conventional economic interventions. In the rhetoric of the World Bank and the IMF, the fight against corruption is just another 'necessary' technical instrument employed in the bundle of other technical measures, such as accounting and budgeting systems, to transform the state into an efficient machine that creates the 'enabling environment' needed by private enterprise to boost economic growth.

A characteristic feature of conditionality is what I term the 'normativity of numbers'. Quantified economic data plays a vital role in the policies of the IFIs. 'Getting the numbers right' is at the core of what staff and consultants do, and the sheer amount of data collected by the IFIs is staggering. A policy document of the World Bank and the IMF would be incomplete without extensive statistics and tables on every aspect of a country's economy, ranging from data on the Gross Domestic Product to social indicators such as school enrolment. These numbers enable policy planners to make determinations of the state of the national economy and predict future development (Harper 1998: 24).

By means of being incorporated in the conditions of the loan agreements, numbers are transformed into norms or standards. Numbers may acquire normativity in two ways. First, the number itself can transform into a norm as a prior action, performance indicator or benchmark and, second, the collection of specific numbers using standardised methods can constitute a condition of the loan. Typical examples of the former are targets for economic growth, inflation and public expenditure. The second type of normativity of numbers exemplifies the neoliberal trend toward systems of self-control. The operation of the new systems of management and control depends on the collection of reliable and standardised data. For example, the installation of computerised personnel and payroll management, expenditure planning and accounting are conditions of the civil service reform programme. These systems are supposed to function as instruments of self-control that are operated by the government without any direct intervention from the World Bank and the IMF. Ideally the role of the IFIs is limited to the supply of the tools, the training of local staff to operate them and occasional 'technical assistance' when needed. This self-representation is at variance from actual practices. The following section presents evidence on the extent to which World Bank and IMF experts are involved in drafting supposedly government-owned documents.

Sequencing of documents and the role of missions in the drafting process:

The two foregoing sections present the splitting of the Letter of Policy (World Bank) or the Letter of Intent (IMF) as a means to place the responsibility for the conditions of a loan with the borrowing government. As important as the splitting of the different documents is their sequencing (Harper 1998). Of course, a government has to request support before an agreement or arrangement can be signed. And before a loan is granted the President of the World Bank or the IMF has to endorse a request. Here I analyse the sequencing of the documents in the light of information that the loan documents reveal about the actual involvement of World Bank and IMF staff and consultants during the drafting of supposedly government-owned documents.

The following documents have to be distinguished: the Draft Staff Appraisal Report and the Memorandum and Recommendation of the President of the IDA to the executive directors. The latter is normally heeded by the executive directors. The president's recommendations are based on the Draft Staff Appraisal Report, which is based on data collected by visiting missions and provided by the government. It is meant to assess the policy objectives listed in the Letter of Policy. Malawi's Minister of Finance sent a Letter of Policy to the World Bank on 3 May 1994, stating the government's intention to implement a range of policy measures to reform the civil service. The Staff Appraisal Report, which is dated 17 May 1994, referred to this Letter of Policy from 3 May 1994 and endorsed the planned measures.

Formally, the sequencing of the documents was correct, the Letter of Policy is dated 3 May 1994 and the Draft Staff Appraisal Report is dated 17 May 1994. It is odd, though, that the Draft Staff Appraisal Report and the Memorandum and Recommendation of the President of IDA are both dated 17 May 1994. A comparison of the three documents further undermines the impression created by the sequencing of distinct documents. First, it is striking that the wording of large parts of all three documents is identical. Second, the data referred to in the documents was already collected during the appraisal mission of World Bank staff in October and November 1993 and updated by World Bank staff and consultants in subsequent years. The same observation applies to the policy prescriptions. All documents refer to recommendations discussed during the same visit of the World Bank mission in October and November 1993.

Consultants and experts of the World Bank were not only involved in the collection of data. They were also actively involved in drafting policy documents of the government. According to a report of a consultant of the accounting firm KPMG, one of the conditions for disbursement of the second tranche of US$30 million for the 1996 Fiscal Restructuring and Deregulation Programme was the submission of a Civil Service Reform Action Plan to the World Bank. However, the first draft of this action plan was rejected by the World Bank officials because it did not meet the World Bank standards for civil service reform. At this point several experts of the British Overseas Development Administration (ODA)[14] were involved 'to develop an acceptable action plan and more generally to meet the conditions for the release of the second tranche of funds from the Bank' (KPMG 1996: 3). They wrote a new draft which was submitted in March 1996 and duly accepted by the World Bank officials.

The rejection of loan applications that do not meet World Bank and IMF standards is common practice. The Interim PRSP was submitted to the World Bank and the IMF in 2000. It was discussed with the various missions visiting Malawi. Then four draft versions were written in the course of the following two years, a process in which various donor agencies and external consultants actively participated. Especially important was ownership. During the Consultative Group Meeting in 2000, a representative of a donor country commented on one of the drafts of the PRSP: 'It gives some reason for concern that the document [interim PRSP] states at the outset that the PRSP process is simply a response to requirements of the IMF and the World Bank' (*The Nation* 18 March 2000). Of course, the criticised passage was duly removed from the following draft. After four drafts had been rejected, several World Bank and IMF consultants participated in the writing of the government document and eventually the Final Draft was submitted and endorsed by the donors represented in the Paris Club[15] in April 2002.

I hope to have shown how the splitting of the loan documents, their legal status and their sequencing are all aimed at reinforcing country ownership. This image, however, is undermined by the extent to which consultants hired at the instigation of the Bretton Woods institutions ensure that the letters and documents of the government of Malawi are 'acceptable' and meet the standards of the two institutions for project proposals. Hence, the official presentation of ownership should be interpreted for what it is: a legitimising strategy for a particular political ideology.

CONCLUSION

It has not been my intention to lament the loss of political and economic sovereignty of Third World governments due to the neo-colonial and neo-imperial policies of the Bretton Woods institutions. Instead, I have attempted to transcend the conceptual division between the international financial institutions and the borrowing government that succeeds only in reifying the worn-out dominator–dominated dichotomy. The image of the undivided political and economic sovereignty of a nation-state that is at the core of such a conceptualisation does not correspond with the contemporary integration of Malawi's state institutions into a global system of interdependent self-regulating technologies. Hence, my analysis is not primarily concerned with the question whether the reforms are 'owned' by the government or the Bretton Woods institutions. Maybe the question has to be rephrased as: who is owned by the rationality of conditionality and Good Governance? By zooming in on the veil or surface of mundane legal detail and scientific rationality that seems to hide conspiracies of Manichean proportions from our gaze, it is possible to open a path of inquiry into the subtle ways in which power operates in this era of a global consensus on Good Governance and development.

This consensus is phrased in the language of economic theory and legitimised by scientific rationality. Good Governance and ownership are not presented as superior ideological concepts or desirable goals, but as inevitable solutions or tools to address problems that are of a technical nature. One set of tools, conditionality, creates possibilities to insert another set of tools, such as civil service reform or measures against corruption. Together they form an interlocking ensemble of self-controlling sub-systems that make other alternative forms of policy making impossible and even unthinkable. In this sense, they operate not unlike computer programmes that require the installation of other programmes by the same manufacturer and are incompatible with products from other manufacturers. In order to 'download' Good Governance reforms, a borrowing country has to 'install' specific conditions by signing the loan documents with the World Bank and the IMF. In order to optimise the operation of these tools, the recipient country has to 'download' upgrades and new programmes continuously, ensuring future orders.

So what ought one to conclude? On paper, an encompassing system of control and surveillance of panoptical dimensions seems to operate. However, one should not jump to conclusions. Documents do not necessarily correspond with the messy reality of policy implementation and it should not be overlooked that the flexibility and the absence of parliamentary control that characterise the credit and loan agreements or 'arrangements' are often greatly appreciated by political leaders who publicly denounce the lack of accountability of the World Bank and the IMF. The rhetoric of Good Governance and ownership not only affords Third World leaders safe passage to the financial resources of the Bretton Woods institutions, it also legitimises the continued existence and growth of huge bureaucracies that depend on the financial contributions of the rich member states and, therefore, have to be reinvented from time to time when they are threatened.

NOTES

1. Good Governance is written throughout with capital letters to indicate that the term refers to the brand promoted by the World Bank and the IMF. Good governance is not the exclusive domain of the Bretton Woods institutions. Two traditions have to be distinguished: the first can be traced to various initiatives in the context of the Stockholm Initiative (see van Gastel and Nuijten, this volume) and puts the emphasis on democracy and citizens' rights, whereas the second tradition derives from the neoliberal paradigm of the World Bank and the IMF. This chapter is limited to the concept as it is interpreted and used by the World Bank and the IMF. *Shibboleth* is a Hebrew word used in the Old Testament (Judges XII: 1–6) to denote a password for safe passage. According to modern usage it denotes both a password and the mindless repetition of a phrase uttered without inner conviction.
2. Unless stated otherwise, the word 'government' is used in the conventional sense referring to the executive branch of the state apparatus.
3. On Foucault's discussion of the Chicago School see Lemke (2001). On the role of economists of the Chicago School in national politics in Latin America see Dezalay and Garth (2002).
4. The concept of juridification or '*Verrechtlichung*' was developed with regard to Germany, a country with a highly legalistic tradition, although similar trends are reported for other countries (Teubner 1987; Voigt 1983). It was

first used to criticise the legal formalisation of labour relations in the Weimar Republic, which neutralised genuine class struggle (Kirchheimer 1972). The term usually has negative connotations and is associated with the 'explosion' or 'flood' of norms in modern society. Since the 1970s the juridification of labour relations, social welfare, corporate structures and competition law has been observed (Habermas 1981; Voigt 1980, 1983).

5. Art. V Sect. 10 [Art . V Sect. 6 with regard to the IDA] *'Political activity prohibited* – The Bank [The association] and its officers shall not interfere in the political affairs of any member; nor shall they be influenced in their decisions by the political character of the member or members concerned. Only economic considerations shall be relevant to their decisions, and these considerations shall be weighted impartially in order to achieve the purposes stated in Article I [of this agreement].'

6. IDA is the branch of the World Bank that is concerned with the poorest member states; the president of IDA is identical with the president of the World Bank Group.

7. The executive directors are responsible for the day-to-day decision-making of the World Bank and exercise all powers delegated to them by the Board of Governors under the Articles of Agreement. Every member government is represented by an executive director. Representation depends on the size of the shareholder's economy: The five largest shareholders (Germany, France, Japan, the United Kingdom and the United States) appoint an executive director. All other members are represented by 19 executive directors.

8. It is disputed whether credit agreements with entities other than governments of member states, such as companies in member states, are governed by public international law or domestic law (Head 1996). Here my analysis is limited to agreements signed with the government of Malawi.

9. Sir Joseph Gold played a crucial role in the legal development of the IMF in his function of General Counsel between 1960 and 1979.

10. On the legal aspects of IMF conditionality in general see Denters' comprehensive study (1996).

11. 'IMF arrangements are not international agreements and therefore language having a contractual connotation will be avoided in arrangements and program documents' (IMF 2002b).

12. Overlap or conflict between World Bank and IMF conditionality is known as cross-conditionality.

13. The discovery of the 'C word' has to be seen in the context of growing critique of the World Bank and its policies in the early 1990s. A heterogeneous assemblage of scientists, NGOs and lobbying groups had criticised the Bretton Woods institutions for a long time, drawing the attention of public and politicians to the failures of the World Bank and the IMF. Both organisations were held responsible for the deteriorating living conditions of people who were supposed to benefit from their programmes and for the deterioration of the environment due to large-scale infrastructure projects. Pressure on the World Bank became an existential threat when major donor countries, led by the United States, became increasingly critical of World Bank projects and began to reduce their contributions. By discovering the 'C word' Wolfensohn succeeded in reinventing the World Bank as an organisation fighting

corruption, diverting at least some of the attention of its critics to corrupt and parasitic African civil servants. This was not the first time that the World Bank had been reinvented. When the Bank was threatened by donor fatigue in the 1960s McNamara succeeded in reinventing it when he identified poverty alleviation as the primary policy objective of the World Bank in 1968 (Finnemore 1997).

14. ODA was the precursor of the Department for International Development (DFID).

15. The Paris Club is a yearly conference of the major donor organisations at which the general trends of a country's performance and future policies are discussed.

REFERENCES

Abrahamsen, R. (2000) *Disciplining democracy: development discourse and good governance in Africa* (London: Zed Books).

Barry, A., T. Osborne and N. Rose (1996) (eds) *Foucault and political reason: liberalism, neo-liberalism and rationalities of government* (London: UCL Press).

Botchwey, K., P. Collier, J. W. Gunning and K. Hamada (1998) *Report of the Group of Independent Persons Appointed to Conduct an Evaluation of Certain Aspects of the Enhanced Structural Adjustment Facility* (Washington, DC: International Monetary Fund).

Broches, A. (1959) International legal aspects of the operations of the World Bank. *Recueil des Cours (Collected Courses of The Hague Academy of International Law)* III, vol. 98: 301–409.

Bröckling, U. (2000) Totale Mobilmachung. Menschenführung im Qualitäts- und Selbstmanagement. In U. Bröckling, S. Krasmann and T. Lemke (eds) *Gouvernmentalität der Gegenwart: Studien zur Ökonomisierung des Sozialen*, pp. 131–67 (Frankfurt a.M.: Suhrkamp).

Burchell, G., C. Gordon and P. Miller (eds) (1991) *The Foucault effect: studies in governmentality* (Chicago: University of Chicago Press).

Collier, P. (2000) Consensus building, knowledge and conditionality. Paper presented at the 12th Annual Bank Conference on Development Economics, Washington, DC, 18–20 April, <http://siteresources.worldbank. org/INTABCDEWASHINGTON2000/Resources/collier.pdf>, visited on 16 June 2005.

Cruikshank, B. (1996) Revolutions within: self-government and self-esteem. In A. Barry, T. Osborne and N. Rose (eds) *Foucault and political reason: liberalism, neo-liberalism and rationalities of government*, pp. 231–51 (London: UCL Press).

Delaume, G.R. (1982) Issues of applicable law in the context of the World Bank's operations. In N. Horn and C. Schnitthof (eds) *The transnational law of international commercial transactions*, vol. 2, pp. 317–28 (Deventer: Kluwer).

Denters, E. (1996) *Law and policy of IMF conditionality* (The Hague/London/ Boston: Kluwer Law International).

Dezalay, Y. and B. Garth (2002) *The internationalization of palace wars: lawyers, economists, and the contest to transform Latin American states* (Chicago/ London: University of Chicago Press).

Dia, M. (1993) *A governance approach to civil service reform in sub-Saharan Africa* (Washington, DC: World Bank).

Escobar, A. (1995) *Encountering development: the making and unmaking of the Third World* (Princeton, NJ: Princeton University Press).

Ferguson, J. (1993) De-moralizing economies: African socialism, scientific capitalism and the moral politics of 'structural adjustment'. In S. Falk Moore (ed.) *Moralizing states and the ethnography of the present*, pp. 78–92 (Arlington: American Anthropological Association).

Ferguson, J. (1994) *The anti-politics machine: 'development', depoliticization, and bureaucratic power in Lesotho* (Minneapolis/London: University of Minnesota Press).

Ferguson, J. (1998) Transnational topographies of power: beyond 'the state' and 'civil society' in the study of African politics. In: H. Secher Marcussen and S. Arnfred (eds) *Concepts and metaphors: ideologies, narratives and myths in development discourse*, pp. 45–71 (Roskilde: International Development Studies Roskilde University).

Ferguson, J. and A. Gupta (2002) Spatializing states: toward an ethnography of neoliberal governmentality. *American Ethnologist* 29(4): 981–1002.

Finnemore, M. (1997) Redefining development at the World Bank. In F. Cooper and R. Packard (eds) *International development and the social sciences: essays on the history and politics of knowledge*, pp. 203–27 (Berkeley/Los Angeles/London: University of California Press).

Foucault, M. (1991) Governmentality. In G. Burchell, C. Gordon and P. Miller (eds) *The Foucault effect: studies in governmentality*, pp. 87–104 (Chicago: University of Chicago Press).

Gold, J. (1980) *The legal character of the IMF's stand-by arrangements and why it matters* (Washington, DC: International Monetary Fund).

Government of Malawi (2002) *Malawi Poverty Reduction Strategy Paper: final draft April 2002* (Lilongwe: Government of Malawi).

Greco, M. (1993) Psychosomatic subjects and the 'duty to be well': personal agency within medical rationality. *Economy and Society* 22(3): 357–72.

Habermas, J. (1981) *Theorie des kommunikativen Handelns. Band 2: Zur Kritik der funktionalistischen Vernunft* (Frankfurt a.M.: Suhrkamp) [*Theory of communicative action: a critique of functionalist reason*, vol. 2 (Cambridge: Polity Press, 1989)].

Harper, R. (1998) *Inside the IMF: an ethnography of documents, technology and organisational action* (San Diego/London/Boston: Academic Press).

Head, J.W. (1996) Evolution of the governing law for loan agreements of the World Bank and other multilateral development banks. *American Journal of International Law* 902: 214–34.

International Monetary Fund (1997) *Good governance: the IMF's role* (Washington, DC: International Monetary Fund).

International Monetary Fund (2001) *Structural conditionality in IMF-supported programs.* 16 February.

International Monetary Fund (2002a) *IMF conditionality – a factsheet*, 4 December.

International Monetary Fund (2002b) *Guidelines on conditionality*, 25 September (Washington, DC: International Monetary Fund).

International Monetary Fund/World Bank (2001) *Strengthening IMF–World Bank collaboration on country programs and conditionality* (Washington, DC: International Monetary Fund).

Kirchheimer, O. (1972) *Funktionen des Staats und der Verfassung* (Frankfurt a.M.: Suhrkamp).

KPMG (1996) *Malawi civil service reform: report of KPMG visit 27 May –1 June*. 21 June, unpublished report.

Lemke, T. (2001) 'The birth of bio-politics' – Michel Foucault's lecture at the Collège de France on neo-liberal governmentality. *Economy and Society* 30(2): 190–207.

Miller, P. and N. Rose (1990) Governing economic life. *Economy and Society* 19(1): 1–31.

The Nation (2000) The PRSP process. *The Nation* (Blantyre) 18 March.

O'Malley, P., L. Weir and C. Shearing (1997) Governmentality, criticism, politics. *Economy and Society* 26(4): 501–17.

Porter, T. (1995) *Trust in numbers: the pursuit of objectivity in science and public life* (Princeton, NJ: Princeton University Press).

Power, M. (1997) *The audit society: rituals of verification* (Oxford: Oxford University Press).

Rose, N. (1996) Governing 'advanced' liberal democracies. In A. Barry, T. Osborne and N. Rose (eds) *Foucault and political reason: liberalism, neo-liberalism and rationalities of government*, pp. 37–64 (London: UCL Press).

Rose, N. and P. Miller (1992) Political power beyond the state: problematics of government. *British Journal of Sociology* 43(2): 173–205.

Shihata, I. (1990) *Issues of 'governance' in borrowing members – the extent of their relevance under the Bank's Articles of Agreement*. Memorandum of the Vice-President and General Counsel, 21 December (Washington, DC).

Shore, C. and S. Wright (eds) (1997) *Anthropology of policy: critical perspectives on governance and power* (London/New York: Routledge).

Strathern, M. (ed.) (2000) *Audit cultures: anthropological studies in accountability, ethics and academy* (London/New York: Routledge).

Teubner, G. (ed.) (1987) *Juridification of social spheres: a comparative analysis in the areas of labor, corporate, antitrust and social welfare law* (Berlin/New York: Walter de Gruyter).

Voigt, R. (ed.) (1980) *Verrechtlichung: Analysen zu Funktion und Wirkung von Parlamentisierung, Bürokratisierung und Justizialisierung sozialer, politischer und ökonomischer Prozesse* (Königstein/Ts.: Athenäum).

Voigt, R. (1983) (ed.) *Abschied vom Recht?* (Frankfurt a.M.: Suhrkamp).

World Bank (1989) *Sub-Saharan Africa: from crisis to sustainable growth* (Washington, DC: World Bank).

World Bank (1991) *World development report: the challenges of poverty* (Washington, DC: World Bank).

World Bank (1992) *Governance and development* (Washington, DC: World Bank).

World Bank (1994) *Adjustment in Africa: reforms, results, and the road ahead* (Oxford: Oxford University Press).

World Bank (2003) *Issue brief on adjustment lending, 2003* (Washington DC: World Bank).

3 TIMING, SCALE AND STYLE: CAPACITY AS GOVERNMENTALITY IN TANZANIA

Jeremy Gould

Students of development and international political economy largely agree that we are witnessing the emergence, to borrow Jim Ferguson's (1999: 248) sobering characterisation, of a 'new modality of global inequality.' Recent events in the Middle East are a brutal reminder that violence and coercion remain a central feature of the 'new' regime of international relations. Yet there is also widespread consensus that the current dispensation of global inequity – including a rapidly widening gap between the richest and the poorest, and the marginalisation of large sections of humanity from mutually beneficial international exchange – is increasingly maintained through more refined mechanisms.

One could argue (e.g. *Roape* 2003) that the ethos of the new modality is embodied in the notion of 'partnership' – certainly not a new term in the rhetoric of international relations (cf. Pearson 1969), but never so pervasively invoked to describe the normative ideal of North–South relations as in the new millennium (Abrahamsen 2003). Explorations of the political ramifications of aid acknowledge a dramatic reconfiguration of the aid domain over the last 10 years. The earlier rhetoric of competition, confrontation and ideological contestation that characterised the era of structural adjustment has given way to a language of convergence and mutual complicity. Donor–recipient partnership and the local ownership of aid programmes have become the normative ideals upon which aid relations are justified. In their dealings with one another, the major donors extol the virtues of coordinating and harmonising their policies and programmes. The new rhetoric has not been seamlessly transmuted into practice – the extent of harmonisation and ownership varies widely both within and between specific sites. Still, close-up empirical study of the ideas, practices and relations of aid management indicate that changes in the relationships among donor, state and non-state actors are taking place, at least toward the end of the alphabet (e.g. Tanzania, Uganda, Vietnam).

Similarly, the ways that money is moved, and the various contracting and security arrangements that the multi-billion dollar aid industry relies on, are undergoing a metamorphosis as sectoral basket funds (sector-wide programmes) and direct budgetary support replace the traditional development project.

If the new aid regime is organised around corporativist principles of partnership and harmonisation, its substantive policy thrust is rooted in populist norms of poverty reduction and grassroots empowerment. Within the aid industry, these developments are lauded as a major intellectual breakthrough. The new aid management regime is widely believed by its practitioners to resolve the major problems constraining the efficacy of aid in the past and to be of unquestionable benefit for all stakeholders – a 'win-win situation' in native parlance.

And indeed, after a deep crisis of credibility and disbursements in the 1990s, aid has recovered a modest momentum in the new millennium. Public attention to debt relief and the highlighting of poverty reduction programmes have no doubt contributed to aid's moral resurrection, as has the growing awareness of the role of endemic poverty and inequality as a security threat for rich people. Whatever the reasons, there has been a remarkable convergence in vocabulary among the key actors in the aid domain. Indeed, the prevailing philosophy of aid expounded by national and transnational public donors, recipient governments and private agencies alike might be reasonably termed hegemonic.

Especially at the level of country-specific programmes, where 'poverty reduction strategies' have become the overriding framework for policy goals and public asset disbursement in aid-receiving countries, bilateral agencies work docilely under the stewardship of the massive multilateral aid bodies, while private aid agencies (transnational organisations like Oxfam, Care, Save the Children and World Vision) have been fully integrated into the poverty reduction campaign spearheaded by their former arch-rivals, the World Bank and the International Monetary Fund. Most dramatically, perhaps, boundaries between sovereign national government and self-governed external agencies have become blurred beyond definition as a select cohort of external aid managers and local technocrats assumes joint responsibility for designing parameters of poverty reduction policy and the associated algorithms of asset allocation (see Harrison 2001).

Not everything has changed, however – conditions relating to 'trade liberalisation', 'macro-economic stability' and 'fiscal discipline' are still at the core of the development assistance framework agreements overseen by the International Monetary Fund (IMF).

But many 'soft' or 'processual' conditionalities have been added in the form of Poverty Reduction Strategies (PRSs), Public Expenditure Reviews (PERs) and Mid-Term Expenditure Frameworks (MTEFs), all embedded in an ethos of 'stakeholder consultation'. Few would claim that 'partnership' is an aid conditionality, but most of the things that donor–state partnerships seem to imply are. The rhetoric of partnership thus signals a strategic shift in the management of North–South relations away from the carrot and stick of credits and conditionalities to a subtler dynamic of alleged mutual complicity.

BRACKETING PERFORMANCE

The purpose of this chapter is to contribute to the theorisation of the ways that aid contributes to the maintenance of a regime of global inequality. While the empirical evidence reproduced here is largely based on ethnographic work on Tanzania's aid relationship,[1] this very provisional attempt at more theoretical formulations draws on the lessons of a recent comparative study of the politics of Poverty Reduction Strategy formulation, in which our Tanzanian study was one of five cases (Gould and Ojanen 2003). The comparative study sought to analyse and compare how the emerging regime of aid management grounded in partnership has affected the relationships between aid donors, recipient governments and non-state actors in the local (e.g. local government), national and transnational arenas.[2] The (non-)normative point of departure of this exercise was to bracket conventional concerns with 'performance' – we were relatively uninterested in assessing whether the respective PRSs were 'genuinely pro-poor', or whether government consultations were 'truly representative' – and focus instead on the political dynamic of the relationships among actors (alliances, modes of access, mechanisms of inclusion and exclusion) that emerged in the course of the PRSP (Poverty Reduction Strategy Paper) policy processes.

It is not possible to go into the substantive findings of the broader project in this connection, but one important point bears underscoring. Carrying out comparative research on the new modalities of aid in five very different countries and diverse contexts confirmed that wherever one studies aid and aid relationships these days, one runs into the same characters. It is possible to speak, albeit loosely, about a transnational 'aid domain' populated by a large number of relatively isolated recipient country governments and public agencies, all interacting intensively with a relatively small group of transnational actors – public and private aid agencies – run by a transnational breed of managers with very similar middle-class backgrounds, vocabularies and lifestyles. Unsurprisingly, the agencies they run also exhibit very similar organisational properties. These agencies are highly complex entities with opaque political dynamics that function on several different levels of operation and pursue their strategic aims via concrete actions (projects) at a multitude of parallel sites. A number of scholars and theoreticians working within a field that might be loosely termed the 'ethnography of globalisation' (e.g. Arjun Appadurai, Philip Cerny, Jim Ferguson and Akhil Gupta, George Marcus, Janine Wedel) have been calling attention to the multi-level and multi-sited nature of these powerful transnational actors. Beyond this rather general characterisation, however, we have precious little empirically based knowledge about the political dynamics, management regimes and strategic behaviour of these organisations. This is especially true of those actors constituted as private agencies (cf. Stubbs 2003).

Recognising these facts about the dominant actors in the aid domain carries important methodological implications. Foremost among these is the need for more ambitious and coordinated multi-scholar research efforts in order to grasp the dynamic properties of the aid domain and its inhabitants. Understanding the specific operations of any major player or process, and its relations with other players and processes in the domain, requires empirical analysis at a number of sites on different organisational levels.[3] In order to make sense of observations at these diverse sites data must be put in context, requiring a substantial log of site-specific knowledge. Such a complex and laborious task is clearly beyond the grasp of most mortal academics. This suggests a pressing need for more team-based research efforts in order to grasp the overall patterns and mechanisms at work. But teamwork places heavy demands on the methodological and theoretical arsenal. The comparative analysis of data gathered at different sites and levels can only make sense if the parallel data sets are organised around similar premises, concepts and hypotheses. Where should one look for elements of a theoretical framework that could meet these rigorous demands?

There are obviously many possible points of departure for such an endeavour. More out of a will to provoke debate than from unwavering self-confidence in the path chosen, I try and explore one such theoretical option in what follows.

AID AS GOVERNMENTALITY

An ideology of mutual interest has achieved hegemonic status in the rhetoric of aid across the board – from the megalithic multinational financial institutions (like the IMF and the World Bank) through transnational private aid agencies (like Care and Oxfam) to bilateral donors (like SIDA and USAID) and national NGOs (non-governmental organisations) in dozens of northern and southern countries.

This suggests that the new modalities of managing inequality are infused with some sort of 'governmentality'. This is a reference to a line of political theory (derived from rather provisional remarks of Michel Foucault) that highlights the exercise of hegemonic authority through internalised disciplines of power (Burchell et al. 1991; Dean 1999; Rose 1999). According to this line of thought, a 'partnership mentality' might be seen as a mode of governing key actors populating the aid domain, of ensuring their complicity in a policy regime that reflects the aims of external creditors (as against those of a nationalist entrepreneurial class, for example). Within the emerging modality of global equality, according to this perspective, the new mechanisms of aid encompass a 'liberal' regime of government, in the distinctive sense elaborated by Foucault for whom the 'liberal arts of government' implied ruling not through coercion but through complicity – by instilling a self-discipline in subjects that serves the interests of 'government' broadly understood (Cruikshank 2001).

Such liberal practices of governing the aid domain would include the basic mechanisms through which aid partnerships are engendered: policy dialogue, local ownership, harmonisation, consultation, participation. Of prime interest for a research agenda based on this perspective is to identify the practical and rhetorical means by which actors in societies receiving aid assume responsibility for ensuring the smooth operation of policies (such as 'trade liberalisation,' 'poverty reduction' and 'good governance') engineered and imposed by external players.

The governmentality perspective attracts interest above all because of its seductive fit with the contours of the research problem itself. It promises to provide insights, and empirical research tools, into the elusive foundations of 'partnership' across the yawning gulf of global inequity. That said, it is only one approach among many, strong on vigorous and vocal advocates, but somewhat weak in empirical track record. Its programmatic – and suspiciously functionalist – tendencies draw curt critique even from those sympathetic to its basic premises. Much care must be taken to ensure that a framework for multi-levelled, multi-context comparative analysis is flexible enough to allow for a great diversity in contexts. Otherwise, 'comparative analysis' rapidly degenerates into the functionalist accumulation of premise-confirming anecdotes dressed up in uniform conceptual garb. With so much at stake, there is clearly a need for a rigorous critical assessment of its theoretical claims.

This is not the place for such a systematic assessment. Yet it is worth spelling out some of the risks associated with adopting a governmentality approach to the issues at hand. The most obvious reservation one might express about applying this perspective to the study of aid in the South concerns the context-specificity of the governmentality framework. According to its primary exponents, from Foucault to Rose, governmentality is a property of late capitalism. It is specifically a feature of 'advanced' liberal democracies in a Western cultural context. Few, if any, students of African politics classify contemporary African states within the category of advanced liberal democracies. Many would claim that the Tanzanian state (for example) is not only *not* an example of the 'advanced capitalist' species, it doesn't necessarily even belong to the same genus.

Second, the governmentality approach is predicated on the identification of 'technologies of (self-)discipline', defined as governmental practices which create 'compliant subjectivities'. Yet in Tanzania (as elsewhere in Africa) it is hard to see how the achievement of a hegemony of partnership could be the outcome of the actions of 'the state' or any other form of public authority. The wielder of such technologies would have to be an actor of another order.

One possible way around this problem might lie with the analytical tradition (e.g. Abrahamsen 2000) that identifies the multilateral financial institutions, above all the International Monetary Fund and the World Bank (together these comprise the Bretton Woods institutions – the BWIs) as the predominant source of hegemonic discourses and practices in the aid domain. Following this line of thought, one could circumvent the theoretical problems concerning the taxonomy of the 'African state' by locating the seat of governmentality in the BWIs and their fellow travellers in the aid industry. The empirical data discussed below lends credibility to such a view for, as we shall see, the aid domain in Tanzania clearly revolves around the initiatives of the BWIs.

There are, however, problems with an analysis that derives the empirical mechanisms of the prevailing order from the alleged interests of the BWIs and their accomplices. What, in the first case, are the interests of the BWIs? In the final analysis, these resolve to the mundane imperatives of creditor institutions everywhere – profit, maintaining/expanding one's capital base, access to financial markets, portfolio management and loan recovery, etc. But the BWIs (and their allies) are also deeply enmeshed in complex political processes which introduce non-financial imperatives into their strategic formulae – career development issues among ambitious managers, concerns with organisational credibility, competition with other creditors in the same ecological niche, public relations skirmishes with national and transnational advocacy groups, pressures from national delegations to their Boards, and so on. Short-term financial considerations can and do conflict with longer-term non-financial concerns in a way that complicates any simple calculation of BWI interests as an explanatory factor.

While the BWIs are obviously the single most powerful player in the aid domain, it is risky to simply assume that they constitute the source of a transnational regime of governmentality that systematically ensnares southern governments in its web of complicity. Rather, the Tanzanian evidence conjures up a vision of a constructed community of interests that transects the borders of agencies, bureaux and nations, constituted by an identity of epistemic, educational, class and lifestyle/taste distinctions. This community of interests is the main site of the social construction of partnership, and is the source of a specific *logic of engagement* within which specific 'technologies of subjectification' are at work. Tanzania, as we shall see, is a prime candidate for such an analysis by virtue of the extent to which responsibility for donor-designed social agendas have been taken over by various local agents.

Before proceeding to elaborate on some mid-range conceptual tools for interrogating the central registers of aid as governmentality, a bit of descriptive narrative on the roots of Tanzania's aid 'partnership' will be useful.

THE MYSTERY OF PARTNERSHIP

The foundational moment of Tanzania's insertion into the regime of partnership was the publication of the so-called Helleiner report in 1995. Written by 'five wise men' (including a future World Bank Deputy Country Director and the leader-to-be of Tanzania's largest opposition party), the document was commissioned by a group of Nordic donors as a fix to the aid-freezing stalemate that the government of Tanzania (GoT) and donors had haggled themselves into. According to the analysis of the Helleiner group, the core problem was one of 'capacity', in particular that of the GoT. The government was unable to meet donor expectations for good governance because its undeveloped administrative system could not bear the 'transactions [sic] costs' of receiving aid; the same people who were supposed to supervise and monitor policy implementation were stuck in interminable and repetitious meetings with donors and their consultants. The thin veneer of technocratic expertise required to manage Tanzania's end of the aid relationship was over-burdened and under-rewarded. What's more, the Helleiner report claimed, the behaviour of the donors, and the World Bank especially, was 'self-confident to the point of arrogance' towards the GoT (Helleiner et al. 1995: 13).

Helleiner's solutions to the problem were (and are – Helleiner 2002) partnership and greater local ownership. The basic message of the foundational partnership narrative is that GoT must be *trusted* in order to be brought into the fold of the well-governed. This is the

initial signal that alerts our analytical sensors to a 'liberal' project
of state-making. The subject is not to be coerced, but relied upon
– the maintenance of order and stability is contingent on the self-
discipline of the citizen/subject – in this case Tanzania as the citizen
of a 'supranational governmental regime in which the international
system of states plays a fundamental role' (Hindess 2002: 136).

In its act of preaching trust, the Helleiner report became a symbol
of the mutuality upon which the new partnership is based. 'Helleiner'
is constantly evoked within the Tanzanian policy community, a
meta-event of the now-established regime of partnership.[4] It is not
hard to discern in this account elements of a mythic narrative of
national salvation. The most intriguing feature of the narrative,
and an important guarantee of its compellingness, is its constitutive
paradox of partnership. Others have noted the paradoxicality of
partnership. True partnership between rich powerful donors and poor,
subordinate Tanzania can only be a sham, it is claimed, implying
that there must be a hidden agenda at work. For our purposes, the
bewildering paradox of partnership rhetoric is not in the imputed
disingenuousness of motives, but in the irresolvable contradiction of
the fact that so many people have actually bought into it.

At the root of the paradox is the contradiction of pledging trust
in an entity that is notorious for its untrustworthiness, as manifest
in endemic corruption, inefficiency and abuse. Donors do not trust
'the state' in Tanzania – or much anywhere else either – but they do
identify select individuals upon whom they rely for implementing
their development goals. In Tanzania, these include the President
(who is also the president of the ruling 'Revolutionary Party', the
Chama cha Mapinduzi (CCM)), some senior (Principal Secretary-level)
technocrats at the Treasury, the Vice-President's Office, Planning and
Statistics (the list changes slowly over time – trust is long in the
winning, but can evaporate in a blink of the eye).

Trust is personal – it is not squandered on very junior officials,
and alliances are always established with specific individuals at
the fulcra of power. The personal qualities and motivation of such
trustees of the partnership are extensively (if informally) scrutinised
among senior aid managers. The consolidation of partnership is
thus, in practice, a starkly individualising process. The 'selfless' civil
servant transmogrifies into a personalised trustee – a guarantor of
the partnership and of the specific policies it entails, but also a model
of self-discipline for others.

There is admittedly an element of insincerity in the rhetoric of
partnership, but there is also a profound *mystery*: disingenuous or
not, the whole enterprise – comprising annual aid disbursements in
Tanzania of over a billion dollars, a substantial hunk of Tanzania's
domestic product – relies on the paradoxical rhetoric of partnership,

ownership and consultation. Hundreds of people in Dar es Salaam, Washington, London, Stockholm and elsewhere work long hours to ensure that this system is maintained. A not entirely explicable force seems to maintain this order. To challenge the mystery could mean disrupting this disbursement pattern, upon which everyone in the local aid community – and much of the Tanzanian political elite – depends.

One should not underestimate the pull of material incentives, or their instinctive, collective defence by real and potential beneficiaries. But efforts to promote 'local capacity' – by, among other things, consolidating the status of the trustees – also respond to compelling spiritual needs of the aid manager. It not only gives expression to the deep-seated will to civilise, it does so in a way that reaffirms sacred values of the aid domain: modernity, rationality and political neutrality. An agenda of 'capacity-building' may not inflame idealistic passions, but it is a rallying point upon which normative coherence, and a collective unity of purpose, can be constructed. This perhaps goes some way toward explaining why it is incredibly important to donors, especially, that vigorous efforts to improve 'capacity' lie at the core of and legitimise the aid relationship – thus increasing the likelihood that the somewhat flimsy trust now invested will one day redeem itself. Rather than having conspiratorial beginnings in an explicit strategy of manipulation and control, the ideology of 'capacity' performs a sense-making function in the normative order that makes aid a reasonable, justifiable endeavour for its perpetrators.

A SELF-REFERENTIAL ORDER

The aid domain in Tanzania (and perhaps more generally) can be characterised as a self-referential order, in two distinct senses, grounded in a set of governmental practices that serve, above all, to perpetuate the aid relationship. As argued above, a commitment to enhancing 'capacity' (the way its main features are defined, and the way that different players and stakeholders are assessed in light of these definitions) can be considered a primary ordering principle of the Tanzanian aid regime. A corollary of this thesis is that, contrary to native claims (that is, those of the inhabitants of the transnational aid industry and their local clients), the workings of the aid domain would not seem to be primarily geared toward 'poverty reduction', 'growth' or 'development'. Rather, the practices and relations of aid are first and foremost about reproducing the prevailing order in the face of considerable internal and external pressures. This is the first sense of the self-referentiality noted above.

The self-referentiality of the aid domain also implies that the construction of social meaning within the aid domain is relatively insular. The definition of pivotal terms like 'governance', 'partnership', 'ownership' or 'capacity' within the aid discourse draws almost exclusively on meanings with which these concepts are imbued in the course of the routine interactions, negotiations and contestations among the actors populating this exclusive community. These meanings can, and do, diverge significantly from the way such concepts are used and understood in 'society at large', or in parallel specialist domains (e.g. among soldiers, lawyers or accountants).

The argument about how 'capacity' translates into governmentality goes something like this: 'Capacity-building' is a constitutive part of, and works through, a logic of engagement that largely (though not with any great strategic consistency) serves to instil self-governmental disciplines in the client-subjects of the aid relationship: state and non-state actors alike. These practices do not explicitly aim at, nor do they achieve, organisational cultures that are fully adapted to the contours of the transnational policy agenda, able to perform reliably the (self-) management routines required by the exigencies of the aid industry. Yet much of what goes on in the name of capacity-building seems driven by precisely such a logic of engagement. While instilling internalised disciplines of good self-governance is, in fact, an explicit aim of donors and their subcontracting agents, neither the purveyors nor the objects of these interventions see the broader pattern of 'governmental' engagement or its wider effects.

The core point about capacity-building is that it is embedded in interventions with specific goals that are almost always about conforming to formal demands or expectations of aid-related actors and processes. There are many forms of attention to capacity, and many assemblages of practices are justified via the need to improve the performance of 'local' actors – policy-making ministries, public revenue authorities, front-line administrative structures, private service-delivery organisations, policy advocacy groups, legislative institutions and law-enforcement agencies, etc.

Capacity-building is not carried out for its own sake, but is linked to specific policy agendas of the aid community. Efforts at reforming the state have been the central platform of capacity-enhancement – good governance and democracy support, legislative reform, public service and local government reforms, etc. The 'pro-poor poverty partnership' has ushered in a new generation of demands for which capacity must be created, such as stakeholder consultation, poverty monitoring, macro-economic literacy and public expenditure tracking. The dissemination of such skills and capacities is seen as a lubricant without which the poverty reduction process will seize up.

The ideology of capacity-building has a wide range of power effects, all the more effective due to its niche in development-speak as a pervasive, virtually uncontested normative ideal. The rhetoric of capacity identifies a lack which needs to be corrected, an emptiness to be filled that can provide entry into virtually any domain or arena: any subject, irrespective of other qualities, can be described with reference to its (lack of) capacity. The ideal norm of capacity implies a hierarchy of authority and expertise, overseen by aid managers. It also affirms the infinite improvability of the subject; there is no end to the extent to which one can acquire new capacities.

As useful as capacity-enhancement measures would appear to be for fashioning compliant subjectivities, one must also take into account its dialectical nature. Capacity-building can instil both discipline and empowerment. Capacity implies the exercise self-disciplines that can provide access to the resources of the aid domain. But beyond this, capacity-building implies long-term exposure to the inner workings of the aid domain. The skills necessary to conform to the rules of the aid game can be applied creatively or subversively. While I have never heard of a course or workshop dedicated to exposing the informal dynamics and decision-making procedures of aid agencies to potential clients, many recipient players attend capacity-building lessons in search of precisely such strategic information.

REGISTERS OF CAPACITY

The ordering power of capacity works on the ground through negotiation and contestation. That is, the self-referential and hegemonic qualities of the aid partnership in Tanzania are not givens – they represent the outcome of intense social interaction. While some players see the emerging order as one ripe with opportunity, others challenge the premises of the order in countless, largely uncoordinated, ways. Tanzania's partnership relations have a distinct history, a genealogy of concepts and practices, and struggles about them and what they mean.

My main contribution to this discussion is to suggest that the will to instil a certain mode of capacity works through three substantive 'registers' – *timing, scale* and *style* – and that an analysis of aid practices in these three registers reveals essential truths about the arts of government underpinning the new modality of global inequality. Where we hope to break new ground is in linking the ordering principle of capacity to specific disciplinary discourses and practices, and thus rendering the govern-mental apparatus more transparent 'all the way down'.

One could obviously slice the pie in other ways as well. No claims are made for the 'ontological' validity of these three registers – they are purely heuristic tools that may well give way to richer and more incisive categories. For the time being, they seem to provide the means to convey the most revealing moments and suggestive incidents encountered in the course of our ethnographic investigation of the Tanzanian partnership.

Timing

Timing is perhaps the most effective instrument for controlling the operations of the aid domain. The most important instrument of control is the sequencing of events, when agendas and agreements are finalised. The power to control the quintessential practices of the aid domain derives, largely, from quick reaction time and sufficient 'human resource' to participate in meetings, draft memos, draw up minutes, keep correspondence up to date, partake in informal discussions over lunch or drinks, and so on. Such time management capacity is the World Bank's overwhelming advantage over all other players in the domain. This was strikingly evident in connection with the PRSP process.

Poverty Reduction Strategy Papers (PRSPs) are prepared by aid-recipient governments in order to qualify for debt relief under the HIPC (Heavily Indebted Poor Countries) debt relief initiative. PRSPs are based on a new genre of 'process' conditionality designed by the BWIs. According to the new rules of behaviour, it is not enough merely to meet certain benchmark goals (privatisation, deregulation, macro-economic stability) – although these conventional neoliberal conditions are still in place.[5] The new requirement is that recipient governments involve non-state actors in the design of the policy framework. In order to qualify for debt relief, the Tanzanian government was required to carry out 'consultations' with a 'wide range of stakeholders', in particular representatives of 'civil society' and 'the poor'.

The Tanzanian government and its ruling party, the CCM, had no difficulties meeting these conditions in record time. The political leadership has a long tradition of political consultation via its grassroots organisational infrastructure, and donors (above all the United National Development Programme, UNDP) were eager to provide support to ensure that the exercise was successful. Time was of the essence; the BWIs and GoT were equally eager to complete the PRSP process as quickly as possible.

GoT/CCM had their own pragmatic reasons for promoting the PRSP process. The government passed the first hurdle ('decision point') by completing an 'interim-Poverty Reduction Strategy Paper' just before the October 2000 elections. The I-PRSP was prepared in a couple of months by a small group of government economists with no popular input ('consultation'). Regardless, it sufficed for the BWIs to certify Tanzania's eligibility for debt relief. This provided CCM with invaluable campaign munitions, as its candidates were able to announce their success in securing $200 million in donor funds for national development on the eve of the elections.[6]

The core of the PRSP process was the consolidation of a strong, mutually beneficial alliance between GoT and the BWIs. The course of alliance building was punctuated by a number of critical events (decision point, elections, consultative workshops, completion point) around which the players legislated their strategic manoeuvres. President Mkapa was instrumental in pushing the PRSP process forward within the government apparatus, and a core group of economists at the Ministry of Finance and the Vice-President's Office were his chief lieutenants in this campaign. As a result the control of the technocrats over public policy processes was much enhanced. Indeed, one can claim that a transnational guild of poverty technocrats, based in government ministries as well as in public and private aid agencies, were major 'political' beneficiaries of the PRSP process. Their collaboration across national and organisational boundaries deepened as their influence grew. In contrast, elected politicians had little say over the contours of Tanzania's Poverty Reduction Strategy, and over the public resource allocation algorithms it defines. In other words, depoliticised, administrative procedures supplanted the exercise of power by elected officials in the determination of policy frameworks.

The PRSP crowded out other policy agendas and alliances. Prior to the advent of the HIPC/PRSP process, and the resulting upper-echelon alliance with the BWIs, GoT was deeply involved in formulating a 'home-bred' Tanzania Assistance Strategy (TAS) which UNDP had been vigorously 'facilitating'. There are many reasons why Mkapa and his lieutenants abandoned the TAS and jumped on the PRSP bandwagon. For one, since about 1997 UNDP had ceased to be a spending organisation. Its main assets come in the form of expatriate advisers and there was no promise of financial assistance to put the TAS into implementation. The PRSP process was another matter. First of all there was HIPC money; second, partnership with the Bank was a sure guarantee of new credits. Beyond this, the PRSP process was the natural culmination of the patching-up of relations with the BWIs following the virtual breakdown in relations between the donors and Tanzania in 1994 that led to the Helleiner report. Given the extent of Tanzania's dependence on aid, and the disastrous consequences of earlier disputes with the donor community, the government's decision to throw in its lot with the BWIs is not surprising.

The incentives used by the World Bank to cement its partnership with GoT/CCM are similarly complex, and one must be cautious about imputing intent on the basis of outcome. For the BWIs and the Bank in particular, the HIPC/PRSP process consolidated their position as the chief architect of Tanzania's aid portfolio. World Bank managers are rewarded on the basis of the volumes of their loan portfolios, and the renewed partnership with the government – encompassing a deepening intimacy with a much-empowered Treasury – promised a streamlined loan-processing environment. Taken together, the compendium of new aid-management measures established in sync with the HIPC/PRSP arrangements – the rolling Public Expenditure Review, the Medium Term Expenditure Framework, numerous sectoral baskets, the expansion of direct budget support – all improved the opportunities for the Bank to conspire with GoT officials to process loan agreements quickly. Timing and sequencing are crucial here as well, since other financial institutions (like the African Development Bank, or bilateral donors) often have grants available on softer terms for the same purpose.

In addition to lowering the transaction costs of maintaining a large loan portfolio, other factors also made partnership with Tanzania important for the Bank. Recall that the foundations of the current partnership were laid at the peak (between 1997 and 1999) of a relatively coordinated global attack on the credibility of the BWIs as poverty-oriented institutions. In Africa – where the poverty-inducing effects of the neoliberal policy orthodoxy were most vivid – Tanzania and Uganda became important laboratories/flagships for a new user-friendly approach to development finance. One could reasonably argue that the rhetoric of mutual interest cultivated by the Bank and President Mkapa was instrumental in subduing Jubilee 2000's criticism of the conservative (and wholly inadequate) debt-reduction model that was eventually ratified. Through the careful sequencing of its manoeuvres related to HIPC and the PRSP, the Bank was able to reconstitute its public image in a relatively short time from that of soulless agent of transnational financial interests to one of a compassionate partner in global poverty eradication.

Time management capacity is obviously critical. The BWI coalition with Treasury technocrats constitutes a watertight system for coordinating policy processes and credit negotiations. Oversight of the budget is the single most important element in this register of practices. An ability to identify specific funding gaps, coupled with the capacity to prepare the requisite studies and documentation ahead of other potential donors is a good guarantee of successful portfolio enhancement. The ironclad policy-making coalition forged by the BWIs and GoT technocrats left other players with few options. Only the British aid agency, the Department for International Development (DFID), was in a position – by virtue of its extensive in-country technical expertise and its intimate familiarity with the workings of the Tanzanian government – to compete with the Bank in the timing and sequencing of critical moments in the budgetary process.

DFID, however, opted to support the BWI/GoT partnership, taking on responsibility for coordinating 'the building of NGO capacity' so that 'civil society' might internalise the demands of the new policy regime. The smaller bilaterals, not unlike the hollowed-out UNDP, were obliged to tail along with the partnership.

Scale

The importance of scale as an instrument of governmentality derives, to a great extent, from the transnationalised character of the aid domain. Success in playing the aid game (as a client-subject or, potentially, as a bona fide 'partner') presupposes a capacity to operate translocally, to 'jump scales' (Seppänen 2003) and link strategic action at different sites and scales of aggregation. The inability to do so renders one relatively powerless to defend oneself in the face of encroachment by actors with greater scalar endowments.

This observation resonates with lively debates among social-theoretically inclined scholars concerned with social and political space and relations concerning the 'politics of scale' (Smith 1992; cf. de Sousa Santos 2002: Chapter 8). These debates have stressed the commonsensical fact that 'scale' (level of resolution) is never an 'ontological' given; rather, the scale of analysis (and that invoked in policy discourse) is always a social construction. The 'social construction of scale', as Marston (2000, 221) notes, should be understood as 'a political process'; indeed, 'scale-making is not only a rhetorical practice; its consequences are inscribed in, and are the outcomes of, both everyday life and macro-level social structures.'

Much of the recent scholarly interest in the politics of scale reflects the increased visibility of 'global' social movements. Analysts have been fascinated by how local lobbies and movements confronting a large-scale opponent like a state or a transnational corporation have sought to jump scale in order to muster the greater political resources incumbent in agents and organisations at higher levels.[7] Whether or not local movements are successful in their campaigns, the basic message is clear: scale may be a social construction, but it is also a tangible political resource. Here, too, the BWIs have an incomparable advantage over all other players in the field.

Further evidence of the BWI's leverage at the fulcrum of the aid domain can be seen in the way that the HIPC/PRSP gambit harnessed the transnational private aid agencies that had been at the forefront of Jubilee 2000 in the service of the new aid order. Agencies like Care International, Oxfam and Save the Children Fund were initially drawn into the PRSP process in the role of 'capacity-builders' of allegedly weak Tanzanian advocacy groups. Their task was to beef up the input of the domestic advocates into the consultative process. When the

Tanzanian organisations failed to keep up with the fierce pace of the PRSP process (a 'timing' issue), the transnationals found themselves covering for the domestic advocates as a kind of proxy civil society, by preparing, for example, a 'civil society position paper' for the 2001 Consultative Group meeting (Gould and Ojanen 2003). A common outcome of the politics of scale in the Tanzanian PRSP process was thus the 'crowding out' of small-scale actors like the Tanzania Coalition on Debt and Development and their 'inappropriate' (anti-liberalisation, anti-privatisation) agenda.

The politics of scale are also played out in the dynamics of 'networking'. Part of the campaign to enhance Tanzanian capacity to internalise the demands of the new policy regime involved encouraging small civic groups at the sub-District level ('community-based' and other 'non-governmental' organisations) to establish 'umbrella organisations'. This task was also contracted out to the transnational NGOs.

One such capacity-building endeavour sought to midwife a District NGO network in Masasi District, on Tanzania's southern border with Mozambique. The Masasi Non-Governmental Organisation Network (Mangonet) was established in 2000 under the facilitation of Concern Worldwide, an Irish/international private aid agency. The establishment of Mangonet was an outcome of a Civil Society Development Programme through which Concern had established 'partnerships' with 17 CSOs (civil society organisations) in Masasi District with the aim of 'enhancing their organizational development' (Concern Worldwide 2001a: 46).

Concern's HQ is in Dublin, with subsidiary offices in Belfast, London, Glasgow and New York, a country office in Dar es Salaam (and 26 other countries), as well as regional offices in Mtwara and Kigoma. Concern mobilises a little more than half of its resources (a total of 62 million euros in 2001) through public fundraising drives in Ireland, the UK and the US. Roughly 40 per cent comes from public donors (EU, Irish Aid, DFID and UNHCR are the largest public contributors, while Irish Aid provides a hefty block grant). The Masasi Civil Society Development Programme ran on funds from Irish Aid, DFID and Concern's private contributions.

Facilitation and support to Mangonet is managed by Concern's Mtwara office. Support has comprised a range of services from convening Mangonet's founding meeting to the provision of an office building in Masasi. Much 'capacity-building' has also taken place along the way, both to Mangonet and to the member organisations which are also Concern's partners. Concern's partnership with Mangonet and its member bodies is portrayed in reports and verbal accounts in politically neutral, technical terms. The focus of capacity-building is to promote 'self-sufficiency' and make civic associations more 'effective'. 'Future work', promises Concern's *Annual report* (2001a: 46) will include 'the facilitation of strategic planning and constitutional development'.

Concern's current policy is to work with and through local non-state organisations. There are powerful interests at work influencing this emphasis. As development aid loses its popular appeal, private transnational agencies are in intense competition for donations and support from both public agencies and private donors. *Credibility* is the pivotal asset (after financial responsibility) in this struggle for survival. Direct links to the grassroots via viable partnerships and networking with 'local civil society' contribute decisively toward consolidating valuable credibility. Local non-state organisations often have strong clientelist ties to the political elite, and establishing grassroots linkages with politically untarnished bodies may require creating from scratch the very organisations one needs to 'partner' with. In any event, much organisational development is needed, since, as a Concern manager in Mtwara put it, 'Local NGOs don't reach the poor.'

Another important source of credibility is a demonstrated ability to influence national policy (promoting the 'pro-poor agenda'). In Masasi, Concern is clearly working to establish credentials as a champion of grassroots policy advocacy; one of its first actions after 'facilitating' the foundation of Mangonet was to assign this new 'Learning Network' (Concern Worldwide 2001a: 46) with the task of evoking feedback on the popularised (Swahili-language) version of the PRSP through member organisations. The intent may have been to provoke critical debate among 'the poor'. In practice what happened was that Concern was subcontracted to disseminate a thinly veiled World Bank policy document through its 'grassroots networks'.[8] All in all, engagement with a 'District-level CSO network' serves the function of legitimising Concern's image as an 'NGO of choice' (Concern Worldwide 2001b: 6) in its particular market niche – thus helping to maximise its attractiveness for potential recruits and for public and private donors.

It is certainly *not* true that Concern's activities only reflect self-interested considerations of pragmatic corporate strategy. All is not just about political ecology and resource mobilisation. Concern's professional staff are competent, committed and often highly sensitive to the political complexities of their role as brokers between a multiplicity of diverging interests. Yet the political effects of all this organisational engineering are not a direct reflection of any given actor's intentions and aspirations. Corporate strategic considerations will commonly act as overriding imperatives when assessing alternative options. As in any development intervention, unintended consequences often overshadow desired objectives.

This narrative of the politics of scale in rural Tanzania reveals a whole slew of governmental practices. Concern, a transnational advocate of 'global civil society' finds itself functioning as local gatekeeper for the BWI-driven policy agenda. Local civic groups in remote Masasi find themselves being inserted into an ambiguous 'network organisation' with a predesignated agenda of someone else's design. Capacity-building is undertaken in an effort to empower, but its most tangible outcome is one of regulation and control. The consolidation of local groups into a district network under Concern's patronage represents vertical containment alongside integration into a 'global' network. Attractive as this latter option may appear as a means to mobilise upscale political resources, it is only hypothetical: individuals can jump scale, but civic groups and movements muddle through the quagmire of trying to keep up with the shifting goalposts and latest demands of the aid domain, many of which relate to style.

Style

Legal anthropologist Annalise Riles (2000) takes the critical analysis of empowerment and capacity-building into previously uncharted areas in her study of NGO networks. Riles undertook an ethnography of women's organisations in the Pacific region and especially Fiji as they prepared for the Beijing 'Women's Decade' Conference in 1995. The establishment of many of these organisations was heavily 'facilitated' by donor agencies, and they were also the target of much transnational 'capacity-building'. Riles became interested in the way routines and formalities dominated the agency of Network members, and in the way that these networks appeared to be a self-referential mode of political action. Her conclusion was that participating in the Network was an end in itself. Members had little in common: nationality, values, background, even education. Despite the pervasive rhetoric of equality and participation, most activities of the 'focal points' in the Network organisations were about inclusion and exclusion, that is, about who could claim membership in the Network.

Networks were purportedly about 'sharing information', yet key players in the Network worked hard to restrict the spread of certain kinds of knowledge. Instead of sharing (or even networking), key participants in the Network were obsessed with what Riles refers to as the 'aesthetic' dimension of action. Much of this had a textual referent: countless hours were spent debating and refining procedure as well as the style, semantics and graphics of documentation. These aesthetic standards provide the Network with its transcendental logic – a concern with stylistic elements rather than policy substance – which ordered and patterned the behaviour of those in the Network.

In Riles' view there was no secret or hidden logic behind evidentiary patterns of action – the routines, procedures and aesthetic concerns. Women in the Network did not come to govern themselves and one another in order to achieve some higher, more valid goal (justice, equity, empowerment). Rather the aesthetic of the network *was* its substance. If there was an ulterior motive underlying the obsession with style, it was to enhance access to funding, to aid-rents. Yet the two were inseparable: experience demonstrated that the 'proper' aesthetic was most successful in attracting funding.

Reflecting on Riles' observations, it is evident that a mastery of stylistic, aesthetic elements is a vocation. It implies a certain professional habitus, a certain mode of utilitarian calculation, one for which rhetoric is substance; presentation is output; quantity (of funding) is quality, etc. Thus, through the mechanisms of capacity-building and empowerment, self-organised, largely unregulated forms of socio-political action adhere to mechanisms of self-governance that are relatively uniform across multiple sites (and at multiple levels or layers). These mechanisms of self-regulation emerge largely without the coercion of a central authority. It is through them that indigenous social movements, or innocuous service delivery groups like the members of Mangonet, become (self-)disciplined clients of donor agencies. The incentive to perform according to an aesthetic pattern is largely linked to national and multinational public and private aid agencies, to recognition and funding. The mode of reward-delivery is in the form of a 'project'. The Concern/Mangonet example corroborates this view and suggests that transnational private aid agencies are becoming an instrumental link in establishing these disciplinary mechanisms.

As aid-rent extraction surpasses local resource mobilisation as the main source of value, clientelism multiplies. Increasingly, these rents are extracted through NGOs created to access aid flows, many of which are patched into transnational networks. Resources flowing 'down' from transnational donors to CSOs are by far a more important asset than block grants from a central government to a local authority; often higher than, for example, the state's sectoral expenditures within a given constituency. At this level, it is often considerations of style that determine success in securing a project and thus ensuring the availability of assets for elite accumulation. These include meticulous audits and a complex array of formalised reporting procedures: stakeholder analysis, project documents based on logical framework analysis, standardised monitoring and evaluation reports, financial summaries based on strictly prescribed formats. Indeed, the internalisation of a rigorously formalised aesthetic for the production of such documents is considered a prime indicator of improved capacity.

Because 'aesthetic' discipline is about form as against content, there is little overt conflict between the rhetoric of 'empowerment' and demands to conform to externally imposed criteria of style (including standards of leadership and management structure). This form of disciplinary power can comfortably coexist within a patron organisation alongside an empowering self-image and the rhetoric of partnership.

CONCLUSIONS

Judging from the rhetorical surface of policy discourse, the achievement of a new, hegemonic ordering of ideas, practices and relations in the aid regime has been astoundingly successful. Seldom is heard a discouraging word out on the pro-poor policy range. But two important forms of disjuncture are apparent amidst the emerging order.

On the one hand, a closer scrutiny of accounts and practices indicates that the rhetorical harmony of interests is parsed together from very disparate elements. Actors at different social sites, or in different camps may, for reasons of instrumentality, pragmatism, opportunism or solidarity, perform the vocabulary of partnership. Yet it is obvious that the connotations (and practical implications) attributed to pivotal notions like consultation, capacity, empowerment, etc. can and do vary widely from one site to another. An interrogation of the blatant and subtle differences between divergent glosses can reveal latent or potential political fault lines.

Second, in a more speculative vein, one can sense a deep mismatch between the explicit goals and justifications of the emerging 'pro-poor partnership' (state reform, poverty reduction and grassroots empowerment), and the longer-term political consequences of these practices and alliances. Specifically, the question emerges of the extent to which the particular practices through which partnerships are being forged among these various sets of actors is commensurable with the achievement of political agency geared toward the organised articulation, mobilisation and promotion of popular (as against elite/ creditor) rights and interests. To whit: does the way in which the new aid management regime enables and constrains specific forms of political agency promote a political order in which citizens are better positioned to extract fundamental services and responsible leadership from their government? It doesn't quite look that way.

The foregoing analysis has interlaced rather abstract conceptual elaboration with very concrete empirical exposition. It would clearly be risky to propose very bold conclusions on the basis of such an imbalanced foundation. A number of tentative points of theory might nonetheless be chalked up in lieu of conclusion:

1. From the user's point of view, the governmentality perspective is quite productive. It facilitates mid-range concept formulation and theory construction on the basis of complex empirical data. The alleged non-normativity of the approach is an obvious attraction in an area of study (development aid) over-saturated with self-referential moralising vocabulary. Viewing aid as governmentality encourages one to sidestep a sprawling thicket of cynicism, hypocrisy and rhetoric and to focus on the basic facts of power and its exercise. This can be enormously refreshing intellectually. A governmentality perspective also promotes an impression of moral detachment. This derives from bracketing the apparatus of moral self-justification and rationalisation that undergirds the aid domain as a whole. Strip away the moral buffers of 'poverty reduction' and 'good governance' and the aid domain appears as a game-like struggle among competing actors and interests (e.g. Ostrom et al. 2001). While this can be of utility to advocates and politicians, it is possible that the alleged non-normativity of a governmentality perspective on aid merely substitutes one moralism for another. What replaces the normativity of 'capacity-building' and 'partnership' is a populist moralism of the subaltern.

According to this view, large and powerful agencies are intrinsically sinister and consistently mistaken in their policy prescriptions simply by virtue of their commanding position in the hegemonic regime of partnership. This may be a reasonable and just response to an order of global inequality predicated on the sovereignty of creditor interests. Yet, taken too literally, a populist moralism may lead us to miss what Foucault termed the 'productive' side of power – sites where mechanisms of 'partnership' generate 'capacities' – forms of awareness and modes of mobilisation and organisation – that actually do empower and entitle. Without productive power, politics in the service of virtuous ends (however defined) cannot consolidate and flourish.

2. What if this analysis of trends in politics of aid in Tanzania is accurate? What might be the effects of making the mechanics of a regime based on the complicity of donors, technocrats and NGOs transparent to both its governors and its subjects? There are obvious ethical risks involved. Assigning individual responsibility for perpetuating aid dependence (and debt-slavery) to self-serving political leaders and senior technocrats (as implied in our analysis) can easily lead to the (self-)alienation of a powerful, insular elite. Undermine the self-image of technical expertise in the national service of this elite, and the legitimacy of their actions and alliances becomes highly questionable.

If, to put it another way, 'debt relief' simply perpetuates servitude to transnational creditor interests, and 'poverty reduction' merely institutionalises the marginalisation of the masses, the political outcomes of the 'pro-poor partnership' could encompass increased fragility, instability and capriciousness. With no popular controls on public policy formulation, a perverse upward accountability becomes the only mode of checks and balances. Eyes turn to 'global civil society' as a proxy for bottom-up democratic control. Transnational organisations have the capacity to jump scale, but are they equipped with productive power commensurate with the political challenges and the context?

3. It must be left to the reader to decide whether this analysis has succumbed to the functionalism and cynicism which are never far from the Foucauldian legacy. In truth, the partnership regime is not hegemonic, it is flimsy. Tanzania, like Uganda and Mozambique, is a showcase. Fostering partnership in these countries has been an expensive public relations exercise, contingent on immense levels of aid-dependency. Vietnam and Honduras, for example (see Gould 2005), have shown themselves capable of retaining far greater degrees of policy sovereignty in the face of donor pressures. Some forms of freedom are not (yet) subject to the allures of governmental disciplines.

NOTES

1. Caveat: Tanzania can be taken as an extreme example of a system of government dominated by aid practices. The observations and analysis advanced here cannot be automatically taken as generic propositions about the ordering of aid. On the other hand, parallel studies undertaken in the quite different configurations of Honduras (Seppänen 2003) and Vietnam (Nørlund et al. 2003) reveal a very similar pattern (see also Gould 2005).
2. Funding for the studies was provided by the Ministry of Foreign Affairs of Finland, Norad and SIDA. The other cases were Honduras, Malawi, Vietnam and Zambia. Further information on this research programme and its findings is available at <www.valt.helsinki/kmi/policy>.
3. For reflections on the methodological problems of studying multi-level, multi-sited aid agencies see Gould (2004).
4. Helleiner subsequently became a 'process' and eventually stabilised into an institution: the semi-official Independent Monitoring Group managed by the Economic and Social Research Foundation, one of two major private think-tanks that survive on such donor commissions. ESRF is publishing the collected documents of the 'Helleiner process' in one volume.
5. Albeit hidden away in the IMF's semi-secret Poverty Reduction Growth Facility agreement, also a requirement for HIPC eligibility; see Gould and Ojanen (2003: 51).
6. In fact, HIPC debt relief does not bring in additional aid. Under the HIPC arrangement, qualifying for debt relief allows the eligible government to redirect budgetary funds that would have been used for servicing its debt to other, poverty reducing, ends.
7. Marston (2000) summarises a number of examples of such research.

8. The main contradiction in marketing the PRSP to 'the poor' lies in the fact that a rigorous set of macro-economic conditions for debt relief and further credit-worthiness was part of the PRSP/HIPC package, but these conditions were not among the items included in the 'consultations' organised to legitimise the PRS. Feedback was not evoked on whether the government should privatise public utilities, remove import barriers or curtail civil servant salaries, despite the fact that these conditions for HIPC eligibility had a direct negative impact on poor Tanzanians.

REFERENCES

Abrahamsen, R. (2000) *Disciplining democracy: development discourse and good governance in Africa* (London: Zed).

Abrahamsen, R. (2003) Development partnerships and liberal governance. Paper presented at the Annual Conference of the International Studies Association, Portland, Oregon, February.

Burchell, G., C. Gordon and P. Miller (1991) *The Foucault effect: studies in governmentality* (Hemel Hempstead: Harvester Wheatsheaf).

Concern Worldwide (2001a) *Annual report* <http://www.concern.ie/news/annual.htm>, visited March 2003.

Concern Worldwide (2001b) *Financial statement* <http://www.concern.ie/news/annual.htm>, visited March 2003.

Cruikshank, B. (2001) *The will to empower: democratic citizens and other subjects* (Ithaca, NY: Cornell University Press).

de Sousa Santos, B. (2002) *Toward a new legal common sense*, 2nd edn (London: Butterworths).

Dean, M. (1999) *Governmentality: power and rule in modern society* (London: Sage).

Ferguson, J. (1999) *Expectations of modernity: myths and meanings of urban life on the Zambian copperbelt* (Berkeley: University of California Press).

Gould, J. (2004) Positionality and scale: methodological issues in the ethnography of aid. In J. Gould and H.S. Marcussen (eds) *Ethnographies of aid – exploring development texts and encounters* (Roskilde: Roskilde University Centre – Occasional Paper 24).

Gould, J. (2005) *The new conditionality. The politics of poverty reduction strategies* (London: Zed).

Gould, J. and J. Ojanen (2003) *'Merging in the circle': the politics of Tanzania's Poverty Reduction Strategy* (Helsinki: Institute of Development Studies – Policy Paper 2/2003).

Harrison, G. (2001) Post-conditionality politics and administrative reform: reflections on the cases of Uganda and Tanzania. *Development and Change* 23: 657–79.

Helleiner, G. (2002) Local ownership and donor performance monitoring: new aid relationships in Tanzania? *Journal of Human Development* 3(2): 251–61.

Helleiner, G., T. Killick, N. Lipumba, B. Ndulu and K.E. Svendsen (1995) *Report of the Group of Independent Advisers on Development Cooperation Issues Between Tanzania and its Aid Donors* (Copenhagen: Royal Danish Ministry of Foreign Affairs).

Hindess, Barry (2002) Neo-liberal citizenship. *Citizenship Studies* 6(2): 127–43.

Marston, S.A. (2000) The social construction of scale. *Progress in Human Geography* 24(2): 219–42.

Nørlund, I., Tran Ngoc Ca and Nguyen Dinh Tuyen (2003) *Dealing with the donors: the politics of Vietnam's Comprehensive Growth and Poverty Reduction Strategy* (Helsinki: Institute of Development Studies – Policy Paper 4/2003).

Ostrom E., C. Gibson, S. Shivakumar and K. Andersson (2001) *Aid, incentives and sustainability: an institutional analysis of development cooperation* (Stockholm: SIDA Studies in Evaluation 02/01).

Pearson, L.B. (1969) *Partners in development: Report of the Commission on International Development* (New York: Praeger).

Riles, A. (2000) *The network inside out* (Ann Arbor: University of Michigan Press).

Roape/Review of African Political Economy (2003) Africa: partnership as imperialism. Conference announcement <http://www.africainformation.co.uk/roape1.htm>, visited January 2003.

Rose, N. (1999) *Powers of freedom: reframing political thought* (Cambridge: Cambridge University Press).

Seppänen, M. (2003) *Transforming the concessional state? The politics of Honduras' Poverty Reduction Strategy* (Helsinki: Institute of Development Studies – Policy Paper 3/2003).

Smith, N. (1992) Geography, difference and the politics of scale. In J. Doherty, E. Graham and M. Malek (eds) *Postmodernism and the social sciences*, pp. 57–79 (London: Macmillan).

Stubbs, P. (2003) International non-state actors and social development policy. In B. Deacon, E. Ollila, M. Koivusalo and P. Stubbs (eds) *Global social governance: themes and prospects* (Helsinki: Globalism and Social Policy Programme).

THE GENEALOGY OF THE 'GOOD
GOVERNANCE' AND 'OWNERSHIP'
AGENDA AT THE DUTCH MINISTRY
OF DEVELOPMENT COOPERATION

Jilles van Gastel and Monique Nuijten

For a long time anthropologists have contributed to the formulation of new development policies and programmes to improve the living conditions of the underprivileged. Today, however, academic interest in policy making has also become concerned with the felt 'limits of governing' and the accompanying need to rethink 'the relationship between social theory, policy analysis and politics' (Hajer and Wagenaar 2003: Preface). The context of policy making is changing as new political spaces emerge and traditional institutions lose legitimacy (Hajer 2003). The need to re-think policy making within these new institutional realities is strongly felt, not only within anthropology but within development studies too (Duffield 2001). In this chapter we contribute a 'practice perspective' which focuses on the inherently contextual nature of policy making. It makes use of an interpretive perspective, which places the historical development of policy discourses and the stories of practitioners at its centre (Hajer and Wagenaar 2003). In attempting this, we analyse the workings of the Dutch Ministry of Development Cooperation[1] by reconstructing and analysing the processes of policy formulation around ideas of 'good governance', 'self-reliance' and 'ownership'. The chapter is based on ethnographic and documentary research at the ministry in the Netherlands.[2] The main focus is on the life histories of ministers, the shaping and re-shaping of different documents around key concepts and their accompanying institutional dynamics.

THE ROLE OF POLICY IN DEVELOPMENT

We begin with a discussion on different views on policy in development studies. Broadly speaking, two dominant approaches to policy in the field of development can be distinguished. First, there is an 'instrumental' approach, which aims to generate knowledge and action for the solution of developmental problems through the application of scientific methods. Policy is perceived as a rational problem-solving instrument, and as a neutral, technical means to steer social processes. Since policy is progressively improved through better knowledge, much attention is paid to the monitoring and evaluation of projects and programmes – a specialisation in itself – so that lessons can be learned for future policy making. Within this perspective, organisations tend to be understood as machines, divided and compartmentalised into hierarchical levels, functions and people (Morgan 1997; Quarles van Ufford 1999; van Gastel 2001). Within the hierarchy, higher levels, such as the management board, are expected to develop policy which flows down to and is implemented mechanically by the lower levels, in the form of specialised civil servants. As Urban suggests, 'the bureaucratic hierarchy manifests itself as a technical necessity (to co-ordinate the subdivided tasks) [and] as a rational organizational arrangement for the accomplishment of collective ends' (1982: 23–4). Since managerial control over the process is central, this model is especially prevalent among ministers and high-level public officers. Yet, as we will show, the actual relation between policy and organisational dynamics is very different.

The 'instrumentalist' approach can be criticised on several grounds. First, it does not satisfactorily explain the relationship between formal policy discourse and implementation. Indeed, Mosse (2004) argues that notwithstanding the vast amount of money and time spent on creating new policy models, very little attention is given to the relationship between these models and the effects that they bring about. Instead, these mechanical, linear models of the relationship between policy, implementation and outcomes greatly oversimplify what is in fact a complicated set of processes involving the continuous re-interpretation and transformation of policy ideas (Long 2001: 31). Second, the model has a tendency to reduce even the highly complicated and multi-dimensional phenomena of political culture, democracy and poverty reduction to mere 'variables' to be inserted within rational design and planning models (Duffield 2001: 9).

The second strand of policy analysis comes from critical studies of the development industry and the continuous generation of so-called new models. Critical approaches analyse development bureaucracies and aid policies in the context of a hegemonic global order. Rather than offering new development models, they try to reveal underlying processes of domination in the construction of policy solutions and the working of development bureaucracies (Escobar 1991, 1995; Ferguson 1990). As Mosse argues, from the critical perspective, policy is seen 'as a rationalizing discourse concealing hidden purposes of bureaucratic power or dominance,

in which the true political intent of development is hidden behind
a cloak of rational planning' (2004: 641). In this view, organisations
are constituted by the macro-structures of power and control under
whose influence they are located. Development policies 'have both
institutional effects (maintaining relations of power) and ideological
effects (depoliticization)' (Mosse 2004: 643, citing Ferguson 1994).
But while critical analysis rightly points to the *effects* of development
discourses (e.g. de-politicisation), they fail to examine how policy
is socially *produced* and transformed at the different sites and levels
of development aid. Indeed, one of the central limitations of both
instrumental and critical approaches is that they pay little attention
to the working environments of public officers, whether at the level
of the headquarters or the field offices of bilateral and multilateral
donors. They fail, in other words, to examine the tension between
theoretical rationality and the practical rationality of civil servants
(Hajer and Wagenaar 2003: 19).

The two broad approaches also regard the apparent failure of
rationally planned development projects differently. From an
instrumentalist perspective, the lack of reliable knowledge and the
uncontrollable nature of events are to blame. The critical perspective
points to structural power relations that will always work against
efforts to create a more egalitarian global order. In our study, we
follow the critical approach in arguing that the problem of policy
failure in development results not from a lack of knowledge, but
rather from the relation between policy, institutional dynamics and
politics. But we distance ourselves from the idea that this failure is
based on deliberate or centralised hegemonic processes of control.

Finally, we conceive of policy as a political as much as an analytical
or problem-solving process (Shore and Wright 1997). As we have
seen, the instrumental view neglects the fact that policy is never only
about objective problems and the 'facts of the matter', but inevitably
always about politics and the dynamics of credibility in a contested
political world (Hajer and Wagenaar 2003: xiii). On the other hand,
the critical approach 'replaces instrumental rationality of policy with
the anonymous automaticy of the [hegemonic] machine' (Mosse
2004: 644). In fact, both views are weak in providing insights into
the relationship between policy and practice, and in problematising
policy itself. Therefore, we propose instead a practice approach
towards the policy process (cf. Hajer and Wagenaar 2003).

A PRACTICE APPROACH TOWARDS THE ANALYSIS OF AID POLICIES

Some anthropologists of development have studied the processes
around the implementation of development projects in detail (Arce
1993; Long 2001; de Vries 1997). Others have played an active role

themselves in the framing and implementation of development policies and projects and then reflected on these experiences (Apthorpe and Gasper 1996; Green 2000; Mosse 1994). As we have seen, within a practice approach (Hajer and Wagenaar 2003; Nuijten 2003) policy is understood not as the outcome of a rational, linear process but as 'embedded practices' that are directed by both national and international politics and by negotiations and networks that cross-cut formal institutional boundaries (Rhodes 2000; Yanow 1996). An organisation is seen not as a system or a machine, but as the precarious outcome of actors' interactions, ideas and strategies (Law 1994; Yanow 1996). Our focus is on how organisational realities are constructed, sustained and changed through processes of interaction and enactment (Dawson 2003; Reed, 1992, 2001). Organisational changes are shaped by ideological as well as political forces and the practices of policy formulation are driven less by rational and analytical thinking than by the need for institutional and personal survival. As Hajer and Wagenaar point out, a focus on practice roots interpretive analysis within the concrete objects, experiences and constraints of the world around us (2003: 20).

A vital ingredient of policy analysis is the tracing of interactions and linkages between different organisational sites and levels (Quarles van Ufford 1988: 13). It is necessary to study a variety of arenas where struggles and negotiations around development policies take place, focusing in particular on the 'connections between different organisational and everyday worlds, even where actors in different sites do not know each other or share a moral universe' (Shore and Wright 1997: 14). Following de Ruijter's approach (2000) we therefore pay attention in this chapter to the actors who are involved, the space in which the actions take place, the structure of the negotiations, the different positions of actors and spectators, the division of roles and the techniques that are used. We argue that interdependence, competition and uncertainty about the outcome of the process characterise the interactions, negotiations and struggles of policy making. Policy, then, is to an important extent the unpredictable outcome of embedded practices in multiple arenas. The focus within this practice framework is on the ways in which relations between actors, institutions and discourses are created across time and space in different arenas. We will clarify and demonstrate this perspective through an analysis of policy making at the Dutch Ministry of Development Cooperation.

THE NEW AID STRATEGIES

Since 1990, the concepts of 'good governance' and 'ownership' have been in vogue in development, with agencies such as the World Bank and United Nations Development Programme (UNDP) using 'good governance' as a key concept in their poverty reduction frameworks. For instance in April 1992, Lewis T. Preston, former President of the World Bank, argued that 'the World Bank's increasing attention to issues of governance is an important part of our effort to promote equitable and sustainable development' (World Bank 1992). United Nations (UN) Secretary-General Kofi Annan even stated that 'good governance is perhaps the single most important factor in eradicating poverty and promoting development' (1998: 114). Governance is equally central in the international political arena – 'the genuine common interest in a new global order of co-operation today is such as to rationally motivate nations to build a system of global governance' (Stockholm Initiative 1991: 5) – as well as in Western institutions, the EU White Paper on 'European Governance' (2001) being a prime example. The Commission identified the reform of European governance as one of its four strategic objectives in early 2000, stating that 'the Union should seek to apply the principles of good governance to its global responsibilities' (2001: 5). Together with the focus on good governance, anti-poverty efforts in development cooperation focus on 'equitable partnership' and changing 'donorship' into 'ownership' (OECD 1996; World Bank 2000).

The Dutch policy document *A world of difference: new frames for development co-operation in the nineties* (Ministry of Foreign Affairs [MFA] 1990) demonstrates a shift from 'self-reliance', to 'participation' and then to 'autonomy', and indicates increasing emphasis on Third World people determining their own destiny, and making their own choices with respect to production structure, the socio-economic order and the political system. The common idea on which these concepts are based is 'giving development back to the people' (MFA 1990: 40). Hence Dutch development cooperation exemplifies these latest fashions in development aid. Yet, as we will show, although the concepts may be the same, the content and operationalisation (if any ...) of these notions can differ greatly from one minister to another. In order to understand these differences, both the institutional dynamics and the personal life histories of key actors need to be taken into account. But before reconstructing the life history of an influential Dutch minister of development cooperation, we go back in history, and to Africa.

BACK IN HISTORY ...

How can we depend upon gifts, loans and investments from foreign countries and foreign companies without endangering our independence? How can we depend upon foreign governments and companies for the major part of our development without giving to those governments and countries a great

part of our freedom to act as we please? The truth is that we cannot. (TANU
[Tanganyika Africa National Union] [Arusha Declaration] 1967: 10, 11)

At the foot of the Kilimanjaro on 5 February 1967, the party leadership
of TANU, headed by Julius Nyerere, set out the legendary Arusha
Declaration, a view on the socialist ideology of the TANU and on the
road to development for Tanganyika (Tanzania). It was stated that one
of the keys to achieve development in Tanganyika was 'self-reliance'.
The TANU policy principle of self-reliance went hand in hand with
socialism. The TANU argued that they had previously focused on
the wrong instruments for development: on money – which they
did not have – rather than on people, land, good policies and good
leadership. In order to avoid an increase in taxation, Tanganyika had
relied to a great extent on external aid. However, it was argued that
from now on foreign finance had to be rejected for two reasons. In
the first place, the country would never get all the money that would
be required for real development. Second, even if this were possible,
the nation would not want it because of the loss of its independence.
It was stated that:

Independence means self-reliance. Independence cannot be real if a nation
depends upon gifts and loans from another for its development. Even if there
was a nation, or nations, prepared to give us all the money we need for our
development, it would be improper for us to accept such assistance without
asking ourselves how this would affect our independence and our very survival
as a nation. (TANU [Arusha Declaration] 1967: 9)

In the 1970s, these ideas about self-reliance and socialist revolution
became very popular among European progressive youth, intellectuals
and Third World activists, bolstered by Western obstinacy in the
UNCTAD (United Nations Conference on Trade and Development)
consultation, which hampered the rise of a new international
economic order; by the American war in Vietnam; and by the
involvement of the USA in the military coup against the socialist
regime of Salvador Allende in Chile in 1973 (Hoebink 1988; Nekkers
and Malcontent 1999). Jan Pronk[3] was one of these people, to whom
the ideas of Julius Nyerere and the TANU clearly appealed.

THE LIFE HISTORY OF A DUTCH MINISTER: JAN PRONK

The son of a teacher at a lower technical school, Pronk had studied
economics and worked for a few years as scientific assistant to
Professor Jan Tinbergen at the Centre for Development Programming
at the Netherlands Economic University at Rotterdam. He was a
member of the Dutch labour party, the PvdA, and linked up with
its reform movement called the 'New Left', which wanted to replace
a political system based on the ruling class with a more democratic
one. On the advice of Tinbergen, Pronk stood for a safe seat in

parliament in 1971. In 1973, at the age of 33, he became Minister of Development Cooperation.

In his official budget speech, Pronk argued that the development question had arrived at an impasse and reorientation was necessary. The government policy statement for the period 1973–77 declared that the analyses and models used to approach questions of development were inadequate since they did not consider power relations between and within states (MFA 1973). New development policy would concentrate on the improvement of the position of the economically and socially weak, by bringing about true freedom of these countries (MFA 1973). Self-reliance was viewed as the key to development.

Self-reliance, however, should not be understood as a policy focused on autarky. The meaning of 'self-reliance' was that developing countries' primary base is their own strength, that they themselves research and decide which social structure they think is best for their country; and that they want to rule out the exercise of power by means of economic and political pressure from outside. From that position, it is argued, economic integration by means of trade can take place, and development aid can be used to overcome shortfalls, where self-support is not possible. (MFA 1973: 28, translated from Dutch)

Unlike TANU's idea, the Dutch policy of promoting 'self-reliance' did not mean that development aid should decrease. On the contrary, Pronk reformulated 'self-reliance' such that more intensive development cooperation was necessary in order to realise 'self-reliance' and overcome the difficulties that developing countries faced in poverty alleviation. Furthermore, Dutch policy should try to increase economic autonomy by altering the international economic structures and by adjusting aid through a conscious choice of channels for the transfer of capital and the conditions of this transfer. A policy that supported self-reliance would therefore prefer public aid without preconditions over commercial private investments; untied aid to tied aid, gifts to loans, and programme aid to project aid (MFA 1973). Thus, unlike Nyerere's view that development aid should be limited, and possibly even rejected, 'Pronk's self-reliance' – a country's freedom to chose its own political system as long as it intended to implement structural reforms that would benefit the whole population – could be combined with 'donorship'.

PRONK'S RETURN

In 1976, at the end of his four-year term in the Cabinet, Pronk returned to parliament. In 1980 he left parliament for Geneva where he became Deputy Secretary-General of UNCTAD. He returned to parliament in 1986 and in 1989 again became Minister for Development Cooperation, a position he held until 1998. As Pronk himself said in an interview, he 'didn't just stick with the ideas ... [he] had in the sixties and seventies' (Bekuis 2003: 6). He renewed development policy, both because his ideas had changed and because the world had changed (an argument that is often used by policy makers to change policy): 1990 marked the end of decolonisation and the Cold War and the start of an era of globalisation. 'When I returned as minister for development in 1989', Pronk said:

I took it on myself to renew the whole policy, which resulted in three memoranda: *A World of Difference*, a major study which appeared in 1990; *A World in Dispute*, which was followed a year later and incorporated the conflict dimension, which was becoming more manifest in the early 1990s; and *Aid in Progress*, which was smaller and a kind of implementation follow-up of the other two. Those documents presented a long-term view which I think is still valid today ... (Bekuis 2003: 5)

'Development by the people' was still the basic idea, however the narrative of 'the fall of the Berlin Wall and the collapse of the socialist system' now gave it a different significance. 'Development by the people' was now conceptualised as democratisation and participation *within* the recipient country, instead of a matter of the recipient country itself choosing its own socio-economic and political system (MFA 1990). These ideas were in line with ideas Pronk developed in one of the international arenas in which he was active.

During this period, Pronk was one of the initiators of the Stockholm Initiative, originating from four different commissions: the Independent Commission on Disarmament and Security (also known as the Palme Commission); the World Commission on Environment and Development under Brundtland; the South Commission, chaired by the former President of Tanzania Nyerere; and the Brandt Commission. These commissions all focused on interdependence and the mutual interest and solidarity of people and nations. In 1990, just after the historic changes of 1989, Brandt assembled members of his own commission, among them Jan Pronk, who was treasurer of the Brandt Commission, together with several representatives of other commissions to meet. As a result, among others, Minister Pronk was asked to form a working group that led to the Stockholm Initiative, consisting of people who held high positions in governments or international organisations all over the world. The political-ideological ideas of the Initiative were published in a booklet on governance called *Common responsibility in the 1990s: the Stockholm Initiative on global security and governance* (Stockholm Initiative 1991). It gave focus to the need for a 'new world order', a new principle based on the norms of justice and peace, democracy and development, human rights and international law. These ideas were all to be found in Dutch development policy under Pronk.

FRAMING 'GOOD GOVERNANCE'

In order to understand how policy models come into being, we need first to understand the historical context and political networks in which they were framed. Pronk's ideas were clearly related to his international connections and past experiences in other contexts – shaped and negotiated by Jan Tinbergen, the labour party, the United Nations and the Stockholm Initiative. Pronk's national policy paper, *A world of difference* (MFA 1990), falls in line with the ideas propagated by the Stockholm Initiative. It describes a changing world with blurring borders, smaller margins and greater risks. His statement that 'within policy documents of international organisations a stronger emphasis is put on the central place that the human being occupies in the development process' (MFA 1992: 75, translated from Dutch) clearly follows the United Nations view that development should be 'human development', that is development of, for and by people themselves.

Pronk had a sixth sense for politically hot issues and a strong 'leftist' ideology. Aware that 'globally good governance and human rights increasingly got more attention' (MFA 1992: 75) he introduced the 'good governance' idea in 1991. Yet he framed this development policy in what may be called a 'humanitarian-ideological way', that is, having a focus on the individual, on human rights and on participation in democratic systems. According to Pronk, good governance asks for:

A government that limits itself to those tasks that can be done best by the government, and which will be fair, effective, and sustainably achieved; that does not waste means to non-productive purposes; that focuses attention on the human being and therefore promotes human rights and the principles of the constitutional state. (MFA 1992: 75, translated from Dutch)

And Pronk continues on good governance as follows:

To some extent this is an administrative matter and an extension of public sector management, for example as a necessary part of programmes of structural adjustment to support the market economy in developing countries. But to a larger extent it is a politically much more sensitive issue, since it involves emphasis on human development, on the crucial value of the individual in a sustainable process of development. There has been a growing realization of the need for a style of government which does not reach out across the people but which instead meets their own needs, is accessible and predictable for them and which they themselves can influence. In general, governance of this kind is promoted by a political system based on the separation of powers and the democratic transition of power, by guarantees of an independent judiciary and the rule of law, and by respect for civil rights and freedoms. In addition, good governance means an absence of corruption and excessive military spending, which works to the detriment of the development process. (MFA 1993a: 21–22)

In 1996 Pronk institutionalised these ideas on 'good governance' by setting up a department called Human Rights, Good Governance and Democratisation (DMD), thereby interlinking the three concepts at a bureaucratic level. The department was staffed by policy makers from the social sciences, such as history, sociology or political science, who had to promote a strong and consistent bilateral and multilateral policy on the three themes.[4]

That same year, Pronk also introduced the 'ownership' approach in the *Explanatory memorandum of the assembly year 1995–1996*.[5] The official, rational argument here was that experience had shown that where the target groups were involved in both the planning and the implementation of projects and programmes and took active responsibility for them, effectiveness and sustainability were increased. It followed that 'ownership is the point of departure' (MFA 1996: 144). Here the needs and wishes of the recipients should receive a central place in development cooperation instead of those of the donor. These recipients were seen not so much as the governments as the poor themselves. It was argued that, although initiative should come from policy formulators and programme implementers, extra effort was needed to enable the poor to participate in preparation and implementation (MFA 1996). Again a 'humanitarian-ideological' view was propagated by Pronk.

NEW MINISTER: NEW STRATEGIES

In 1997, new elections were held and, although the second cabinet of the liberal and labour parties was formed, Pronk was not appointed Minister of Development Cooperation. Instead, Eveline Herfkens was appointed. Herfkens, daughter of a Shell director, spent part of her youth in Venezuela. She studied law in Leiden and, immediately after graduating in 1976, began working in the Ministry of Development Cooperation. With a grandfather and father who were engaged in the PvdA, she became a member of the PvdA herself (Lockhorn 1998). From 1981 until 1990 she was a Member of Parliament. She was also a member of the board of directors of the World Bank for six years (1990–96), during which time Wolfensohn became President.[6] About her relationship with Jan Pronk she said:

Of course there is a difference in style. We are just two totally different people. Jan always had visions and blueprints on how the world in and after 2000 should look like, while I focused my energy more on how the real world could be put forward half a centimetre. (Landman 1999: 48, translated from Dutch)

Since Herfkens came from the same political party as Pronk, she could not criticise her predecessor too strongly. Instead, she declared that Pronk had written many policy documents and now it was time to put them into practice. Some of the views in Pronk's documents appealed to her, so she could easily claim to continue Pronk's work, while at the same time setting her own agenda. She selected a number of priorities for her development policy, among which were 'good governance' and 'ownership'.

In her first budget speech, Herfkens put forward the view that efficiency in international aid is greatest where developing countries pursue good macro-economic policy and that therefore development cooperation will focus primarily on countries with good governance. This policy of aid selectivity was not in fact new. Pronk's document, *A world in dispute*, had stated that 'donors are justified for reasons of development policy in reducing or even completely stopping the provision of aid in cases of flagrant or systematic violation of human rights, serious reductions in democracy and protracted and excessive military expenditure' (MFA 1993b: 23, translated from Dutch). However, the policy became stricter. 'Current cooperation policy takes the effective government as point of departure: attention is focused more than ever on good governance, institutional capacity and strong coordinated action by donors' (MFA 1999a: 38, translated from Dutch). In this she followed the World Bank (1998) which, in its publication *Assessing aid: what works, what doesn't, and why?*, argued that aid could only be effective when there was 'good governance', and thus that donors should be more selective in giving aid. This change in 'good governance' policy was accompanied by a re-ordering of countries that received Dutch bilateral development cooperation. In fact, however, the argument of 'good governance' was used as a legitimisation for the (financial) cutting back and re-ordering of the list of aid-receiving countries. For example, Koch shows that the selection of countries was more inspired by historical ties than by the quality of governance in the countries (2003: 75).

'Ownership' became an even more central concept in Dutch official development policy. As stated in the *Explanatory memorandum of the assembly year 2001–2002*, 'decades of development cooperation have taught that people who take their destiny in own hands are fastest back on their feet' (MFA 2002: 35, translated from Dutch). It is said that 'Dutch aid is interpreted on the basis of the demand and the responsibility of the developing countries themselves' (2002: 35). As shown above, 'ownership' was not new, as Pronk had introduced the concept into Dutch policy in 1996. Though 'ownership' under Herfkens was equally vaguely conceptualised, it was clear that she distanced herself from the 'humanitarian-ideological' Pronkian perspective. Under her ministerial administration 'the Netherlands link up with the poverty reduction policy as formulated by the recipient government' (MFA 2002: 75–76, translated from Dutch).

With this idea she conforms with the Poverty Reduction Strategy framework developed by the World Bank and the sector-wide approach used by major donors such as DFID. It is claimed that an intense policy dialogue with developing countries is the main instrument in this approach (MFA 2002: 89).

INTERNAL FRICTIONS AND THE STRUGGLE AROUND A POLICY DOCUMENT

From the new policy statements it was clear that minister Herfkens also wanted 'good governance' to have a central role in development cooperation. Policy makers in the Department of Human Rights, Democratisation and Good Governance (DMD, established under former minister Pronk) took it upon themselves to try to turn ministerial statements into a policy paper on good governance. As one put it 'We attempt to follow the minister, but the policy framework is not always clear. We, policy makers build on casual statements by the minister, [and] the media which discuss the opinion of the minister, or documents within the organization.' But, there was another reason for DMD to write a policy paper on good governance, and this was institutional survival. The department's position depended upon its ability to capture, consolidate and control a policy agenda that had been widely dispersed by Pronk across other departments (including those responsible for administrative matters, public sector management and institutional development) under many different names and involving units scattered over the ministry and embassies. Although Minister Herfkens used the concept of 'good governance' mainly as a legitimisation for her policy, the DMD department used the policy paper to gain a position in which they could develop and control the thematic management of 'good governance'.

DMD policy makers argued that there was unclear understanding about good governance and how it could be translated into practical initiatives. As a result, early in 1998, a number of exploratory workshops were organised focusing on governmental policy, civil initiatives and the private sector, and on the lessons learned from practical experiences with good governance. Many policy makers from different divisions took part in these workshops. In addition, in the first half of 1998, ten embassies were consulted on their perception and implementation of good governance, and an inventory was made of activities undertaken.

In the summer of 1998, the first good governance policy paper was developed by DMD with cooperation from the staff of other units, the embassies and a number of external consultants. Good governance was defined as 'the transparent and accountable use of political authority and control of power to direct social developments in dialogue with the people' (MFA 1998). According to this paper, the purpose of Dutch good governance policy became the promotion of transparency, efficiency, and effectiveness of public administration, accountability of the government and promotion of dialogue between the government and the society. In other words, the 'good governance' paper described the same policy fields, in the same way as Pronk's three memoranda – *A world of difference, A world in dispute* and *Aid in progress* (as well as another on human rights).[7] Good governance was based on a 'humanitarian-ideological' vision, or, as one interviewee said, 'it was framed in a Pronkian way; it bore close resemblance to his ideological views'.

It was apparent that there were conflicts between the more 'technocratic-governmental' approach held by Minister Herfkens and the 'humanitarian-ideological' approach to good governance inspired by former minister Pronk. The public officers tried to combine both discourses to mobilise support and at the same time influence the minister's view on good governance. A number of influential people from ECDPM (European Centre for Development Policy), the World Bank and the Van Vollenhoven Institute (for Law Governance and Development) were invited to a workshop, together with a so-called 'reference group' representing almost all policy departments within the ministry. A report with clear message from this workshop was sent to the minister. First, it was argued that governance was not only about governments, rather the quality of governance is established as a balance between the demands of the people, the private sector and governmental tasks. Second, the report warned against a narrow financial, technocratic approach to good governance directed towards aid implementation, and asked for attention to the economic benefit of participation. Third, it said that the ethical dimension demands a supportive rather than a strictly normative approach. The minister, however, was difficult to influence. She commented that, although she agreed with the second point, she wanted (bilateral) good governance policy to focus on governments. With this statement she clearly distanced herself from her predecessor Pronk, and a section of her own staff.

In reaction to this, the department suggested writing a short *operational* policy paper. The minister agreed, but expressed concern that DMD had paid little attention to economic and financial aspects. A second, third and finally fourth draft was written. These versions still contained concepts such as democratisation, human rights, decentralisation, the fight against corruption, public finances, and later also the rule of law, transparency and legitimacy. After several months without a reply on the latest paper (MFA 1999b), the departmental official wrote of the urgency of the minister's approval, given both that it was a mainstay of her policy, and that the reorganisation of the whole department depended on the response. Minister Herfkens agreed to authorise the text, but did not at all accept that this policy paper would be a basis for making governance policies operational. The meeting to discuss this response never took place and the document never received official status.

THE INSTITUTIONAL FUNCTIONS OF DOCUMENT-WRITING

How can we understand this struggle between a minister and her staff over a good governance policy document? What is the significance of the documents and being involved in their drafting? For those who rate themselves among the 'real policy makers', it is important to be included in one of the many reference or working groups that are created to write policy papers. These policy makers do not want to be marginal. Not only does the writing of policy documents exert influence over the topic concerned, it also gives some power to direct other related policy issues. There are the important motives of personal survival and career progress. As was said many times at the ministry, *'those who write remain'*. Within the ministry – at headquarters and embassies and other divisions – it is considered essential to be 'visible'. Producing policy papers is a strategy among civil servants to create and maintain 'visibility', especially for those who count themselves among the real policy makers and aspire to a diplomatic career and the highest post of ambassador. The more people within the ministry who read policy papers, documents or memoranda from one's own hand, the more 'visible' one becomes. Furthermore, policy reference or participation in working groups enlarges a person's informal networks, which are also crucial for any career. When applying for a new position every three of four years, it is necessary to lobby colleagues and superiors, and, since certain jobs are in high demand, a good network is essential.

The creation of documents therefore has other functions besides content. This partly explains the fact that public officers have quite a pragmatic approach towards the models they have to work with. For example, within the Dutch ministry, some argue that the gap between theory and practice cannot be bridged, since, as one person told us:

... it is the difference between our poor attempts to capture reality in a workable model and reality itself, that is infinitely more complex, varied and so on than our most complete mathematical, sociological or organizational model.[8]

Others at the ministry stated that *'we should beware that serious discussions on visions and concepts do not knock us out of action'*. Conceptual discussions are often avoided in order not to impede action. Public officers recognise the political and bureaucratic intricacies of policy formulation, and try to achieve workable solutions in this context. Since policy makers do not define concepts precisely, it becomes difficult to comment on whether practice differs from policy statements. Vague and under-defined concepts such as 'ownership' or 'good governance' cannot easily be criticised. Under Minister Herfkens, 'good governance' and 'ownership' became central in development policy. However, in comparison with Minister Pronk's rule, these concepts were more vaguely defined and operationalised. One reason for this was the disagreements which took place between the minister and her officers (Gastel 2001).

A NEW MINISTER: PARTNERSHIP!

Recently, the Ministry of Development Cooperation has fallen into the hands of a Christian Democrat, van Ardenne. She comes from a Catholic family and studied to be a pharmaceutical assistant. She was a member of the party board of the Christian Democrats from 1988 to 1992, and a Member of Parliament from 1994 to 2002, immediately prior to becoming minister. In a number of her introductory speeches for the ministry and her officers, she stressed that she would follow her party's line. As she put it at the ambassadors' conference on 20 January 2003, 'As a Christian Democrat, I believe that in development policy civil society should be central. Development cooperation is not only with governments.' With this statement, she clearly distanced herself from Herfkens, who had focused mainly on governments. Furthermore, under van Ardenne's administration, 'partnership' had now replaced 'ownership' as a central concept. But more important than policy content was the profile of the new minister. Although she claimed in the policy paper the idea of 'mutual interests, mutual responsibilities', and argued that 'essentially, partnership is an attitude, a working method and a means' (MFA 2003a: 8), the key to her policies could also be found in the image or the 'public face' of the minister herself. As the Department for Public Relations stated in an (internal) document on communication strategy:

In communication it is not only of importance to make choices on contents, but in combination with this also to steer a profile that is to be built by the minister: her personal image in Dutch society. Because, whether we like it or not, image precedes policy ... (MFA 2003b: 4)

The replacement of ownership by partnership was one of the instruments to create a new profile for the minister. So, van Ardenne stated in a letter to parliament that 'partnership' is the newest policy theme: 'development cooperation requires intensive cooperation between people, organisations, and countries: partnership. Development cooperation is therefore a multi-sided responsibility:

from government to government and from society to society.' Now
let us have a closer look at the contents of this 'partnership' policy
since the claim is that 'shape and content go together ... otherwise
the packing will be an empty shell'.[9]

The view expressed in the main policy document of van Ardenne,
with the promising title *Mutual interests, mutual responsibilities?* (MFA
2003a) is telling in this respect. Partnerships are formulated as a
situation in which 'two or more parties combine their knowledge,
skills and resources to achieve a common goal' and in which the
added value that is generated is used to work towards poverty
reduction (MFA 2003a: 8). What is new here is that the partners are
not necessarily donor and recipient, but that partners have a common
goal and the emphasis on added value. The precise definition of what
does or does not constitute a partnership is largely to be defined by
the ministry. In the minister's view, the ideal partnership is based on
three elements: government, private sector and civil organisations.
Everyone has to take responsibility. So, the notion of partnership has
been opened up and can creatively be given a range of meanings by
the Dutch ministry, according to circumstances.

CONCLUSION: AID POLICIES AND LONG-STANDING
CONNECTIONS OVER TIME AND PLACE

We have used a practice approach for the analysis of policy concepts
in development. In order to understand how the notions of 'good
governance' and 'ownership' were framed in the Dutch context, we
reconstructed aspects of the life history of Jan Pronk, for many years
Minister of Development Cooperation in the Netherlands. Besides
clearly showing how Pronk's personal career influenced the shaping
of the development policy agenda of the Netherlands, this personal
history also brought to light the influence of some key actors from
the past. Although past figures are no longer explicitly mentioned,
some of them directly guided the agenda-setting in development. In
the case of Jan Pronk, it was Julius Nyerere who made a significant
impact in the 1970s, with his socialist plans for Tanzania and his
stress on the self-reliance of receiving countries. When Pronk became
Minister of Development Cooperation for the first time in 1973, his
policy statements breathed the spirit of Nyerere's visions.

In addition to showing the importance of personal networks
and experiences in development agenda-setting, this analysis also
reveals how good governance and ownership policies, which are often
presented as new agendas, in fact possess long histories. The struggle
for democracy, independence, freedom to act, self-reliance, are not so
different from the agendas that are now presented under the labels

'good governance' and 'ownership'. The difficulties involved with each of these themes are not so different either. In fact, the central dilemma involved in the ownership agenda today was already well formulated by Julius Nyerere in 1967, when he asked: 'How can we depend upon gifts, loans and investments from foreign countries and foreign companies without endangering our independence?' (TANU [Arusha Declaration] 1967). Policy ideas in development are rarely new, but tend to be simply re-presented as part of an ongoing 'reinvention of the wheel'. As part of this process, policy makers hijack concepts and give them new meanings in the context of their particular policy direction. Concepts such as self-reliance, ownership and good governance, serve these purposes well because they have positive connotations and can be interpreted in multiple ways (Nuijten et al. 2004). Since one of the most important objectives of policy formulation is the mobilisation of political support, this process makes perfect sense.

Our study of the Dutch Ministry of Development Cooperation showed that policy formulation is not so much about problem solving as it is about personal or organisational agendas, institutional survival and political interests. This becomes clearer with each change of minister, each of whom wants to assert his or her position by breaking away from the policy agenda of their predecessor. If policy was not seen to change, it could be argued that there was no need for a new minister in the first place. So, new policy does not necessarily articulate a different view but a strategy for political profile and survival. Personal sympathies and antipathies between succeeding ministers weaken or strengthen this general tendency.

Public officers often deliberately keep policy concepts vague since they have to be negotiated and discussed with other offices at different sites and levels. They fear that more precise definitions and discussions about operationalisation will cause differences of opinion and hamper the policy process. It is much easier to agree on vague normative concepts. This again arises from the fact that policies tend to have less an instrumental function of problem solving, and more a political-symbolic function of mobilising people and institutions around a new agenda. The use of vague, non-controversial metaphors and concepts can be a potent strategy to mobilise people (Nuijten et al. 2004; Smircich and Morgan 1982; Yanow 1996). When concepts are defined in detail, much more disagreement is likely to arise.

Policy making at the Dutch Ministry of Development Cooperation cannot therefore be reduced to a technical, linear top-down operation, or to a process pre-determined by dominant forces. Many elements across time and place influence policy making. A practice approach, which studies the historical linkages between situated actors and events from an interpretive ethnographic perspective, can reveal the central factors in the policy process.

NOTES

1. We will refer in this article to the Ministry of Development Cooperation, although the organisation structure is more complicated: development cooperation is one of the tasks of the Ministry of Foreign Affairs. The Minister of Development Cooperation is one of the three ministers of this ministry. For that reason, development cooperation falls under the organisational regime of the Ministry of Foreign Affairs.
2. Jilles van Gastel worked at the Ministry of Development Cooperation from August 2002 to July 2004.
3. Pronk was Minister of Development Cooperation from 1973 to 1977, and from 1989 until 1998.
4. Remarkably, although project support for 'good governance' was the task of this department (DMD), responsibility for thematic policy work lay jointly with DMD and the Department for Social and Institutional development (DSI). To demarcate the activities related to 'good governance', DMD dealt with activities that concerned the wider protection of human rights by the government, while DSI focused on activities concerning the democratisation of public administration structures within recipient countries (with the exception of electoral support, which was a DMD task) (Plan of formation, Ministry of Foreign Affairs 1996). In 1999 the Human Rights, Good Governance and Democratisation Department and the Crisis and Humanitarian Aid Department (DCH) merged into the Human Rights, Good Governance and Peace Building Department (DMV). The aim was to increase policy coherence between conflict prevention, peace building, crisis situations and good governance. Democratisation as a distinct policy issue disappeared, and good governance and peace building were brought together in one division.
5. This budget was handed to the Queen on 19 September 1995, when Pronk was still minister.
6. Wolfensohn started as World Bank president on 1 June 1995. He introduced the Country Development Framework and the Poverty Reduction Strategy, and ownership as a central concept in these frameworks.
7. Third Continuing Policy Paper Human Rights.
8. These quotes are based on an internal discussion on results-based management in one of the regular meetings of the project team on Planning, Monitoring and Evaluation at DGIS (Directorate-General for International Cooperation, where Jilles van Gastel was working) in February 2003.
9. The quotes in this paragraph are from van Ardenne's letter to parliament, 'Ontwikkelingssamenwerking in meerjarig perspectief' [Development cooperation in long-term perspective] (17 June 2003).

REFERENCES

Annan, K. (1998) *Cooperating for development: Annual report of the Secretary-General on the work of the organization* (A/53/1) (New York: United Nations).

Apthorpe, R. and D. Gasper (1996) *Arguing development policy: frames and discourses* (London: Frank Cass).

Arce, A. (1993) *Negotiating development: entanglements of bureaucrats and rural producers in Western Mexico*. Wageningen Studies in Sociology (Wageningen: PUDOC).

Bekuis, R. (2003) Interview with Jan Pronk. *Development Issues* 5(1): 4–6.

Dawson, P. (2003) *Understanding organizational change: the contemporary experience of people at work* (London: Sage).

Duffield, M. (2001) *Global governance and the new wars: the merging of development and security* (London: Zed Press).

Escobar, A. (1991) Anthropology and the development encounter: the making and marketing of development anthropology. *American Ethnologist* 18(4): 16–40.

Escobar, A. (1995) *Encountering development: the making and unmaking of the Third World* (Princeton, NJ: Princeton University Press).

European Union (2001) *European governance, a white paper*. Brussels, 25.7.2001 COM (2001) 428 final (Brussels: European Union).

Ferguson, J. (1990) *The anti-politics machine: development, depoliticization, and bureaucratic power in Lesotho* (Cambridge and New York: Cambridge University Press).

Gastel, J. van (2001) Governing good governance: an analysis of the policy process from sociological and anthropological perspective. Unpublished MSc thesis, Wageningen.

Green, M. (2000) Participatory development and the appropriation of agency in southern Tanzania. *Critique of Anthropology* 20(1): 67–89.

Hajer, M. (2003) Policy without polity? Policy analysis and the institutional void. *Policy Sciences* 36(2): 175–95.

Hajer, M. and H. Wagenaar (2003) *Deliberative policy analysis: understanding governance in the network society* (Cambridge: Cambridge University Press).

Hoebink, P.R.J. (1988) *Geven is nemen: De Nederlandse ontwikkelingshulp aan Tanzania en Sri Lanka* [To give is to take: Dutch development aid to Tanzania] (Nijmegen: Stichting Derde Wereld Publikaties)

Koch, D. (2003) Herfkens'selectiviteitsbeleid onder de loep: een beoordeling en voorstellen te verbetering [A study of Herfkens' selection policy: an evaluation and proposal for improvement]. *Internationale Spectator* 57(2).

Landman, J. (1999) Eveline Herfkens: Het idealisme van een korte termijnspeler. *Bijeen* 32(1): 47–51.

Law, J. (1994) *Organizing modernity* (Oxford: Blackwell).

Lockhorn, E. (1998) 'Ik ben nooit een timide meisje geweest': De dadendrang van minister Eveline Herfkens ['I've never been a timid girl': the action drive of Minister Eveline Herfkens]. *Opzij* December: 32–7.

Long, N. (2001) *Development sociology: actor perspectives* (London: Routledge).

Maxwell, S. (2003) Heaven or hubris: reflections on the new 'new poverty agenda'. *Development Policy Review* 21(1): 5–25.

Ministry of Foreign Affairs (1973) *Rijksbegroting voor het dienstjaar 1974; Hoofdstuk V- Buitenlandse Zaken*. Memorie van Toelichting [Explanatory memorandum of the assembly year 1974, National Budget Foreign Affairs] (The Hague: Ministry of Foreign Affairs).

Ministry of Foreign Affairs (1990) *A world of difference: a new framework for development cooperation in the 1990s*. (The Hague: SDU Publishers).

Ministry of Foreign Affairs (1992) *Explanatory memorandum of the assembly year 1991–92, National Budget Foreign Affairs 1992* (The Hague: Ministry of Foreign Affairs).

Ministry of Foreign Affairs (1993a) *Explanatory memorandum of the assembly year 1992–93, National Budget Foreign Affairs 1993* (The Hague: Ministry of Foreign Affairs).

Ministry of Foreign Affairs (1993b) *A world in dispute* (The Hague: SDU Publishers).

Ministry of Foreign Affairs (1995) *Aid in progress: development cooperation and the review of Dutch foreign policy* (The Hague: SDU Publishers).

Ministry of Foreign Affairs (1996) Plan of formation. Internal document (The Hague: Ministry of Foreign Affairs).

Ministry of Foreign Affairs (1998) Internal policy paper on good governance (The Hague: Ministry of Foreign Affairs).

Ministry of Foreign Affairs (1999a) *Explanatory memorandum of the assembly year 1998–99, National Budget Foreign Affairs 1999* (The Hague: Ministry of Foreign Affairs).

Ministry of Foreign Affairs (1999b) Promotie van goed bestuur in het Nederland buitenlands beleid [The promotion of good governance in Dutch foreign policy]. Internal document (The Hague: Ministry of Foreign Affairs, Good Governance and Peace Building).

Ministry of Foreign Affairs (2002) *Explanatory memorandum of the assembly year 2001–2002. National Budget Foreign Affairs 2002* (The Hague: Ministry of Foreign Affairs).

Ministry of Foreign Affairs (2003a) *Mutual interests, mutual responsibilities: Dutch development cooperation en route to 2015* (The Hague: Ministry of Foreign Affairs).

Ministry of Foreign Affairs (2003b) Communication strategy 2004–07. Internal document (The Hague: Ministry of Foreign Affairs).

Morgan, G. (1997) *Images of organization* (Thousand Oaks, CA: Sage).

Mosse, D. (1994) Authority, gender and knowledge: theoretical reflections on the practice of participatory rural appraisal. *Development and Change* 25(3): 497–526.

Mosse, D. (2004) Is good policy unimplementable? Reflections on the ethnography of aid policy and practice. *Development and Change* 35(4): 639–71.

Nekkers, J.A. and P.A.M. Malcontent (1999). Do something and don't look back. In J.A. Nekkers and P.A.M. Malcontent (eds) *Fifty years of Dutch development cooperation 1949–1999* (The Hague: SDU Publishers).

Nuijten, M. (2003) *Power, community and the state: the political anthropology of organisation in Mexico* (London: Pluto Press).

Nuijten, M., G. Anders, J. van Gastel, G. van der Haar, C. van Nijnatten and J. Warner (2004) Governance in action: some theoretical and practical reflections on a key concept. In D. Kalb, W. Pansters and H. Siebers (eds) *Globalization and development: themes and concepts in current research*, pp. 103–30 (Dordrecht, Boston and London: Kluwer Academic Publishers).

OECD (Organization for Economic Cooperation and Development) (1996) *Shaping the 21st century: the contribution of development co-operation* (Paris: OECD).

Quarles van Ufford, P. (1988) The hidden crisis in development: development bureaucracies in between intentions and outcomes. In P. Quarles van

Ufford, D. Kruijt and T. Downing (eds) *The hidden crisis in development: development bureaucracies*, pp. 9–38 (Amsterdam and Tokyo: Free University Press and United Nations University).

Quarles van Ufford, P. (1999) The organisation of development as an illness: about the metastasis of good intentions. In J.R. Campbell and A. Rew (eds) *Identity and affect: experiences of identity in a globalising world*, pp. 275–93 (London: Pluto Press).

Reed, M. (1992) *The sociology of organizations: themes, perspectives and prospects* (New York: Harvester Wheatsheaf).

Reed, M. (2001) Organisation, trust and control: a realist analysis. *Organisation Studies* 22(2): 201–28.

Rhodes, R. (2000) Governance and public administration. In J. Pierre (ed.) *Debating governance: authority, steering and democracy* (Oxford: Oxford University Press).

Ruijter, A. de (2000) De multiculturele arena: rede [The multicultural arena: inaugural lecture], Katholieke Universiteit Brabant, Faculteit Sociale Wetenschappen.

Shore, C. and S. Wright (eds) (1997) *Anthropology of policy: critical perspectives on governance and power* (London: Routledge).

Smircich, L. and G. Morgan (1982) Leadership: the management of meaning. *Journal of Applied Behavioral Science* 18(3): 257–73.

Stockholm Initiative (1991) *Common responsibility in the 1990s: the Stockholm Initiative on global security and governance* (Stockholm: Prime Minister's Office).

TANU (Tanganyika African National Union) (1967) The Arusha Declaration and TANU's policy on socialism and self-reliance, paper written for TANU by Julius Nyerere (Dar es Salaam, Tanzania: TANU).

Urban, M.E. (1982) *The ideology of administration: American and Soviet cases* (Albany, NY: State University of New York Press).

Vries, P. de (1997) *Unruly clients: a study of how bureaucrats try and fail to transform gatekeepers, communists and preachers into ideal beneficiaries* (Amsterdam: CEDLA).

World Bank (1992) *Governance and development* (Washington, DC: World Bank).

World Bank (1998) *Assessing aid: what works, what doesn't, and why?* (New York: Oxford University Press).

World Bank (2000) Poverty reduction strategy papers: internal guidance note, 21 January (Washington, DC: World Bank Group, operations Policy and Strategy).

Yanow, D. (1996) *How does a policy mean? Interpreting policy and organizational actions* (Washington, DC: Georgetown University Press).

Internet

www.parlement.com
http://activepstbus51.nl/nar.asp?rsc=VRM_Pronk.htm 07–18–03

5 WHOSE AID? THE CASE OF THE BOLIVIAN ELECTIONS PROJECT

Rosalind Eyben with Rosario León

> Rather than being merely ornamental, a dab of local colour, protagonists' narratives about their own conduct merit serious attention as forms of social analysis. (Rosaldo 1993: 143)

It has been suggested that the anthropology of development is shifting from critical understanding to moral reflection, with development conceived 'as daily rout and relationships that cope with disjunctures' (Quarles van Ufford et al. 2003: 19). Accompanying this shift is a corresponding interest in development as 'power', not so much in the Foucauldian sense, already extensively explored in the 1990s, but rather in terms of actual relationships between differently positioned development actors (Groves and Hinton 2004; Pasteur and Scott-Villiers 2004). This chapter is based on one such relationship, between two middle-aged women differently positioned in the aid nexus. I was British and head of the Bolivian country office of the Department for International Development (DFID) and Rosario was Bolivian, an academic researcher and consultant sociologist for aid agencies.[1]

Whose aid? Through multiple encounters and struggles over roles and responsibilities, staff working for donor and recipient governments constantly reformulate and reinterpret their answers to this question. Rosario and I were protagonists in one such struggle over a project to support the 2002 national elections in Bolivia. This experience led to our understanding aid as a gift, problematic and ambiguous in meaning, in which relations of power are imbued with moral purpose.

The material for our narrative is not based on formal, designed-in-advance research but on our lived experience – an experience that initiated our subsequent friendship. Each took rough notes and has copies of some official documents. Nevertheless, our principal source is a recollection of events through structured conversations in July 2003 and based on principles of second-person inquiry (Reason and Bradbury 2001). This encouraged a further process of first-person inquiry, individually and separately examining our actions, ideas, values and emotions at that time, seeking to position ourselves as subjects of our own analysis.

It is difficult enough to describe and explain ourselves. How much harder it is to represent third persons, those who were not consulted about our writing of this story and who, if asked, might provide a very different analysis of their and our roles. We hope that, should they read what follows, they will be provoked to make their own analysis of the dilemmas of aid, recognising that our choices are shaped not only by bureaucratic policy requirements but by our own history, values and social relationships.

This chapter is in two voices. Mine is the main one with a complementary perspective and reflection from Rosario, written in Spanish and translated by me. (Rosario's voice is represented in italics.) In the first section, we reflect on our own positionality at the time of our story and then describe our role as protagonists in a project we helped design. We conclude by considering the possibilities and quandaries in the aid relationship that this story reveals to us.

SETTING THE SCENE

Introducing ourselves

In October 2001, the DFID office in Bolivia commissioned an external review of its performance. It found that DFID was strong in analytical capacity and willingness to engage in difficult or emerging issues, but that some partners believed it sometimes misjudged the timing and pace of its actions: 'pushing too hard and insensitive to the political moment' (DFID 2002: 8). It was a crucial moment in the design of a project to support the right of socially excluded populations to vote in the June 2002 national elections. The reviewers' oblique comments reflect the first, but not the last moment of crisis.

That October, I was coming towards the end of my second year in Bolivia, after 13 years in DFID's London headquarters leading a group advising on the societal dimensions of development (Eyben 2003b). The 1990s had appeared very positive for someone like me, with the recognition of rights-based approaches and the international decision to define poverty reduction as the principal purpose of aid. Nevertheless, by the end of the decade I was bored. It seemed time to return to living in the 'developing world'. I chose Bolivia because it was one of the pilot Poverty Reduction Strategy countries and because Latin America would be a new experience. With a relatively small budget to manage, an intriguing aspect of my future work was whether relationship-building would be more significant for effective aid than the transfer of resources. Yet, my Spanish was sufficiently poor to be unable to appreciate many of the subtleties in the web of relationships of which I was to become part.

I had been considering other options, including two that would have promoted me to a more senior and influential position in the international aid system. My ultimate decision to turn my back on relative power and status may have led me to a sense of irresponsibility and a desire for fun – possibly a preparedness not to behave in a normal bureaucratic manner wearing a mask of impersonal discretion. However, my interest in personal power did not disappear. I enjoyed making a difference. Very rapidly after my arrival, I identified the opportunity for exerting influence offered by the management of the relatively small DFID programme in Bolivia.

For eleven years I, Rosario, had coordinated the Bolivian component of the Forests Trees and People Programme (FTPP) of the Food and Agricultural Organisation (FAO), a global programme supported by nine international donors. FTTP's role was to create links between local populations and state institutions to support the realisation of people's rights to manage their natural resources.

In one sense I was also a donor because I managed funds and could decide with whom the programme would work. I could influence and sometimes define the agenda. Nevertheless, within my managerial role and because of FTTP's underlying philosophy, this experience had encouraged me to develop a participatory approach of facilitation and respectful relationships in the construction of development projects.

I experienced also the pain of introducing innovation and of not following established procedures. I discovered in this programme the tension between the potential for introducing change and the tendency for nothing to change should existing privileges be put at risk.

These tensions translated into pressure from some of our donors and, for the first time, I witnessed the 'clothing of power' when we sat at the negotiating table in Rome with powerful donors, who, while recognising the success of the programme and its innovatory character, failed to understand the participatory management model in which funds went straight from FAO to civil society organisations, bypassing the usual procedural relations between an international agency and the state.

When FTTP came to an end in 2001 I returned to CERES (Centro de Estudios de la Realidad Económica y Social), of which I had been a member since it was founded in 1981. CERES is committed to the pursuit of social justice and, like any institute doing social research in Bolivia, is entirely dependent on foreign financing for its work, hoping to persuade donors to support programmes that the researchers believe are important.

THE AID CONTEXT

In 2000, DFID expanded its office with Bolivian and UK-based specialists; we also hired Bolivian consultants for specific tasks. In this respect our office was similar to those of most official aid agencies in La Paz. Because expatriate staff stay in the country for a short time, an agency's capacity to influence policy depends considerably on the knowledge and political connections of its Bolivian staff and consultants. Some, such as Rosario, are from academia, but many have been in government service under a previous administration and will return there again in the future. Most are part of a white elite that has traditionally run the country. They are connected through ties of kinship and affinity. Retolaza (2004) argues that their interest in the donor presence in the country is both to enhance their present and future career opportunities, as well as to pursue their own political agendas inside and outside government. Through their social networks they fund each other, exchange information and, as the case may be, provide or propose short consultancies. 'Whatever is required to maintain the patronage and *compadrazgo*[2] system flowing: keeping the new patron happy, maintaining the *status quo*' (Retolaza 2004: 15).

We expatriates had our own social network, one that covered the world. It is a community of values and practice, knitted together in a global web of personal relationships that had a local dimension in La Paz. (Eyben 2003a) In La Paz, we lived in the same neighbourhoods, meeting socially in the evenings and picnicking at the weekend. While each had their own networks, the two elites, Bolivian and expatriate, were socially connected. We lived and shopped in the same part of town, used the same sports clubs and schools, and met at parties. The global trend towards donor coordination and recipient government ownership helped reinforce these connections and the sentiments of friendship and trust that came with them.

Bolivia was an exemplar of the new style of international aid relations, based on 'partnership' that had evolved at the turn of the century. It pioneered the Comprehensive Development Framework (CDF) for donor–recipient relations (World Bank 2003) and was among the first highly indebted poor countries to produce a Poverty Reduction Strategy Paper (PRSP) to secure debt relief.

The theme of the PRSP and the associated CDF was that the recipient government decided priorities for poverty reduction and the donors supported these. The donor-led initiatives and donor-inspired projects of the 'bad old days' would no longer be acceptable. The democratically elected government, rather than donors, should decide on public expenditure; aid would only be welcome if integrated into the public expenditure decision-making process.

The Vice-Ministry for Public Investment and External Assistance (VIPFE) coordinated foreign aid. VIPFE enthusiastically promoted the new donor rhetoric that the recipient government be 'in the driving seat'. The year 2001 had been a high point for VIPFE, when the World Bank and the International Monetary Fund (IMF) endorsed the PRSP. I had played a significant role in the PRSP process. Drawing on my headquarters experience of international negotiations, I took the lead in convening the bilateral aid agencies in Bolivia to secure a PRSP that reflected our concerns (Eyben 2004).

One of these concerns, close to my heart, was social exclusion, of which one aspect related to the fact that not all Bolivians possessed identity cards, which prevented them voting in the 2002 elections. While pondering whether DFID could do anything about this, Rosario, someone whom I knew by repute but had never met, came to see me. It was a moment of political crisis, when one of the recurrent *campesino* (peasant) protests was threatening to blockade La Paz. In my journal I noted that Rosario mentioned how these events were an expression of problems of citizenship.

POLITICAL DISENCHANTMENT

My return to CERES occurred at a time when civil society, particularly NGOs, was exploring how to overcome the political disenchantment increasingly evident in Bolivian society. Bolivian NGOs were in crisis. Their historical position as organisations of intellectuals at the service of social justice, democracy, social change and the development of knowledge, had been reduced, in the majority of cases, to the role of providers of services and implementers of policy on behalf of the state bureaucracy and funded by international development agencies.

*

The shortage of resources for NGOs to fight against poverty and nurture democracy confirmed our feelings of impotence, dependency, domination and exclusion when we saw how the donors created a closed circle of negotiations with the bureaucratic and technocratic elites, with very few spaces opened for civil society. Through Bolivia's Comprehensive Development Framework, codes of interaction and conditions of accessibility to external financing were created that were little known or understood by those of us outside that circle.

The NGOs had neither resources nor political means to influence the shaping of the new configuration between government and development aid. Rather, we were recruited as consultants to produce knowledge for validating the policy proposals of the bureaucracy. This created feelings of frustration and inspired actions to call attention to and reject the new order established in donor–recipient relations, in which donors appeared to be playing a too-powerful role in shaping and implementing policy. The disillusion, the feelings of impotence and disenchantment with the forms of doing politics, had also influenced many others in Bolivian society.

Bolivia was preparing for its elections with everything that this implies in Bolivia. As usual, different interest groups were mobilised by political parties. However, this time something could be felt in the air and heard on the streets of La Paz and other cities of the country. This was the distrust of the political electoral game, the distrust of the political class, the citizens' indifference to what an electoral process signified. People on the streets would say:

'Nothing changes, it's the same "chola" with a different skirt.'[3]

'It's the same ones as always, with the same tricks.'

'Once more the politicians will use us for their own ends.'

The country had reached dangerous levels of disenchantment with the electoral process. This, combined with the economic crisis, had created a situation of dangerous political destabilisation.

The almost perfect democratic machinery, operated by elitist, clientelist and patrimonial political habits, was challenged once again, after many years, by the emergence of social struggles, social mobilisations, particularly inspired by the demand for political, economic and cultural rights. This all signalled the necessity to recognise the rights of permanently excluded populations; of listening to the voices of the invisible; of broadening the system of political representation; of understanding the causes of absence and abstention from the electoral system, which went beyond an analysis of electoral preferences.

In this context, searching for a way out of the crisis, as well as allies to develop a different approach, I visited various government offices and donor agencies without securing any positive response. My years with the FAO had left me outside the circle of known consultants. During that time I had worked with many grassroots organisations throughout the whole country, but when the time came to negotiate support for a more inclusive election process, it appeared as if I did not know anyone in the country. The development agencies and the manner of negotiating had changed much in the last few years and donors already had their known and trusted 'clients' to whom they listened and gave funds. Eventually I came to the DFID office and, after considerable insistence, the secretary of the head of the DFID office gave me an appointment with Rosalind in July, three months after my original request.

THE DONOR PERSPECTIVE

The extent to which Bolivia had achieved substantive democracy remained questionable (Whitehead 2001). Bolivia's mainstream political parties had organisational structures reaching down to the local level to 'mobilise' votes, including through the use of patronage (Lazar 2004). Rather than the electoral process, however, demonstrations, road blockades, hunger strikes and other forms of direct action appeared to be more effective in gaining concessions and policy change. By 2001, the leaders of the strikes and demonstrations were gaining greater popularity and their recently established marginalised ('asystemic') political parties could be seen as a potential threat to the cosy parliamentary arrangements of the politicians whom the staff of VIPFE served.

Although 'exclusion' was mentioned in the PRSP to satisfy the requirements of the donors, the policy commitment was weak. That DFID had gained a reputation for being interested in exclusion did not necessarily mean, for VIPFE, that DFID should support activities to which VIPFE did not accord priority. Here lay the seeds of future disagreements.

In theory, this new 'partnership' approach did not preclude donors from funding NGOs and other organisations in civil society. They were officially included in the CDF matrix as drawn up in Washington by the World Bank. In practice, this issue had not been resolved in Bolivia. Rather, an unwritten and un-discussed *modus vivendi* had been established, based on the fiction that bilateral donors provided government-to-government aid whereas private citizens, through their countries' NGOs, supported civil society in aid-recipient countries. In fact, most of these northern NGOs were heavily reliant on funding from their governments.

I saw this *modus vivendi* as not only hypocritical but injurious. The Bolivian PRSP had noted that poverty reduction could not be achieved without joined-up efforts by state and society. Yet donors themselves were maintaining two streams of funding relations that could only widen the breach between state and society. Thus, I proposed that DFID's strategy in Bolivia would be to support state and society actors achieve an increased mutual comprehension of their respective roles and responsibilities in achieving poverty reduction (DFID 2002: 9). Through a single budget, DFID would openly fund both government and civil society programmes. Support to next year's elections would be a case in point.

DESIGNING THE ELECTION PROJECT: THE CONSULTANT'S PERSPECTIVE

In my previous conversations with staff in other donor agencies I had always left, disappointed that the theme of exclusion was not on their policy influencing agenda. However, this time there might be more of a chance. I decided to speak directly and forcefully in DFID about my concerns. I told Rosalind I was profoundly disturbed by the invisibility of many people in

Bolivia, that they did not even have the right to be part of – and actually were not part of their own country. In the eyes of the state, they did not exist. They were the people who could not participate in the election and thus change the way democracy played out in Bolivia.

I was surprised that, unlike at some of my other meetings with donors, Rosalind did not dismiss my concerns to establish on which side of the table sat the power. Rather, I saw an enthusiastic face and doubted my own eyesight. We talked for more than 45 minutes. After this meeting, I was invited to carry out a consultancy assignment on this issue. I felt the outcome had been positive, not only for that reason but also for the way in which the relationship was developing.

So, I had joined the circle of the favoured 'few' who received contracts from donor agencies. To justify this to myself I felt I had to do something that would be really useful for the 'many'.

THE ELECTIONS PROJECT

The previous year DFID had designed an elections project in Peru, funding NGOs to provide voters' education. I envisaged something similar in Bolivia. However, the project would have to be designed differently. The Peruvian government had been happy for DFID to select the NGOs it wanted to support, and to fund and manage its own project. Such an approach in Bolivia would have appeared very strange and unwelcome. Interested civil society organisations would need to come together on their own initiative and to approach donors. They had to 'own' the process. How could we get them to own something that they did not know could exist? Organising a seminar might stimulate an interest and be the first step to designing a project.

We also had to make sure there was sufficient money. DFID alone did not have enough. Furthermore, we had to work within the principles of donor coordination. A project funded solely by DFID would contravene evolving good practice. It would also over-expose us in what might prove a risky enterprise with political ramifications. But before approaching other donors, we needed to know whom to invite to the seminar.

*

DFID contracted me to map the civil society networks that were working on issues of exclusion and voice. I noted the frustration and feeling of impotence of many of those I interviewed in relation to their current difficulties in tackling exclusion, and their enthusiasm for finding new ways to do so. The theme of identity cards would immediately come up.

Another factor constantly mentioned was donors' behaviour. Donors supported parallel and diverse activities, making NGOs compete for funds. Grassroots organisations also commented on the state's abandonment of the communities where they lived and worked, joking: 'Now during election season, gifts will start coming into the rural areas so that the poor people will vote for one or the other party.' Then they quickly added that the time had come for people to vote for themselves, rather than for the politicians.

I discovered more than 50 Bolivian civil society organisations that had an interest and experience in education on citizens' rights and obligations. I found that the work of these organisations was diminished through a lack of coordination of resources. At the same time, I found a keen interest among a number of these organisations to join their efforts into a more strategic approach. My meeting with these organisations, and starting to bring them together to work collectively, gave me back my sense of power.

ENLISTING SUPPORT IN LA PAZ

I asked other donors whether, in principle, they would like to join a basket fund[4] for a civil society project for the elections. Two agreed – the Dutch, with whom the DFID office had been working very closely on a number of shared activities, and the Swedes, who were interested in social exclusion. We were still unclear about our precise objectives. Thus, we met in August to draft a project document and logical framework to establish some common agreement. We also agreed the amount of money we would put in the basket. Ironically, for a project that was meant to be owned by an as-yet-unaware civil society, we had apparently already firmly set the parameters. Our draft project document accompanied the invitation to the civil society organisations – identified through Rosario's mapping exercise – to participate in a seminar in October.

It was difficult to draft the invitation letter. I stressed the exchange of experiences with Peru; I indicated that we had already received some indications from civil society that they would like donor funding to support greater citizen participation in the elections; and I stressed that, despite our having drafted a project document, the parameters of the project had not been set. To secure greater legitimacy I noted that the Electoral Commission and the Ombudswoman's office (whom I had consulted) would be participating in the seminar. With some nervousness, I copied the letter to VIPFE on the grounds of transparency concerning our intentions to fund civil society, but *not* asking permission to do so.

VIPFE reacted more angrily than any of us had anticipated. The Vice-Minister wrote a very strong letter accusing all three donor agencies, but particularly DFID, who was in the lead in the matter, of breaking the principles of the Comprehensive Development Framework and designing a 'donor-led' project. It was the responsibility of the government, said the letter, as to how donor money should be spent, and we should not have made this decision to go ahead without VIPFE's agreement. The usual courteous and high-flown language of official correspondence between government and official donor had disappeared.

Reading that letter was one of the nastiest moments in a long professional career. My colleagues in the DFID office were anxious that we might be getting into serious trouble. Was this the start of a diplomatic incident? With fear and trepidation, I exerted my personal authority, based on my previous leadership role in the PRSP process, to convince my Swedish and Dutch colleagues that we should continue with our plans for the seminar.

By unfortunate coincidence, the seminar was to be held the day after the independent team reviewing DFID's country strategy had an appointment with VIPFE, who used the seminar as an illustration of DFID's bad behaviour:

The seminar is unacceptable. We were invited to go but will not do so. The election theme is very important to us but they should have organised it differently, in coordination with the government.

DFID has a donor-driven approach as they don't have confidence in their counterpart [the government] – this is the basis of a partnership, of any relationship. (Ladbury et al. 2002: 19)

ESTABLISHING A CIVIL SOCIETY CONSORTIUM

I do not remember clearly Rosalind's problems with VIPFE. Perhaps at the time I was unaware. On the other hand, I did notice the insecurity felt by the other donors and the challenge of agreeing to innovative methods.

Eighteen of the civil society organisations participating at the seminar decided to form a consortium that was then to take on a life of its own. I was asked to act as facilitator, funded by DFID. Aware of the time pressure, the Consortium agreed to meet again one month later and to use that meeting for developing a programme of work that the donors could fund.

*

At that next meeting, Rosario encouraged them not to proceed with my original idea of a 'challenge fund' model, where they would have had to compete against each other, but to design an overall programme with members responsible for implementation in their respective localities. Thus, they developed a mode of working based on principles of solidarity rather than on the donor-favoured. market-based model. By December, the Consortium and the donors had agreed a project whereby a committee chosen by the 18 members of the Consortium would be responsible for the direction of the project, and an international non-governmental organisation (INGO) would be selected by the donors, in consultation with the Consortium, to administer the funds.

By channelling the donors' money through the INGO's office back in the capital city in the North we could maintain the fiction that this was NGO-to-NGO support and nothing to do with official aid. Tactically, it allowed VIPFE and DFID to maintain their different stance on this issue without the need for a further confrontation. At the same time, DFID, along with the Netherlands, and with VIPFE's blessing, agreed to provide some money to the Electoral Commission through the United Nations. I hoped that such support would serve as some kind of protection for the civil society consortium. Nevertheless, I now realise that VIPFE was working behind the scenes to stop the project.

CRISIS

By December, the project design had been completed. We hoped to start on schedule in early January, allowing six months for implementation before the elections at the end of June. During these final stages of negotiation a fourth bilateral donor, Denmark became interested and joined the donors, increasing the size of the financial basket.

Then, unexpectedly, in the New Year, the Netherlands and Denmark began to show real concerns. Their senior national Bolivian governance specialists identified new conditions for securing their agencies' support. These included ensuring the approval of the government, with letters of support from the vice-ministries of gender, indigenous people and popular participation, as well as from the police, the Electoral Commission and the Ombudswoman. Another condition required that the members of the Consortium demonstrate they were not representing particular political parties. Aware that time was of essence, the Consortium leaders pulled all their personal and political strings to meet these conditions.

By now it was early February. The Dutch and Danish embassies were surprised and, it seemed to us, disconcerted that all the conditions had been met – and that the imposition of these conditions had usefully resulted in a project that was less risky and had broader-based support. Abruptly the Dutch, followed by the Danes, announced their withdrawal from the project and on new grounds. Their Bolivian governance specialists had advised that the project activities would not deliver value for money – that generalised voter education through mass media would be more effective than through the project's on-the-ground activities in marginal and remote areas of the country.

We received the news with amazement, grief and anger. Rumours and allegations flew around La Paz. Accusations were made about the influence and counter-influence of *compadrazgo*. Different kinds of power and understanding were at play in a serious crisis of conflicting loyalties. The Consortium held an emergency meeting with DFID and SIDA. Civil society leaders made emotional speeches about their effort to respond to all the donor concerns. They spoke of their despair and incomprehension that the project was to be abandoned at this late stage. They asked whether SIDA and DFID were prepared to go ahead without the others. Recognising that the budget would have to be seriously cut, the consortium expressed willingness to redesign the project, provided some funding could be guaranteed.

*

For me and my companions in the Consortium it was difficult to understand how aid, destined for reducing poverty, could not be delivered in the most expeditious fashion to the people in society best equipped to use it. We sadly observed and wondered why some Bolivian aid officials were the first to put difficulties in our way. Only now, do I realise that the Consortium, a coming together of a diverse set of organisations, was not a good 'client', and that the aid negotiations in this project had led us down new paths, bypassing patrimonial control.

*

My priority now was to ensure that my colleagues in the DFID office and back in London would continue to support me. I told them that DFID could not take the political risk of being seen to fund this project when all other donors had withdrawn but that we *should* proceed provided SIDA stayed with us. After thinking about it for three tense days, the head of the SIDA office agreed the Swedes would not quit. My sense of relief was enormous.

Within a week, the project document had been signed and the Consortium had started work, with one month lost due to the delaying tactics of the two donors who dropped out. The emotional strain and the need to work together at a time of crisis produced interesting and unexpected consequences. Consortium members said that their alliance had been strengthened through adversity. They felt they now truly 'owned' the project. They also looked at DFID and SIDA in a different light, treating us in a more friendly and informal fashion. They noted, as did we, that they seemed to be better at managing and keeping together *their* consortium than the donors had been with ours. Our fallibility and internal disputes had made us more human. There was more trust among everyone who stayed the course; the crisis formed a firm basis for Rosario's and my friendship.

The rest of the donor community looked on with interest as the head of the Dutch aid section and I, formerly great allies during the PRSP process, avoided each other at official receptions. I was told that people were asking whether I would ever talk to him again. I realised that my cordial relations and personal authority within the donor community had significantly diminished. That I was largely unconcerned by this must be attributable to my already having decided to leave my job in DFID and join IDS (the Institute of Development Studies). If my situation had been different, I might not have been prepared to suffer this damage to my own social and political network.

The project's emphasis was on the right to an identity card. On a visit with Rosario to one of the areas where the Consortium was active, and after listening all morning to how people struggled to obtain these cards, I concluded that the state was making citizens pay with blood, tears and scarce money for the errors it had itself committed. Personal horror stories were told with passion and grief. In a separate paper, Rosario has analysed the exclusionary effects of the lack of identity cards (León et al. 2003: 4). Those for whom the strategy was allegedly designed not only had no voice in the formal political process, they were also denied economic and educational opportunity because of the state's denial of their identity. This project could make a difference.

*

It seemed that I had made the right choice but in the next section, I consider some of the quandaries and quagmires of this decision in the circumstances of a donor supporting civil society against the wishes of the host government.

THE AMBIGUITIES OF DONOR–RECIPIENT RELATIONS

Aid as a gift of patronage?

Bolivia is understood by foreigners and Bolivians alike as a society based on the personal relationship of the gift rather than one of impersonal relations of entitlement. Thus foreign aid that started life as tax on citizens of the North, becomes part of a complex local set of gift relationships and struggles for power and patronage. By deciding to ignore the wishes of the representatives of the elected government, was I not reaffirming DFID's patronage role, giving and taking away aid as I saw fit rather than as the host country government saw fit? My personal discretion was large. If someone else had been head of the DFID office at that time, it is possible that a different decision would have been made.

Aid conceived as a gift has few friends in the world of development practice because it illuminates, through power relations, the personal, the relational and the emotional. While the liberal economist prefers to see it as an investment, the rights-based practitioner and most Bolivians I have spoken to would like it to become an entitlement. Both perspectives subscribe to the idea of 'ownership'. For the World Bank it is an efficiency argument. Governments that own their policies (and the money that supports the implementation of such policies) are more likely to deliver the results that donors want. The rights-based perspective equally prefers 'ownership' because it implies an inalienable entitlement, administered by a rational bureaucracy. Conceiving aid as a gift is particularly upsetting for those working in non-governmental organisations that are seeking to promote social justice and equality: 'As in a relationship between landlord and tenant, at the centre of the donor–recipient relationship is an exchange of deference and compliance by the client in return for the patron's provision' (Crewe and Harrison 1998).

Gifts are ambiguous, with irreducible elements of morality that shape their character (Mirowski 2001). A gift always has an intention behind it – and therefore has an interest. On the other hand, if the intention is moral or sacred, then the gift can be judged as disinterested. Givers, such as priests, see themselves as vehicles or intermediaries in the delivery of a gift from God (Appadurai 1985). I saw myself as such a disinterested giver, an intermediary, acting on behalf of the taxpayer. My donor patronage was both personal and sacred.

Gifts have a further ambiguity. As an expression of the sacred or the moral, they recognise the social bond between donor and recipient. But that same recognition can be imbued with sentiments of power and even aggression. As noted in a recent discussion on this subject with the former Ombudswoman, the recipient may be powerless to refuse the gift (Amariglio 2002; Callari 2002). This paradox is very clear in the aid relationship. No recipient government or NGO wants to be aid-dependent, attributing their status to the unjust way in which powerful countries manage the world's economy.

WHOSE AID?

The strong sentiments of VIPFE staff about 'donor-driven' projects reflected their wish for control – not to be pushed around by donors to whom they have to be polite. Although donors use the language of 'partnership', a gift in practice reinforces or even reinvents the difference between donor and recipient (Stirrat and Henkel 1997). Entitlements, on the other hand, concern impersonal contracts to which both parties subscribe. A PRSP is in theory an attempt to establish such a contract, providing a guaranteed flow of resources to the recipient. That it does not do so in practice is evidenced by DFID's decision in late 2003 to cut back significantly its aid to Bolivia.

Osteen (2002: 233 quoting Weiner) notes that it is possible to 'keep while giving'. Whereas an entitlement is inalienable – once passed over to the other person the original owner no longer has any claims on it – a gift may never leave its owner, although, through giving, it passes into the possession of the recipient. This particular quality of the gift illuminates current anxieties in the aid world concerning 'ownership' and 'partnership'. Jerve defines the former as 'who decides what in the process of aid delivery' (2002: 394).

If the Bolivian government is understood as the arbiter for the aid given to the country, then its ownership of the elections project was minimal. Although the weak vice-ministries of gender and indigenous affairs expressed support, VIPFE in the Ministry of Finance, and the Presidency, objected. DFID's only defence is that the project appears to have had a bigger impact on Bolivia than most other elements of British aid. It was for this reason that, in the special newspaper supplement for the Queen's Birthday in Bolivia in 2003, and twelve months after my departure, it was this project that took pride of place.[5]

The disagreement between DFID and the Dutch embassy exemplified the donor dilemma. The head of the Dutch aid section acknowledged the dubious legitimacy of the regime as one that political scientists would term 'a minimally institutionalised state' (Moore and Putzel 1999). We did not disagree over the analysis but over the appropriate response. I argued that because the Poverty Reduction Strategy was unviable if many poor people were excluded from the democratic political process, donors should be supporting simultaneously not only the elected government but also those civil society organisations that were seeking to give poor people a stronger voice – even if government officials objected to our doing this.

However, that viewpoint exposed DFID to the accusation of over-interference in another country's affairs and of undermining the concept of the government in the driving seat. Both DFID and the Netherlands aid ministry were global leaders in the new 'partnership' agenda. Up until this crisis, I had been working closely and enthusiastically with my Dutch colleague in pursuit of that agenda. The elections project forced us to make choices. By deciding to initiate and then support the Consortium, I had broken the very rules of the game to which I had been actively subscribing. It was a clear case

last chapter
how ownership is defined

of DFID claiming it knew better than the Bolivian government as to how to spend its aid. VIPFE was correct: the elections project *was* 'donor-driven'.

When he appreciated how unhappy VIPFE was with this initiative, I understand that my counterpart in the Dutch embassy decided that national ownership should be given priority. I imagine he saw 'ownership' as a fundamental innovation in the relations between donor and recipient so important it should not be undermined, even for a good cause. As long as donors spent their money as they saw fit, privileging their analysis over that of the government's, then the old patron–client style of relationship between recipient and donor would continue. National ownership was the first step to recipient governments being *entitled* to aid money, rather than being dependent on donors' whims and the capriciousness of the gift. National ownership would strengthen the state's capacity to govern.

CONCLUSION

Reflections of a passionate bureaucrat

A structural analysis might conclude that by seeking to prevent more poor people voting, VIPFE was protecting the interests of the elite that it served. VIPFE's explicit objection to the project had been couched in terms of DFID breaking the CDF principles of national ownership. More informally, I was told that I was interfering naively in political processes about which I knew nothing. This was of course largely the case. I knew very little, other than what Rosario and her friends told me. I had decided to trust their judgement rather than that of the VIPFE.

If I had been less ignorant, would I have been more hesitant? Starting with an ill-informed social analysis that drew on general principles rather than context-specific knowledge, did I continue my commitment by drawing on another form of knowing, what Reason (1998) refers to as experiential knowledge, gained through empathy and resonance? Did this lead me to trust 'intuitively' in Rosario and the Consortium?

Katja Jassey argues that because 'clumsy donors and bureaucrats' are also passionate people who can be as eager at networking, making friends and promoting change as the next person, development agencies need to have some rules so as to protect taxpayers' money and to stop individual staff members using their power without accountability (2004: 132). What the modern civil service calls evidence – Reason's (1998) propositional knowledge – supports such rule-based decision-making. Interestingly, I made the decision to continue with the project without any substantive evidence because no one had been interested in collecting it. It was the project, once implemented, that revealed the fact that very high numbers of people were denied their right to an identity. The information gathered by the Consortium showed that of a total of 26,418 inhabitants of the 618 rural and peri-urban communities where the project was implemented, just 9 per cent had their personal documentation in order, while 91 per cent were facing documentation problems. This not only denied them the right to vote, but also many other of their economic, social and civil rights (León et al. 2003: 10).

While I was driven by passion, it was what Jassey describes as my 'personal and institutional power' (2004: 132) that enabled me to act. I was shocked that VIPFE regarded citizens' political exclusion as a minor matter, allegedly affecting very few people. I was angry, and my resolve was hardened, when an intermediary communicated to me informally (at a cocktail party, where all such business is done) that if people did not have identity cards it was because they were opting out of their responsibilities as citizens.

This chapter started by referring to the emotions of the project's protagonists. The Consortium lived the all too common experience of aid being offered and then withdrawn. The ownership of aid remained with the donor. The gift itself had a bright and a shadow side, expressed in terms of solidarity, trust and affection on the one hand, and betrayal, anger and aggression on the other. Yet, if we were to read the official donor records concerning this project, we would find a logical framework, indicators of achievement and 'neutral' evaluations. A peculiar sanitisation would have occurred that presents a plausible fiction of a rational bureaucracy making informed value-for-money judgements as to the most effective and efficient means of achieving poverty reducing outcomes.

Rosario's reflections

I have found it difficult to think about myself at a certain time and within a certain set of relationships, and above all it is not easy to recollect vivid emotion. There is a persistent tendency to analyse rather than feel the past and only in a passionate conversation with Rosalind was I first able to look at myself. I have continued since then and in other conversations with young researchers here in Bolivia. Only then did my memory start to learn. By recollecting these emotions I can appreciate the implications of those games of donor–recipient relations, games of which at the time we were unaware.

With this project I had the power to think and design proposals. And the Consortium had gained the power to constrain the bureaucracy's clientelist management of foreign aid. Once DFID and SIDA had decided to continue with the project, despite the objections of the government, perhaps the most significant act was their preparedness to change the design of the original project. The Consortium established itself and implemented the project on the principle of collective action rather than competition for funding. Thus, in this instance, donors were prepared to let civil society not only receive funds but also to design the way they would spend the money. If the political responses to the management of aid are born from a reading of reality where the state is intended to continue transforming society, without giving society the choice of transforming itself and the state, I think that systems of exclusion will tend to endure.

My experience with this project has a special significance for me because it demonstrated the possibilities of transforming the relations that knit together the world of development. What happened in the two years after is another story to be told later.

NOTES

1. We are grateful to David Mosse and Cathy Shutt for their thoughtful comments on earlier drafts of this chapter.
2. *Compadrazgo* is the relationship between the parents and godparents of a child, but is used in Bolivia in a wider sense of the affective relationships that characterise the country's clientelistic political and economic system.
3. *'Chola'* is a Bolivian woman of highland indigenous origin who dresses in a long voluminous skirt, with a shawl and bowler hat.
4. A basket fund is when different donors put their money into a single 'basket' so that the recipient has a single fund to draw down on and does not have to report separately to the different donors. They are still relatively rare but very much favoured in principle at that time in Bolivia (see Nickson 2002).
5. I am told that the project is also frequently cited by DFID head office and ministers as an example of how British aid tackles social exclusion.

REFERENCES

Appadurai, A. (1985) Gratitude as a social mode in south India. *Ethos* 13(3): 236–45.

Armariglio, J. (2002) Give the ghost a chance. In J. Osteen (ed.) *The question of the gift: essays across disciplines* (Routledge: London).

Callari, A. (2002) The ghost of the gift: the unlikelihood of economics. In J. Osteen (ed.) *The question of the gift: essays across disciplines* (London: Routledge).

Crewe, E. and E. Harrison (1998) *Whose development? An ethnography of aid* (London and New York: Zed Books).

DFID (Department for International Development) (2002) Country Strategy Paper for Bolivia, <www.dfid.gov.uk>.

Eyben, R. (2003a) Donors as political actors: fighting the Thirty Years War in Bolivia. *IDS Working Paper* 183. Brighton: Institute of Development Studies.

Eyben, R. (2003b) Mainstreaming the social dimension into the Overseas Development Administration: a partial history. *Journal of International Development* 15: 879–92.

Eyben, R. (2004) Who owns a poverty reduction strategy? A case of power, instruments and relationships in Bolivia. In L. Groves and R. Hinton (eds) *Inclusive aid: power and relationships in international development* (London: Earthscan).

Groves, L. and R. Hinton (eds) (2004) *Inclusive aid: power and relationships in international development* (London: Earthscan).

Jassey, K. (2004) The bureaucrat. In L. Groves and R. Hinton (eds) *Inclusive aid: power and relationships in international development* (London: Earthscan).

Jerve, A.M. (2002) Ownership and partnership: does the new rhetoric solve the incentive problems in aid? *Forum for Development Studies* 2: 389–407.

Ladbury, S., L. Appointee and G. Sierra (2002) Bolivia Country Strategy Review for Department for International Development. Final report, January (unpublished), Le Groupe-conseil baastel ltée. C.P. 1874, Succursale B, Hull, Quebec J8X 3Z1.

Lazar, S. (2004) Personalist politics, clientelism and citizenship: local elections in El Alto, Bolivia. *Bulletin of Latin American Research* 23(2): 228–43.

Léon , R., J. Goulden, C. Rea, H. Salinas, L. Medrano and J. Schollaert (2003) Social exclusion, rights and chronic poverty in Bolivia. Paper presented at the Chronic Poverty and Development Conference, Manchester, <http://idpm.man.ac.uk/cprc/Conference/conferencepapers.htm>.

Mirowski , P. (2001) Refusing the gift. In S. Cullenberg, J. Amariglio and D. Ruccio (eds) *Postmodernism, economics and knowledge* (London: Routledge).

Moore, M. and J. Putzel (1999) Thinking strategically about politics and poverty. *IDS Working Paper* 101. Brighton: Institute of Development Studies.

Nickson, A. (2002) Bolivia: a country case study. Paper prepared for the OECD DAC Task Force on Donor Practices, September. Distributed at a workshop held at the International Development Department, University of Birmingham, 17 June 2003 on Aid Effectiveness – How Should Donor Practices Change?

Osteen, J. (2002) Gift or commodity? In J. Osteen (ed.) *The question of the gift: essays across disciplines* (London: Routledge).

Pasteur, K. and P. Scott-Villiers (2004) *If relationships matter, how can they be improved? Learning about relationships in development.* Lessons for Change in Policy and Organisations No. 9. Brighton: Institute of Development Studies.

Quarles van Ufford, P., A.K. Giri and D. Mosse (2004) Interventions in development: towards a new moral understanding of our experiences and an agenda for the future. In P. Quarles van Ufford and A.K. Giri (eds) *A moral critique of development* (London: Routledge).

Reason, P. and H. Bradbury (2001) Introduction. In P. Reason and H. Bradbury (eds) *Handbook of action research* (London: Sage).

Reason, P. (1998) A participatory worldview. *Resurgence* 168: 42–44, <http://www.bath.ac.uk/~mnspwr/Papers/Participatoryworld.htm>.

Retolaza, I. (2004) Bolivian constitutional assembly: a space for transformation? Unpublished paper written for the MA in Participation and Development at the Institute of Development Studies, University of Sussex.

Rosaldo, R. (1993) *Culture and truth: the remaking of social analysis* (London: Routledge).

Stirrat, R.L. and H. Henkel (1997) The development gift: the problem of reciprocity in the NGO world. *Annals of the American Association of Political and Social Science* 554: 66–80.

Whitehead, L. (2001) Chapter One. In J. Crabtree and L. Whitehead (eds) *Towards democratic viability: the Bolivian experience* (Basingstoke: Palgrave Macmillan).

World Bank (2003) *Towards country-led development: a multi-partner evaluation of the Comprehensive Development Framework* (Washington, DC: World Bank).

6 INTERCONNECTED AND INTER-INFECTED: DOTS AND THE STABILISATION OF THE TUBERCULOSIS CONTROL PROGRAMME IN NEPAL

Ian Harper

Order is extracted not from disorder but from orders. We always make the same mistake. We distinguish between the barbarous and the civilized, the constructed and the dissolved, the ordered and the disordered. We are always lamenting the decadence and the dissolution of morals. (Latour 1988: 161)

The protocols, thus, turn practice itself into a laboratory: by prescribing highly detailed sequences of action, they become the means through which facts can be produced and, at the same time, a crucial part of the networks through which the facts can be performed. (Timmermans and Berg 1997: 297)

In 1993 the World Health Organization (WHO), the health arm of the United Nations (UN), made the unprecedented step of declaring the problem of tuberculosis a 'global emergency' (WHO 1994). Following on from this, Directly Observed Therapy Short-course, or DOTS as it is now ubiquitously known, became the WHO advocated policy for nation states to adopt. This policy was, and still is, widely supported by the World Bank, DFID and a range of other powerful transnational, multilateral and bilateral institutions. DOTS, then, is an example of a generic policy that, it is believed, can be transplanted to any nation state in the world. It is perceived as a 'management strategy for public health systems' (WHO 2004) and it consists of the following five main areas: government commitment to the national programme; detection of cases through sputum smear microscopy; short course chemotherapy for all smear positive cases – this includes direct observation of at least the first two months of treatment; a regular uninterrupted supply of all essential anti-TB drugs; and good recording and reporting systems (WHO 1995).

In Nepal, this strategy has been adopted since 1996. By 1999, when the fieldwork upon which this chapter is based was ongoing, it had been expanded to cover over 50 per cent of the country, particularly in the districts that had been able to adhere to the strict protocols for the introduction of Short Course Chemotherapy (SCC) (NTP and HMG/N 1999).[1] By 2001 it was possible for the programme to be represented by the director in the following way:

DOTS was introduced in 1996 after a joint His Majesty's Government of Nepal (HMG/N)/WHO review of the National Tuberculosis Programme (NTP) revealed that only 30% of TB cases were registered under the NTP and of these, only 40% were treatment successes. The cure rate in the first cohort of DOTS patients was above 89%. By July 2000, the programme had been expanded to 183 treatment centres in 69 districts and covers 78% of population. The treatment success rate in the DOTS centres remains at approximately 89%, with the national treatment success rate now reaching almost 85%. Nationally, this year over 28,000 TB patients have been registered and are being treated under the NTP. Out of these, over 75% are being treated under DOTS. (Bam 2001)

This chapter is based on research done around this programme as it was implemented in the district of Palpa, in west-central Nepal, during the period of 1998 to 2000.[2] In it I take as my object of analysis the system that scrutinises the presence of the tubercle bacillus, the bacterial agent whose presence within epidemiological discourse is necessary for the diagnosis of the disease tuberculosis.[3]

The chapter is divided into three broad sections. First, I examine the case of one woman diagnosed with tuberculosis and her attempts at entry into the system. She was one example of how the attempt to stabilise diagnostic categories requires many to fall outside of tightening definitions of who actually has tuberculosis, part of the requirements for entry into the programme. Second, I follow the paper trails necessary for the recording and reporting of the DOTS system as the disease tuberculosis enters broader epidemiological and political orders. The discourses and practices mobilised around the control of the spread of the disease at the level of the reified population, as has been noted for other medical systems, involves the use of protocols (Berg 1998; Timmermans and Berg 1997) and the laboratory (Singleton 1998). I hope to demonstrate that the object of the public health gaze is a different object to that being dealt with by clinicians less informed by this public health gaze. While it may be argued that there is nothing that relates this system management to neoliberalism – that it is not specific to 'development' in this form, but is indicative rather of bureaucratic practices generally – in the third and final section I (tentatively) examine how the reified object of the tubercle bacillus at a population level is also put to work for political ends within discourses and practices that constitute the global in certain ways. It is not coincidental, I suggest, that the rise of such a technocratic programme mirrors the rise of neoliberal reform and all its associated discourses. As the bacilli's relationship with humanity is constituted as one of terror, it is not surprising that its 'elimination' from the population carries a particular resonance today.

A POINT OF DEPARTURE

I first met Dev Kumari nearly a year into my anthropological fieldwork researching a number of local healers, their interaction and networks, and how locally people negotiated and chose particular therapeutic options. I was sitting in the recently opened DOTS tuberculosis clinic of the district hospital in Tansen, Palpa district one day in late September 1999. This public hospital was a dreary place, sitting atop a steep ridge that delimited the edge of town. Buses and 'Trax' jeeps stopped below it, discharging their passengers onto the street sides outside the shop fronts, three or four of them private clinics and pharmacies. The hospital itself, built around an open courtyard, with its wards, clinics, laboratory and operating theatre, was filled mainly with those who were too poor to afford the treatments of a massively expanding private sector or the local mission hospital. The paint was peeling from the walls. The hospital was usually emptied of many staff by early afternoon as they retired to their private clinics and pharmacies. Underpaid health workers referred people for often unnecessary tests to these private clinics, adding costs that many patients could ill afford.

In the clinic on this day sat the DOTS clinic worker, who did the bulk of the work, taking histories, examining the patients, filling out the forms and registers, administering the combination of medicines. He was employed by a mission organisation involved in health work in the district, and was subcontracted to this clinic in the name of partnership with the government. A volunteer community medical assistant (CMA), the product of a year's training at one of the two private technical training colleges in Tansen was also here, gaining experience and 'directly observing' those who came to this clinic each day for their medicines. On this day too, the District Tuberculosis Supervisor was here, checking on the patient registers and cohort forms, and providing advice about treatment regimes. Then there was myself, as anthropologist (and, because of my previous medical experience, in part, TB adviser), as ever scribbling away in my notebook. All of us were, as Mol (1998, 1999) suggests similarly in her philosophical meditations around anaemia and atherosclerosis, in the process of performing, or doing, tuberculosis.

This required the interaction with a number of material objects as well. On the wall of the clinic – which opened through one shuttered window out into the corridor, where the majority of people waiting to be seen sat on benches – was a WHO calendar, a cloth flip-chart used for health education purposes, and a chart describing the three categories for treatment, and registration into the national DOTS programme:

- Category one – new smear positive patients
- Category two – re-treatment cases
- Category three – non pulmonary tuberculosis

Each had a different treatment regime associated with it. Each category and regime had to be rigidly adhered to if free treatment, via the public health system, was to be administered. An old cupboard sat in the corner filled with the anti-tuberculous drugs in large plastic containers, supplied by the NTP, but most of them procured as aid with donor money. Among the registers and papers on the desk sat a jug of water and glasses that patients could use to wash down the tablets that they all had to be observed taking.

Dev Kumari had been sent to the DOTS clinic this day from Dr P's, one of the busiest and most popular of 17 private clinics in town, and one frequented, I was told, by many of the communist supporters in the district. Trained in Russia, like many doctors in Nepal, he was also a member of the United Marxist-Leninist Party and was from a powerful and respected family in town. His father, and grandfather before him, had been well-known Ayurvedic physicians, and their family had originally migrated from Kathmandu several generations previously with the Ranas, members of the then powerful hereditary family of prime ministers. His treatments were more expensive than others, but he was said to have particularly powerful medicines and a source of drugs more reliable than many of the newer drug distributors that had mushroomed in the area in the last five years or so following Nepal's embracing of the free market on the back of structural adjustment policies.[4] As we shall see, the variation in practices performed around tuberculosis in these private clinics and pharmacies is a particular 'problematisation', or field of delimitation, constituted by policies designed to control disease at the population level. Many patients were more than prepared to pay the extra at Dr P's clinic, but Dev Kumari had run out of money for her anti-tuberculous chemotherapy, and so Dr P had sent her to get the remainder of her treatment from the government clinic, where, he had assured her, medicines were free. The National Tuberculosis Programme policy dictates that the provision of tuberculosis treatment should be free and delivered through the public health care system.

Dev Kumari stood quietly in the door, dressed in a working sari, as the supervisor pored over her notes. I, too, was asked to look at these writings to assist in deciphering what was going on. While living in Nepal I scrutinised literally hundreds of such bits of paper, both during my anthropological fieldwork, between September 1998 and March 2000, and previously when I had worked in a tuberculosis clinic and programme in the early 1990s. Objectified as a doctor, I was continually asked to sift through pieces of paper that so many people seemed to hold on to with what seemed at times great reverence, and pass judgement on the treatments prescribed by others, to suggest other possible courses of action. I tried to decipher headed bits of paper – with the name of the clinic, hospital, pharmacy – often from distant places (clinics in India or in other urban centres in Nepal), many covered in incomprehensible scrawl (usually, I think, in an English of kinds). These were inscriptions – histories, examinations, diagnoses – translations from lived experiences into the categories necessary for biomedical treatment. Along with X-rays, ultrasounds and their reports, these were combined with recollections of partially remembered encounters with doctors, merging with other epistemological realities, frequently leading to confusion as biomedical prescriptions became another avenue of hope in the search for cure.

In Dev Kumari's case Dr P had clearly written the two and a half month's medications that she had received, had articulated the diagnosis of TB and had suggested the follow-up regime. Unfortunately, she had not had her sputum examined under a microscope to visualise the tubercle bacillus prior to receiving her treatment. Hari, the TB programme supervisor, could find no evidence of this. He told her that she did not fit the programme categories, and as the NTP regime was different to the one Dr P had given her, he sent her away to buy the medicines. I interrupted at this point and suggested that he put the notes to one side, and listen to her carefully. I drew on my experience as a doctor in treating tuberculosis cases in East Nepal. She had considerably improved on her medicines, put on weight, and it would be clinically prudent to prescribe the remainder of her medicines I suggested. But where does she go on the report forms he asked? Hari pointed out that the regulations and protocols prescribed by the NTP dictate that those who present after having had more than one month of treatment from the private sector, who have not had their sputum tested, cannot be entered into the NTP. It is more than likely that they will have drug-resistant tuberculosis, may have had intermittent therapy – if they have tuberculosis at all, for which there was no evidence, he pointed out. I asked him if the reports were more important than the person. And he quietly replied that they are both important. I demanded that he obtain permission from the National Tuberculosis Centre for this, but he could not contact them and as I waited with Dev Kumari, he returned an hour later saying that his immediate boss had said that she was not to get treatment.

There is a structural violence (Farmer 1998) in administering this bureaucratic medicine, and Hari was in no position to challenge this. He had to manage everyone in such a way that he did not rock the boat, and so that he could keep his job. He managed the records carefully because he was judged/supervised centrally by these reports. Whether they had been filled out correctly, or not, in relation to the programmatic aims was the single most important criterion of assessment. Over the months, I spent many days with Hari – and learnt how tenuous his position was – that transfer was often at the whim of his seniors whom he had to keep happy. Very poorly paid, he was extremely demoralised, like so many others working in the public system. He had at one point been selected to go to Bangalore on a study tour, as reward for his good work in tuberculosis, but it was snatched away from him at the last minute by the Minister of Health himself and given to someone else – something that even the head of the National Tuberculosis Centre was unable to do anything about. Being given a pay rise by one District Health Officer (DHO) had been interpreted as siding with that person's political party; it evoked jealousy, and resulted in his transfer to another, more remote district, a downward career trajectory that most staff, understandably, try to prevent at all costs.

I met Dev Kumari again several weeks later at a health post about six hours from the district centre, still attempting to obtain free drugs. Terrified that she would die if she stopped taking her drugs, she also told me she wanted to die because of her social circumstances. It was at moments like these, listening to narratives of such suffering that I felt most voyeuristic, angry and helpless. The health post in charge told me that he would have given her the medicines in the past, but now with DOTS and the strict control over medicine distribution, he could not do a thing unless he had the referral card she should have brought with her from the district centre. In the meantime she was buying her medicines, a week or so at a time, from another local pharmacist.

Although only in her mid 20s, she already had four sons and was pregnant with a fifth. She had fallen ill, she told me, because of an excess of 'heat', had taken herbs for this, had then decided that she must have been cursed by a witch, and started to dry up. Her husband was in India looking for work and, unable to contact him, she had been persuaded by some neighbours to go to Dr P. She had not asked anyone at the health post or known that the medicines were free, she said. She was initially treated for 'gyastric', the local name for a collection of symptoms requiring dietary change, but did not recover and was then given the diagnosis of tuberculosis. She recovered dramatically on anti-tuberculous chemotherapy, which is a good clinical indication that she had the disease. She just wanted to finish the full course of medicines that she had been told, repeatedly, she must finish. Her husband returned from India and they had to sell half their meagre holding of land to repay the borrowed money needed to buy the anti-tuberculosis drugs. Her unemployed husband had blamed her for their state of indebtedness. When she was at the hospital she told me, she was also charged 150 rupees for an X-ray and a blood test, but had not received any medicines. She was starting to think that, with a poor maize crop this year and less land, the possibility of survival was looking tenuous. Maybe it would just be better if she died, she said. After I got back from this visit I phoned the NTC and used what in Nepal is referred to as 'source and force', went over Hari's head, used my own connections, obtained permission to have her registered, and she collected her free medicines a few days later. I regret that I had not done this as soon as I first met her, yet I desperately wanted the system to accommodate her.

Exploring the machinations of the order of this system into which Dev Kumari had fallen is the interpretive task for the rest of this chapter.

CREATING ORDER FROM TREATMENT CHAOS:
FRAMES, PROTOCOLS AND PAPER TRAILS

Dodier, in his work on occupational medicine in France, has demonstrated how doctors working within different frames – what he calls the administrative and the clinical – draw on different reference points to deliver judgements on specific individuals (Dodier 1998). The administrative frame he sharply delineates from the clinical frame. In the former, the individual is depersonalised, he suggests, as they are treated according to a formalised category, which is determined with reference to the idea of the population, and particularly in relation to notions of risk. These are specifically developed in order to counteract the uncertainties of individual practitioner judgement, contained within the clinical frame. This administrative frame depends on rules coming from the centre, as in other bureaucratic situations, and it is the administrative frame that has developed massively under the combined influence of scientific networks and those of the law, he further suggests. Dodier also highlights that this corresponds to the diffusion of protocols deeply into the system – protocols and guidelines that have to be strictly adhered to.

The protocol has been, in the last 50 years or so, vital to medical expansion and stabilisation (Berg 1998). Berg suggests that the function of the protocol is to attempt to anchor decision moments to areas of stability. In the example I have given – the attempts to stabilise treatment rationale in tuberculosis control programmes in Nepal – we see how this results in deferring authority over clinical diagnosis to the laboratory and the visualisation of the bacilli. As Berg further suggests, the protocol defers to, and attempts to stabilise, a different order to the one in existence (1998). It is a technoscientific script that crystallises multiple trajectories (Timmermans and Berg 1997). A protocol is a '*standard* which intervenes in different trajectories of patients, instruments, drugs, and staff, redirecting their courses' (1997: 276).

This attempted stabilisation of a new order of tuberculosis control, and the tensions inherent in the different frames of reference are clearly at work here in the example I have started with. Many of the ill who presented to the National Tuberculosis Programme in the public hospital in Tansen, like Dev Kumari, had already received partial tuberculosis treatment from the private sector, dependent on diagnostic and treatment regimes quite different to that of the NTP. Dev Kumari's example is just one of many. Herein lay a difficulty the DOTS clinic staff told me: in which category were such patients to be placed? So-called 'New smear positive patients' are supported by a strict definition, dictated by the need for standardised global categories, so that comparison between programmes can be made. One of the things that protocols attempt to create is 'the comparability of activities over time and place' (Timmermans and Berg 1997: 296). Since this district had also been chosen as one in which a large research-based trial was to compare the outcomes of different forms of patient surveillance, the protocols were being particularly strictly adhered to. A 'new smear positive case', therefore, included all new patients who have visible tubercle bacilli in their sputum, or those who had their sputum tested elsewhere and could prove it, *and* had received less than one month's treatment elsewhere. The staff within the national programme spent many hours poring over the bits of paper that these patients brought along, sifting the 'evidence' on paper from the often confused verbal utterances. It is not just that the patient's symptoms, pulse rate, chest sounds auscultated with a stethoscope, 'speak' to the health workers replacing the patient's own so-called 'subjective' interpretation. A double displacement occurs here, in which an individual doctor's interpretations of the symptoms, too, are deferred to the authority of the actual visualisation of the tubercle bacillus, a truth which is then transferred onto paper.

The ambiguities that occur within this shift of order, and the greater adherence to protocols necessary for this shift to be made, were, of course, acutely experienced by the staff working within the NTP. As I discussed the difficulties these staff faced in their work, they frequently reiterated the trainings and seminars that they had been sent to, organised by the National Tuberculosis Centre (NTC) in Kathmandu. Here, for example, is the kind of thinking behind Dev Kumari's problems, namely, that those who may have tuberculosis, may or may not have been 'smear positive'. If they were, and they had taken their drugs intermittently, then they could already be 'resistant' to first-line treatment, the drugs recommended for those in this category. However, they were not strictly 're-treatment' cases either, as for this there needed to be proven defaulting from treatment. It was necessary to know that they had completed treatment and were labelled as 'relapsed' to fit this category. Alternatively, they may not have had tuberculosis at all and been placed inappropriately on treatment. In discussion with the clinic staff, we estimated that up to 20 per cent of all people who presented to the national programme in this district fell outside the categories defined by this internationally sanctioned system of disease surveillance. And given that autonomy of staff to make more individualist decisions (possible within Dodier's clinical frame) had been deferred to the authority of the protocol, combined with the frequent absence of the District Health Officer as arbitrator, all that they could do was refer patients back to the vagaries of the private system. Neither these patients' own interpretation of their condition, nor that of individual practitioners who had not had their patient's sputum examined, was of value to this emerging order.[5]

Bits of paper usually lie in the background of analyses, but I wish here to foreground them in order to trace further this process of attempted stabilisation. For disease 'surveillance', as the WHO calls it, is crucially mediated by what Smith (1984) has called 'textually mediated relations'. As patients presented to the public tuberculosis clinic, the health worker–patient relationship was crucially mediated by pieces of paper. As we have seen, long periods were spent asking the patient to remain silent as these bits of paper were pored over, looking for those vital pieces of 'evidence' indicating whether this was 'really' tuberculosis or not. The laboratory form was particularly important, with the red 'smear positive' mark and the number of +s placed in the appropriate column, indicating the degree of positivity, or the number of stained 'rods' of tubercle bacillus seen in fields of vision under the microscope. Placed into a position of passivity, there was little the patient could do but await judgement. Difficult cases, protocol stated, were to be referred to the District Health Officers, all of whom at the time had medical qualifications, but were often not in the district. One of the DHOs in Palpa district was away for three entire months in Bangkok, ironically at a training course on developing disease surveillance systems.

The protocol stated that for those who had not received a diagnosis elsewhere, more than one sputum had to be examined to guard against 'false positive' diagnoses. Despite this laboratory moment being crucial to the stability of the whole system, for a number of reasons it was also a point of particular instability and anxiety for the National Tuberculosis Programme supervisors I spoke with. The possibility of false positives – that is, the reading of the bacillus when it was not there – was one for which an entire system of quality control had to be developed. But there was also the problem that the slide has to be scrutinised for a long period of time before it could be said that there are no bacilli visible. This was time taken out of lucrative private practice, when these technicians could be earning more money charging for urine tests and doing blood tests. Also, those presenting to the hospital therefore had to hang around for at least two days to receive the diagnosis, and could easily leave in the interim. Singleton, in her work on the role of the laboratory in the UK cervical screening programme, has similarly highlighted this as a point of particular instability in this system (Singleton 1998).

But let us follow the paper trail further for those patients who entered the system diagnosed as 'new smear positive patients'. The laboratory form with the crucial diagnosis is taken back to the clinic. Registration follows in the TB register; a written referral form allows treatment from a decentralised point, one of the nine health posts in this district labelled as treatment sub-centres; finally, there is the filling out of a treatment card to be taken to that sub-centre. Off to the sub-centre next, where re-registration occurs after bringing in the local Female Community Health Volunteer (FCHV). This forms part of discourses both of the national policy facilitating greater 'decentralisation' of service provision (Sigdel 1998) and of DOTS –'direct observation'. These volunteers were then responsible for the direct observation of their tablets being swallowed; and, after each tablet, the box was ticked off on the treatment card. In Palpa, the FCHVs were being used to directly observe therapy as a part of a trial looking at the implementation of this method of treatment supervision against that of a member of the family doing the direct observation of treatment. Districts had been randomly assigned to one or other category, as part of research into DOTS implementation, a part of the research agenda developed by the NTP, the WHO and a network of public health-based research institutions linked to develop evidence on the best way to stabilise the system.

Follow-up visits for the patients to the district centre had to happen twice to have sputum re-tested (a return journey that, even within the district, could take two days, much of it on foot). This occurred after two months and at the end of treatment. This information gathering was necessary for cohort reporting systems upon which the success of the programme is judged, namely the categories of 'sputum conversion rate' and numbers 'cured', defined as sputum conversion at the end of treatment. These data were then entered into the registers. From each sub-centre, every four months, a representative of the treatment sub-centres was sent to the district DOTS meetings. Here all patients were reported on and placed into cohorts. What is recorded is sputum conversion (i.e. a revisualisation of stained sputum to see whether the bacilli had disappeared) at two months and at the end of treatment, as well as an audit of drugs used for procurement purposes. Specially designed cohort reporting forms were filled in, and sent off to the regional centre, where again district-wide results were reported and fed into regional figures taken to Kathmandu. The traces of these categories, charting the presence or otherwise of the tubercle bacillus in the sputum were now entered into the national databases. And off to Geneva, where the figures become part of league tables, manipulated by huge and complex databases and statistical software packages, charting the movement of the national programmes towards internationally defined goals, in which national programmes should find 70 per cent and cure 85 per cent of all its pulmonary positive patients. Further transmogrification occurs from here as predicative mathematical modelling is undertaken to project onto rational and possible futures potential programmatic successes, and the impact on disease prevalence (see for example Dye et al. 1998). This manipulation of data is appropriated and used to insert the current policy into a number of quite different orders, frequently geopolitical.

This is not the tuberculosis that concerns those private and other practitioners unaware of the implications defined epidemiologically in terms of the impact of the disease on reified 'populations'. These practitioners are more concerned with the disease and its manifestations in the individual body, not the body of society as a whole. These tensions between an individualised bio-therapy and the concern with the 'public's' health re-emerge and are re-formed in debates and tensions over individual rights and civil liberties, and the 'protection' of the public, mediated more and more by issues emerging around international human rights discourses (Coker 2000). 'Statistico-tuberculosis', let us call it, is intimately concerned with a global (and national) prevalence of the disease, which, it is believed, will decrease when enough infective patients are found and effectively treated. These reservoirs of infective patients, those who secrete the bacillus into their sputum, are a risk to others when they cough (etc.). This brings me, by way of conclusion, and following Mol's ideas of diseases as multiple objects (Mol 1998, 1999) to the idea of multiple tuberculoses. For the tuberculosis reified as a population problem, 'statistico-tuberculosis', is one that has the spectre of multi-drug resistance hanging over it. If the rifampicin (the key drug in SCC) 'is lost', then the fight against tuberculosis is lost, is how I have heard the problem referred to again and again. The system is developed and managed in an increasingly centralised way to contain and eliminate this threat.

It is to the trace of those allowed into the system, who feed into this globalisation of concern around tuberculosis control, that I now turn.

FEAR AND LOATHING OF THE BACILLUS – ELIMINATION AND PUTTING THE GLOBAL IN

When I first reflected on these encounters with medical practitioners in Palpa district, I theorised that they demanded one type of biomedically defined subject, that of the compliant patient and consumer of multinational drugs and treatments. These encounters between doctor and patient sought to reduce everything to a single biomedical reality, one that in the name of the 'real' cannot cope with difference. This difference, I speculated, was medicine's other, those healing practices of a reified 'traditional' nature, constituted within these discourses as barriers to the correct diagnosis and treatment. Within discourses of tuberculosis control, I assumed a stability and singularity of the object of the gaze, the causative organism of tuberculosis, the tubercle bacillus. I have come to reconsider this position. As Mol and Berg (1998) suggest in the introduction to their edited volume *Differences in medicine*, what I had not really considered was the starting point for their volume, the multiplicity within medicine itself. The object of tuberculosis control programmes, as epidemiologically constituted, is a quite different object to that engaged with in other clinics, as I hope is being made clearer.

At the level of the population, the agency or intention attributed to the tubercle bacillus is the destruction of the human race.[6] Metaphors are generative in that they structure a public health perception and inform its movement and directions. As the bacillus is waging terror on the human population it has a particular resonance in contemporary geopolitical relations. Warfare is the most striking idiom of disease elimination programmes, and it is this that further defines and constitutes the agency attributed to the bacillus. What are the possible consequences of totalising responses to global problems that are deemed to threaten human survival? What is happening here I suggest is not just the re-emergence of diseases like tuberculosis, as has been suggested by some authors within what is described historically as the 'third epidemiologic transition' (Barrett et al. 1998). Nor is it simply the rising awareness in more developed countries of a problem that had previously been invisible, although it is this in part (Farmer 1999). Rather, it is also the (re-)emergence of the tubercle bacillus as a new political object, within an emerging global order. As we shall see, new forms of globalised alliance are forming around the problem of tuberculosis constituted in particular ways, and particularly around DOTS propaganda, which is used as a clarion call to mobilise these forces. The tubercle bacillus, and the need to eliminate it as a threat, is put to work in a range of discourses and practices.

That medicine often relates itself to its object, disease, as 'war' can be little in doubt and this metaphor has been explored in other work (for example Brown 1997; Martin 1994; Sontag 1991). The metaphor is everywhere. It cordons off representations in medical textbooks, advances in the front line of public health literature, explodes into health education, and ricochets into the popular media. Warfare has been an organising metaphor in much primary health care for a long time. Since the 'discovery' of germs, one of medicine's most significant epistemological shifts, this has allowed a more directed warlike focus against these disease-causing organisms. Antibiotic discovery and consequent mass production fine-tuned the ability to attack the targets; indeed it was the accelerated research, testing and mass production of penicillin by the military during the Second World War that facilitated this process (Neushul 1999). The historians Cooter and Sturdy suggest that public health programmes were frequently pursuing war by other means. Following the end of the guerrilla resistance to the American occupation of the Philippines, for example, the struggle shifted to the war waged over the natives' bodies in the 'sustained assault on a cholera epidemic' (Cooter and Sturdy 1999: 9). Brown, too, recognises the centrality of warfare as an organising metaphor in his history of malaria eradication efforts (Brown 1997). He suggests that the use of military metaphors in organising disease elimination programmes fitted models of social organisation of the time, particularly with the discovery of chloroquine and DDT, and the rise of the disease-specific health campaigns after the Second World War. He also suggests that the metaphor of 'community participation' organising primary health care activities is quite different. Nonetheless, vertical disease-oriented programmes have 're-emerged', and significantly in the latter part of the 1990s, with the all-important funding (for malaria too) and the military metaphor with it. Whether there will be another backlash of what Brown calls the '*ideological resistance* that characterised the reaction to the entrapment in the military metaphors of the eradication epoch', remains to be seen (1997: 137). What is certain, however, is that they have re-emerged, and along with them the political visibility of the scourges they are attempting to eradicate. This parallels both 'the return of the disease' into primary health care and the rise of neoliberalism. One significant factor in this decade has been the loss of the promised utopia that the widespread availability of antibiotics hailed, particularly with the rise of 'super-bugs'. The fear that this has generated – reflected in titles like *The coming plague* (Garrett 1994), for example – and the spectre it creates, should not be underestimated. We could conceivably, now, lose the battle. The war against this terror is intensifying.

Historically, as the battles with disease at the level of the individual have moved outwards towards populations, demography, epidemiology and statistics have been particularly important in the 'taming of chance' (Hacking 1990). This has been a movement towards making the world apprehendable, in discerning order in epidemics and offering the possibility of both control and elimination, and producing now at the beginning of the twenty-first century vast global databases caught within huge webs of complex statistics. Gray, in his book on postmodern war, tracks the rise and centrality in warfare of the computer, which is now the primary weapon he argues. What is important, he suggests, is having the most up-to-date information, as well as controlling its flows (Gray 1997). A 'fact sheet' produced by the WHO calls for the development of strong surveillance systems as the means of addressing concerns about communicable diseases (WHO 1998). The WHO calls for the creation of a 'super surveillance system', the development of a 'network of networks', cited now as an area of international collaboration by the G7/G8 member countries, along with the WHO member countries. This, they suggest, should be combined with UNICEF (UN Children's Fund), UNHCR (UN High Commission for Refugees) and military networks like the US Department of Defence and Global Emerging Infections System (DoD-GEIS). All this requires the mapping of geographic and population gaps, as well as addressing deficiencies in expertise. It is supported by the massive expansion in information technology and the Internet, as well as the possibilities of legal mandate, like the International Health Regulations. These require the WHO member states to notify diseases of international import. The need to know, the desire for information, the push for evidence on which to base further policy and planning, is a powerful driving force in this war. At the centre of this, 'information' and its gathering is the organising principle.[7]

A major concern for both national governments and global institutions is that bodies infected with the tubercle bacillus also facilitate the movement of tuberculosis around the globe. As the following quote from Hardt and Negri suggests, this fear of contagion is a particular problem in relation to globalisation.

The contemporary processes of globalisation have torn down many of the boundaries of the colonial world. Along with the common celebrations of the unbounded flows in our new global village, one can still sense also an anxiety about increased contact and a certain nostalgia for colonialist hygiene. The dark side of the consciousness of globalisation is the fear of contagion. If we break down global boundaries and open universal contact in our global village, how will we prevent the spread of disease and corruption? ... The boundaries of nation-states, however, are increasingly permeable by all kinds of flows. Nothing can bring back the hygienic shields of colonial boundaries. The age of globalisation is the age of universal contagion. (Hardt and Negri 2000: 136)

While I am writing here of this in relation to TB control, these ideas came spectacularly to light in the frenzy around SARS.

The *New Scientist* issue of 7 July 2001 had a cover article that illustrates the point, declaring, 'It kills every ten seconds and is heading our way so why don't we care? Because it's called TB' (Coghlan and Conclar 2001: 29). The story, we are told, starts in Newham, East London, 'the tuberculosis capital of the affluent Western World', where there are 3,000 Londoners on treatment, and seven new cases presenting each day (2001: 29). Newham's prevalence of the disease is higher than that of India and Russia, and the disease is thriving among 'the homeless and disenfranchised, among drug addicts and the malnourished, people living in unsanitary, overcrowded houses, sleeping on floors and chairs' (2001: 29). Over half of those with TB are also asylum seekers, from Africa, India, Bangladesh, 'where resurgent TB has been a growing problem for the past two decades' (2001: 29). It's the poverty they encounter in Britain that activates the latent disease they have in their bodies, we are informed. London's worsening TB problem is then portrayed as a symptom of *globalisation* – 'of the fact that in an interconnected world of cheap air travel, one nation's epidemic can quickly become another's. During the heyday of the empire, Britain exported TB. Now it's back and baying for blood' (2001: 29). One of the major factors contributing to the growing and ever more dangerous global epidemic of tuberculosis is the movement of people, with trade, in airplanes, as refugees and the displaced, a WHO fact sheet tells us (WHO 2000). As the WHO declared, announcing its DOTS campaign:

It is no longer possible to eliminate an infectious disease in one part of the world and allow it to run rampant in another. In short, it will be impossible to control TB in the industrialised nations unless it is sharply reduced as a threat in Africa, Asia and Latin America. (WHO 1994)

Globalisation, suggested Small in a plenary lecture at the 1998 World Conference of the International Union Against Tuberculosis and Lung Disease in Bangkok, will result in 'economic inter-dependence leading to co-dependency and cooperation. As the world continues to shrink people will come to realise that we are, in fact, all breathing the same air' (Small 1999). They are described as 'Airborne Killers' in one WHO article, as the bacilli collect frequent-flier miles (Panos and WHO 2000). Germs and viruses now criss-cross continents in a matter of hours, as the world's populations become more mobile – this is the image presented.

This rising awareness of the rapid globalisation of infectious diseases works in two paradoxical ways. On the one hand, it mobilises a greater global (transnational) will to deal with the disease. On the other, it also feeds into foreign policy and immigration policy with a tendency to protectionism, which relates to the conflicts in the way the globe is conceptualised. The right-wing press in the UK is obsessed with asylum seekers, for example, and makes a fetish of their capacity to carry diseases like TB into the country. As a 're-emergent' problem, then, tuberculosis has entered into images, or discourses, of globality. Health, and its management has always been a key political question when the idea of the global is at stake, as images of how the world should be health-wise, implicitly contain underlying images of how societies can and should be structured suggests Keane (1998). Globality, or the consciousness of the world as a single and unitary place, is structured by these images, he suggests. Let me take the US as a further example. Within the US, infectious diseases have become an issue of both US and global security. 'Infectious diseases pose a serious threat to global political stability, and therefore to US national security' it was reported on the CNN website.[8] The US government has been studying the dramatic surge in infectious diseases around the world, we are informed. The problem is a potentially 'catastrophic' threat which complicates US security and will endanger US citizens at home and abroad, and, importantly, threaten the US military, as well as exacerbate political instability where the US has its interests. For John Steinbruner, the global nature of infectious disease allows the possibility of surveillance for both this and the more serious possibility of using pathogens in warfare. He quotes Russia as an example of a state that has lost its ability to deal with tuberculosis in its increasingly 'stressed' population, because of the difficulties following the dismantling of its communist polity. The fact that less than 2.5 per cent of Russia's gross national product is invested in issues of public health, combined with the rise of multi-drug resistant tuberculosis in its prisons, has created a 'dangerous reservoir of disease'. 'The weakening of control over both dimensions of the threat in Russia creates reasons for assertive international assistance that are already strong and could become compelling' (Steinbruner 2000: 190).

As another example, for Robert Kaplan (2000), an American neo-Malthusian academic writing on issues of globalisation, West Africa has come to symbolise worldwide demographic, environmental and societal stress. He perceives the greatest threats, and the 'coming anarchy', as coming from the Third World.

West Africa is becoming *the* symbol of worldwide demographic, environmental, and societal stress, in which criminal anarchy emerges as the real 'strategic' danger. Disease, overpopulation, unprovoked crime, scarcity of resources, refugee migrations, the increasing erosion of nation-states and international borders, and the empowerment of private armies, security firms, and international drug cartels are now most tellingly demonstrated through a West African prism. (2000: 36)

In this world, HIV and tuberculosis are 'fast-forwarding each other' (2000: 40). He finishes his doomsday scenario by highlighting the difficulties he had in getting back through the tougher and tougher security procedures in the US, increasingly tough not least because of fear of imported disease. Similarly for UNICEF, tuberculosis in Asia threatens regional security. It is a 'raging epidemic' that is driving families into poverty and stunting the region's economic development (UNICEF 2000).

Using recent technological advances like genetic fingerprinting techniques it is possible to trace individual strains of the tubercle bacillus through people and ascertain from whom they were infected. This allows outbreaks to be traced back to their origins, and has allowed the articulation that much of origins of the spread of tuberculosis are arising in 'foreign' countries. Do you screen everyone who comes through the borders and treat them, or is the cheaper option to treat everyone on the planet at 'source', regardless of where they come from? Often arguments based on humanist grounds go for this latter option, based on calculations that suggest it is both cheaper, and the more humane thing to do (see for example, Coberly 2000).

Partnerships proliferate out around these problematisations of tuberculosis. In 1998, the Stop TB initiative was launched by the WHO, with a call to develop global partnerships in dealing with tuberculosis. By 2001 there were over 60 partners whose main base is still in the more industrialised nations, but includes multinational companies' philanthropic trusts (for example, the Bill and Melinda Gates Foundation, Soros's Open Society Institute); drug companies; bilateral agencies like USAID; multilaterals like the World Bank and WHO.[9] It is described as a global movement to accelerate social and political (as in the action of national governments, regardless of their ideological underpinnings) action to stop the unnecessary spread of tuberculosis around the world. In 2000 a ministerial conference on 'TB and Sustainable Development' was held in Amsterdam, to politically ratify commitment to DOTS, and to its expansion. Commitment was made to the 'global drug facility' of new international approaches towards ensuring universal access to efficient national systems for procurement and distribution of tuberculosis drugs and DOTS expansion.[10] Four reports on Global Tuberculosis Control had been published by 2001, in which standard data collection from 211 countries via the WHO regional offices had been collated and reported on.[11] A global alliance for the development of TB drugs has been launched, along the lines of public/private partnership. A revised framework for effective TB control has attempted to reframe access to TB care and drugs as a human right, and emphasises the socio-political dimensions of DOTS.[12] The 'Stop TB partnership' evolved into the broader 'global partnership to stop TB' and developed working groups to look at DOTS expansion, new TB drug development and the containment of multi-drug resistant tuberculosis. Its values are of urgency, equity, shared responsibility, inclusiveness, consensus, sustainability and dynamism. The World Bank hosted its first global forum in October 2001. There is, then, an increasing amount of activity around the global threat of tuberculosis.

What is of interest, though, is the emergence of two divergent discourses of implementation. One is 'health sector reform' foisted on Nepal by bi- and multilaterals, which is reflected in the rhetoric about the need for increasingly decentralised implementation to make the health service more responsive to locally defined needs. Yet it is argued that this can only be done if the information systems on the state of a country's health are efficient and able to represent health 'burdens' accurately. Much aid and money in the health sector in Nepal is pumped into developing these systems. At the same time, since the rise of the World Bank's hegemony in defining health, with the dismantlement of the Alma Ata declaration of 'integrated primary health care' and the return to the idea of vertical disease-oriented interventions, coupled with the need for proven cost-effectiveness, the 'burdens' as they are called, are increasingly defined by globalised discourses and interests. Following a series of research studies in Africa by health economists, intervention in tuberculosis is now deemed particularly cost-effective, as treatment also acts to decrease the prevalence and the burden on the country's economy (De Jonge et al. 1994; World Bank 1993). In Nepal, then, the vertical tuberculosis programme has developed its own separate recording, reporting and drug distribution system, which still emphasises the public sector. Simultaneously, privatised medical services articulated in the name of reform – and seen as the answer to many of Nepal's health service inadequacies (Karki 1999) – are deemed a problem for good public health practice. And this disparity, as well as the desire to control the vagaries of the private system, is being played out on the bodies of those who are ill with tuberculosis in Palpa district.

When we look at any individual's relationship to the public health order, we are dealing with the complex interaction of global discourses and state. As Dugdale has pointed out, it is the mixture of materials with bodies that make up subjects; that is, subjectivities are being produced in these material arrangements even before any verbal utterances are made, and these are bureaucratic arrangements that constitute all involved as subjects of a certain kind (1999: 118). As she further elaborates, this also involves 'relationships and trajectories that pertain to government' (1999: 119), citing therapeutic goods, companies, health professionals and consumers as important agents in this process. In the Nepal DOTS example, to name some, we have relationships with anti-tuberculous drugs, microscopes and chemical reagents and their manufacturers; with governments that procure them as aid; with public health workers who advocate their use; with national, institutional and organisational practices that dictate what can and cannot be treated (what is 'normal' or 'pathological', what is deemed most cost-effective to treat) and the strict regimes of surveillance following those put on treatment as cohorts; with research institutions competing for limited funds; and with patients. How patients and health workers enter into these arrangements in the public sector is already tightly pre-defined, and with TB these arrangements comply with internationalist notions of best practice in public health.

CONCLUDING REMARKS

Over the last ten years, tuberculosis programmes have been changed by the development of a policy that, many would argue, has revitalised the control of this awful disease. This has developed at a time – and been held up as a success – when we have similarly witnessed the growth of 'a new architecture of aid'. As the chapters by Coelho and Eyben in this volume point out, this new-style aid is frequently inherently contradictory in its operation. Within the health sector in Nepal, discourses of good governance, decentralisation and reform (private sector involvement) run against the grain of what has become a highly centralised and state-controlled tuberculosis strategy. Programmatic success is judged from the perspective of the elimination of the disease and the direction the programme takes is dictated by the desire to prevent the rise of multi-drug resistance. This utilitarianism, and the direct links with the needs of the state result, however, in a 'narrowing of vision' (Scott 1999); this is inextricably bound to the use of globalised epidemiological disease categories which may unintentionally, yet paradoxically, deny significant numbers of people who have TB access to treatment. The practices and production of an administrative abstraction in the Nepal context – 'statistico-tuberculosis' – has profound material effects.

While I anticipate that many of those involved in the creation of this system would argue that it is better than the 'chaos' before – the low cure rates and lack of knowing what was happening to patients – the attempted stabilisation of the system itself can still significantly marginalise patients and deny their agency. As such, this may also unfortunately exacerbate what Farmer (1998) would describe as 'structural violence'. Social hierarchy in Nepal is reflected in its health systems, where responsibility is all too easily referred to the protocol or to other authorities. This can further compound the unintended effects of policy that we must be aware of. What I am attempting to articulate here is what is at stake epistemologically within this global order. This is a moment in which the patient Nepal, and the tuberculosis sufferers, are pushed to adopt the subjectivity prescribed, must take their treatment, and be directly observed while doing so. We should strive to bring about the situation where this does not further add to the suffering of those most marginalised from the current global order, those whose position makes them most vulnerable to this awful disease.

NOTES

I acknowledge all the hard work of those involved in developing and working within the Nepal TB programme, and particularly those health workers and patients who shared time with me. Their names have been changed for the sake of anonymity. For all those who develop and work within the limitations of the DOTS framework, I hope that these interpretations are taken in the spirit of critical understanding and are not just rejected as being 'anti-DOTS', an unfortunate and all too frequent tendency. I also wish to acknowledge Christopher Davis who, as my PhD supervisor, first suggested that I think of bacteria as political objects. Thanks are due also to James Fairhead who, as discussant for this paper at the SOAS conference 'Order and Disjuncture', gave me the idea for the title, as well as to David Mosse for his continuing encouragement to develop and present this work. I also thank all those who, at various forums, have engaged with the evolution of this chapter and provided feedback.

1. SCC is called 'short course', as it replaced the 'standard' regimes of the past, with an entirely oral regime that substituted the drug rifampicin for the injectable streptomycin, and the regime needed only to be given for six to eight months rather than a year. In Nepal DOTS was adopted as national policy following the gift of free rifampicin from the Japanese government, as part of their aid package, to the National Tuberculosis Programme and amid fears that this would produce an epidemic of multi-drug resistant TB once the markets were flooded with this drug (Fryatt 1995).
2. This was funded by the ESRC, for my PhD in Social Anthropology (Harper 2003) at the University of London.
3. When I first wrote this chapter, I did so to address a conference theme, 'Order and Disjuncture'. Order, first, can be used as a noun or a verb. As a noun, its definitions in the *Oxford Dictionary* include the following: Order, as Arrangement: The way in which people and things are arranged in relation to each other or, the state of being carefully and neatly arranged. Order, as controlled state: The state that exists when people obey laws, rules or authority. Order, as instruction: Something that somebody is told to do by somebody in authority. Order, as system: The way that a society, the world, etc. is arranged, with its system of rules and customs. Order,

as Biology: a group into which animals, plants, etc. that have similar characteristics are divided. Within the terms of the conference, then, order (a combination of these meanings above) is juxtaposed against a particular stage in the series of activities or events – or juncture – within which the order is being established or stabilised. Disjuncture, again a noun, is a difference between two things that you would expect to be in agreement with each other. The order I analyse combines, to varying degrees, all these meanings above – as arrangement, controlled state, instruction, system and taxonomy – within the attempts to manage the health of the people of Nepal.

4. The evolution of neoliberal ideas in the health sector in Nepal can be traced within the five-year health plans (Harper 2002; Maskey 2002).

5. However, after the staff presented their difficulties to a supervisor from the NTC, it was agreed that they could accept a diagnosis made by a private doctor as long as they received, with the patient, a referral letter from that doctor referring them into the system – many, unsurprisingly, arriving after their money had run out, did not have this.

6. I have reviewed recent WHO, scientific and other literature elsewhere to demonstrate this and so will not expand further here (Harper and Tarnowski 2003).

7. This is being questioned, for example by Buse and Walt (2000) in a debate in *Social Science and Medicine* on the World Bank's shift into international health, as millions of dollars are spent in some countries to generate the requisite data. The generation of huge quantities of facts, and the centralising tendencies that those institutional monitors require, also raises questions around what is meant by decentralisation (Harper and Tarnowski 2003).

8. See <www.asia.cnn.com/2000/HEALTH/06/29/infectious.diseases/index. html> (consulted August 2003).

9. See <www.stoptb.org/stop.tb.initiative/index.html> (consulted August 2003).

10. See <www.stoptb.org/GDF/index.html> (consulted August 2003).

11. See <www.who.int/gtb/publications/globre00/summary.html> (consulted August 2003).

12. See <www.stoptb.org/material/revised_framework.Intro.htm> (consulted August 2003).

REFERENCES

Bam, D. (2001) DOTS in Nepal. http://tb.net.vom/tbneet.forum/contents/ forum/issue01/bam.html (accessed December 2001;Tbnet was closed down in 2002).

Barrett, G.C., W. Kuzawa, T. McDae and G. Armelagos (1998) Emerging and re-emerging infectious diseases: the third epidemiologic transition. *Annual Review of Anthropology* 27: 247–71.

Berg, M. (1998) Order(s) and disorder(s): of protocols and medical practices. In M. Berg and A. Mol (eds) *Differences in medicine: unravelling practices, techniques, and bodies* (Durham, NC and London: Duke University Press).

Brown, P. (1997) Culture and the global resurgence of malaria. In M. Inhorn and P. Brown (eds) *The anthropology of infectious diseases: international health perspectives* (Amsterdam: Gordon and Breach Publishers).

Buse, K. and G. Walt (2000) Role conflict? The World Bank and the world's health. *Social Science and Medicine* 50: 177–79.

Coberly, J. (2000) We cannot eliminate TB on one continent: TB crosses borders, <www.hopkins_tb.org/tb_conf/tb_conf_4.html> (accessed November 2001).

Coghlan, A. and D. Conclar (2001) Coming home. *New Scientist* 2298 (7 July): 28–33.

Coker, R. (2000) *From chaos to coercion: detention and the control of tuberculosis* (New York: St Martin's Press).

Cooter, R. and S. Sturdy (1999) Of war, medicine and modernity: introduction. In R. Cooter, M. Harrison and S. Sturdy (eds) *War, medicine and modernity* (Stroud: Sutton Publishing).

De Jonge, E., C. Murray, H. Chum, D. Nyangulu, A. Salomao and K. Styblo (1994) Cost effectiveness of chemotherapy for sputum-smear positive pulmonary tuberculosis in Malawi, Mozambique and Tanzania. *International Journal of Health Planning and management* 9: 151–81.

Dodier, N. (1998) Clinical practice and procedures in occupational medicine: a study of the framing of individuals. In M. Berg and A. Mol (eds) *Differences in medicine: unravelling practices, techniques, and bodies* (Durham, NC and London: Duke University Press).

Dugdale, A. (1999) Materiality: juggling sameness and difference. In J. Law and J. Hassard (eds) *Actor network theory and after* (Oxford: Blackwell Publishers/ Sociological Review).

Dye, C., G. Garnett, K. Sleeman and B. Williams (1998) Prospects for world-wide tuberculosis control under the WHO DOTS strategy. *Lancet* 352 (12 December): 1886–91.

Farmer, P. (1998) On suffering and structural violence: a view from below. In A. Kleinman, V. Das and M. Lock (eds) *Social suffering* (Delhi: Oxford University Press).

Farmer, P. (1999) *Infections and inequalities: the modern plagues*. Berkeley, Los Angeles and London: University of California Press.

Fryatt, R. (1995) Foreign aid and TB control policy in Nepal: commentary. *Lancet* 346: 328.

Garrett, L. (1994) *The coming plague: newly emerging diseases in a world out of balance* (Harmondsworth: Penguin).

Gray, C.H. (1997) *Postmodern war: the new politics of conflict* (London: Routledge).

Hacking, I. (1990) *The taming of chance* (Cambridge: Cambridge University Press).

Hardt, M. and A. Negri (2000) *Empire* (Cambridge, MA and London: Harvard University Press).

Harper, I. (2002) Capsular promise as public health: a critique of the Nepal National Vitamin A Programme. *Studies in Nepali History and Society* 7(1): 137–73.

Harper, I. (2003) Mission, magic and medicalisation: an anthropological study into public health in contemporary Nepal. Unpublished PhD in Social Anthropology, University of London.

Harper, I. and C. Tarnowski (2003) A heterotopia of resistance: health, community forestry and resistance to state centralisation in Nepal. In D. Gellner (ed.) *Resistance and the state: Nepalese experiences* (Delhi: Social Science Press).

Kaplan, R. (2000) The coming anarchy. In P. O'Meara, H. Mehlinger and M. Krain (eds) *Globalization and the challenges of a new century: a reader* (Bloomington and Indianapolis: Indiana University Press).

Karki, D.B. (1999) Some visible changes could be seen in the near future. *Spotlight* 27 August: 21.

Keane, C. (1998) Globality and constructions of world health. *Medical Anthropology Quarterly* 12(2): 226–40.

Latour, B. (1988) *The pasteurization of France.* (Cambridge, MA and London: Harvard University Press).

Martin, E. (1994) *Flexible bodies: the role of immunity in American culture from the days of polio to the age of AIDS* (Boston, MA: Beacon Press).

Maskey, M. (2002) Development of health services in Nepal. Paper presented at a workshop on 'Issues of Research Methodology' (Accompanying activity of the project 'Monitoring Shifts in Health Sector Policies in South Asia'), organised by RIAAG, Maastricht, and JNU, India, in Dhulikhel, Nepal, 23–25 November.

Mol, A. (1998) Missing links, making links: the performance of some atheroscleroses. In M. Berg and A. Mol (eds) *Differences in medicine: unravelling practices, techniques, and bodies* (Durham, NC and London: Duke University Press).

Mol, A. (1999) Ontological politics: a word and some questions. In J. Law and J. Hassard (eds) *Actor network theory and after* (Oxford: Blackwell/Sociological Review).

Mol, A. and M. Berg (1998) Differences in medicine: an introduction. In M. Berg and A. Mol (eds) *Differences in medicine: unravelling practices, techniques, and bodies* (Durham, NC and London: Duke University Press).

Neushul, P. (1999) Fighting research: army participation in the clinical testing and mass production of penicillin during the Second World War. In R. Cooter, M. Harrison and S. Sturdy (eds) *War, medicine and modernity* (Stroud: Sutton Publishing).

NTP and HMG/N (1999) *Tuberculosis control in Nepal 2055–2060 (1998–2003): long-term plan* (Kathmandu: NTP).

Panos and WHO (2000) Airborne killers (adapted from WHO report 1996). In K. Dixit, A. John and R. Gupta (eds) *TB do or die: journalists take a look at how Asian countries are fighting tuberculosis.* Kathmandu: Panos and WHO.

Scott, J. (1999) *Seeing like a state: how certain schemes to improve the human condition have failed* (New Haven, CT and London: Yale University Press).

Sigdel, S. (1998) *Primary health care provision in Nepal* (Kathmandu: Express Colour Press Co. Ltd).

Singleton, V. (1998) Stabilising instabilities: the role of the laboratory in the United Kingdom cervical screening programme. In M. Berg and A. Mol (eds) *Differences in medicine: unravelling practices, techniques, and bodies* (Durham, NC and London: Duke University Press).

Small, P. (1999) Tuberculosis in the 21st century: DOTS and SPOTS. *International Journal of Tuberculosis and Lung Disease* 3(10): 855–61.

Smith, D. (1984) Textually mediated social organisation. *International Social Science Journal* 59–75.

Sontag, S. (1991) *Illness as metaphor: Aids and its metaphors* (Harmondsworth: Penguin).

Steinbruner, J. (2000) *Principles of global security* (Washington, DC: Brookings Institution Press).

Timmermans, S. and M. Berg (1997) Standardisation in action: achieving local universality through medical protocols. *Social Studies of Science* 27: 273–305.

UNICEF (2000) Press release, 23 March, <www.stoptb.org/conference/press/Asia.Pacific/AFP.Unicef.Asia.html> (consulted May 2002).

WHO (1994) *TB: a global emergency – WHO report on the TB epidemic*, WHO/TB/94.177 (Geneva: WHO).

WHO (1995) *WHO report on the tuberculosis epidemic, 1995*, WHO/TB/95.183 (Geneva: WHO).

WHO (1997) *Questions and answers about the DOTS strategy*, WHO/TB/97.225 (Geneva: WHO).

WHO (1998) *Fact sheet no. 200*, June (Geneva: WHO).

WHO (2000) *Tuberculosis, Fact sheet no. 104*, revised April 2000, <www.who.int/inf-fs/en/fact104.html> (consulted August 2003).

WHO (2004) *8th annual report on global tuberculosis control* (Geneva: WHO).

World Bank (1993) *World development report 1993: investing in health* (New York: Oxford University Press).

7 THE WORSHIPPERS OF RULES? DEFINING RIGHT AND WRONG IN LOCAL PARTICIPATORY PROJECT APPLICATIONS IN SOUTH-EASTERN ESTONIA

Aet Annist

Developmental cultures evolve through a complicated set of interests and agendas as well as the concerns of various stakeholders. The ethnographic data I collected during fieldwork in two south-east Estonian communities, and at different levels of a DFID-funded multi-agency participatory Rural Partnerships Programme (RPP) seeking to reduce poverty and social exclusion in rural communities in the Baltic states, is well suited to study this complex scene of global and local development relations.[1] In what follows, I examine the evaluation process of project applications from rural Estonian communities at precisely the stage where the programme's general ideology is tested and translated into practice. The chapter shows how local development agents strictly follow the requirements and regulations that organise the evaluation process in such a way as to create the impression of a trustworthy partner for foreign funders. At the same time, the process serves to conceal a frequent reliance on personal information, such as a suspicion about the motives of certain applicants, when rejecting projects.

These practices run counter to the overall stated objectives of the programme and its empowerment philosophy, since it replaces the idea of 'communities to be helped' with one of individual project applicants who can be accepted or rejected largely on the basis of judgements about whether they are dedicated to or trusted by their communities. The handling of one case in particular, provided here as an ethnographic example, will demonstrate how such 'undeserving' applicants can then be presented as the major cause for any failures encountered by the programme, which is a line of argument that can be seen to satisfy the needs of both local and international development agents. However, there is some indication that the communities may 'even up the score' by suspecting in turn the evaluators of selfish motives, undermining at least to some degree the carefully constructed image of impartiality and fairness.

POST-SOVIET RURAL ESTONIA

Rural poverty and social exclusion on the current scale are new experiences for Estonians, since rural areas enjoyed a relatively high quality of life during the Soviet period from the late 1960s onwards. The rural population of Estonia was relatively unaffected by the difficulties of buying foodstuffs, at least compared with urban Soviets who had to struggle with shortages on daily basis. In fact, Estonian city dwellers often depended upon fresh products, including meat, provided by rural relatives. Since the early 1990s, this form of access has largely vanished as new Western foodstuffs, eagerly demanded by deprived ex-Soviets, have flooded the market; as a result, rural Estonians lost these mutually useful exchanges with the urbanites. Even more importantly, they lost access to the Russian market, now sealed off by new border and hostile market protection mechanisms. Over the last decade, while new opportunities opened up in the cities, they were mostly closing down in rural areas.

Hopes that there would be a rejuvenation of family farming in the late 1980s and early 1990s were short-lived, and turned out to be a figment of the imagination of urban politicians rather than a reality for rural people themselves. While land was rapidly privatised, many new landowners lacked access to the necessary technology and the development of farmers' cooperatives faltered. For many years, politicians then argued that conventional agriculture was entirely unprofitable in Estonia. Opportunities for alternative non-agricultural livelihoods remained extremely limited and have only recently started to develop. However good their business plans, sufficient credit for new productive opportunities remains unavailable to most rural inhabitants, whose average incomes are the lowest in the country. Over the last ten years, the majority of the rural population has fallen to the very bottom of the social hierarchy. This dire picture is confirmed by sources such as national censuses, UNDP reports (1999, 2000), the Economist Intelligence Unit Country Profile (EIU 1999/2000), and by authors such as Abrahams (2002), Alanen (1999), Alanen et al. (2001) and Unwin (1999). Unemployment and the likelihood of suffering from poverty are considerably higher in rural than urban areas; additionally, the steady decline in vital services has motivated a continuous flow of out-migration.

Despite today's adversities and shortages, people with a Soviet past possess strong networks built up over decades. Such a past can provide institutional resources for change in the present (Stark and Bruszt

1998: 7, 122). Indeed, Russian and Romanian peasants and workers have re-established paternalist relations with neo-capitalist ex-Soviet managers, creating neo-feudalist systems (Humphrey 1991; Verdery 1996). Polish peasants have revolted against their fate by defining the changes brought about by the trade liberalisation policies as not only anti-peasant but also anti-Polish, and have enjoyed considerable popularity in the country (Zbierski-Salameh 1999). Bulgarian peasants have voted for socialists (Creed 1999) as their response to social breakdown. No such solutions appear to have been an option for the Estonian rural population, however. While agricultural issues were routinely discussed in the media during the Soviet period, they have now been pushed aside to become specialist issues, and sympathy regarding rural problems is rare. Socialist political parties have not gained popularity within the free and democratic elections in Estonia.

The way collective and state farms were eliminated severely reduced the space for communal activities rather than simply modifying it. Even if it was recognised that it might be safer to build something from the old socialist farming structures, the combined force of the government's hostility to collective farming, the success of the ex-Soviet leaders, and the overall mentality favouring fast and total change, created an atmosphere in which building on the old system was very difficult. Years of restitution and ultra-liberal reforms have brought a loss of trust and confidence, the destruction of families and kin groups, and changes in ownership and rights; they have created hostility, broken relationships and eroded communities which have lost the social capacity to organise themselves for support or for protest (see Annist 2003). Cooperation and communal values – symbols of the Soviet time – have been discredited in the media and in the political arena for several years. All this has contributed to the lack of cooperation and weakening of communal capacity.

THE RURAL PARTNERSHIPS PROGRAMME

The goal of the Rural Partnerships Programme (RPP), active in Estonia from 2000 to 2003, was to 'reduce poverty and social exclusion in the [three] Baltic States through improved rural and regional development', and to 'enhance the capacity of local communities in project areas to improve rural livelihoods on a sustainable basis' (DFID 2000). This aim appeared to deal with a theme vital for the recovery of these areas. In Estonia, the programme operated in all three counties of south-eastern Estonia, an area whose socio-economic indicators signal great difficulties.

The ideology of the programme was an explicitly participatory one. The need for participation from those targeted – that is, the rural people facing hardship, as well as those socially excluded – was repeatedly stressed by those organising the programme. Participatory ideals and values were generally considered an important message, together with inclusive planning and participation at every level of decision-making, and were an important part of what the programme representatives were hoping to distribute among all the Estonians involved. However, it was not the participation of the target communities on the various levels of programme decision-making that was in fact propagated, but rather participation and social involvement at the local level, most importantly within the communities themselves, reflected in the communities' own ability to involve everybody in community-level (village-level) decision making.

The Estonian programme manager frequently pointed out to project newcomers that the word *kogukond* (community) was rarely in use prior to introducing the programme in Estonia – a claim that is difficult to verify, but is indicative of the programme's vision of its role and influence. Through increased inclusion of members of the community in social activities, it was expected that communities would become empowered as social units, which would help them break out of their cycle of poverty, exclusion and social fragmentation and, thus, their inability to bring about change. A strong socially functioning community was considered able to help itself and its members in the longer term by establishing community enterprises and other socially viable activities, as well as by applying for funds, among others, from the various resources opening up to new members of the European Union (e.g. SAPARD 6th measure, Structural Funds Programmes, etc.). In other words, the aim was to help communities create new informal networks to replace what they had lost during rapid and shattering changes.

The RPP was funded by DFID and tendered to an implementing agency via a bidding process in the UK. Both DFID and the implementing agency performed an overseeing role every six months. The ideological base and model for the programme came from Ireland and Northern Ireland (e.g. Partnership in Action 1996), where partnerships for community development have been functioning for several years. Each level of the hierarchy of the RPP in Estonia, except the administrative unit, was intended to reflect the partnership model. This meant involving four sectors of the society – voluntary representatives were engaged from national and local government, from the private and non-profit sectors. It was expected that partnership values would disseminate through various training sessions but also through the individuals involved at different levels of the system. RPP's national administrative team formed the rest of the programme hierarchy in Estonia. They managed the process, coordinating the functions and tasks of the institutions involved in training as well as the local partnership networks. The people working in this unit were hired by the UK and Irish representatives and were paid by them. A voluntary Steering Committee oversaw the process on the national level. The selection of its members linked it to various other programme units, as well as to the social, agricultural, internal and financial ministries of the country. Through those representatives, the programme also hoped to influence national policy decisions concerning rural livelihoods, as well as to disseminate partnership and participatory values among those ministries.

In each of the three south-eastern counties, local voluntary Partnership Boards were set up, bringing together representatives from local government, the state, the private sector and the non-profit sector. Each of the three Boards was autonomous, devising its own county strategy, based on a process of identifying the greatest local needs. In the following, I will mostly concentrate on the programme activities of the L Partnership Board (LPB).

Once the Board had clarified the county strategy, various publishing efforts disseminated it in the county. The Board launched the Small Projects' Fund Competition, which was advertised in local newspapers as well as at various public events, encouraging project applications from communities. As some rural municipalities had been identified as target areas, based on their adverse socio-economic indicators, special attention was paid to advertising the project competition for potential respondents in these areas. The maximum sum for each project was £3,000 in the first round, and £850 in the second round.

The main task of the programme as a whole was to arrange the competition for projects that could lead to sustainable and successful initiatives. The major expectation from the Small Projects' Fund applications was that the applications would reflect the needs of communities that were willing to become strongly participatory, highly inclusive, involving everybody in a given community in the activities proposed. For allegedly 'weak' communities, the programme offered help in writing proposals for communal activities and for local solutions for problems, or in accessing services. All interested communities were able to consult the project coordinator based in their county. In various training programmes, potential community leaders from the target and other areas were carefully taught the participatory, inclusive ideology of the programme. It was explained that they were to take into consideration everyone (i.e. including the socially excluded) in their communities. However, not everybody who applied to the programme had received this training, and not all those who were trained applied for money.

Once the project applications had been received, an Evaluation Committee (EC) was set up for the projects. It consisted of members of the LPB as well as representatives from other units who volunteered and did not have obvious vested interests in any projects. Successful projects were finally considered by another important unit of the programme, the NGO Partnership (NGO). This unit comprised the more active and leading members of each County Board. It was established as a voluntary work-based NGO to act as grant beneficiary for all project grants in cases where the recipient was not an existing NGO. This unit took on all financial and legal obligations in relation to both the projects funded and the foreign partners, signed contracts with the involved parties and monitored the flow of funds. Unlike the LPB, which was usually attended by representatives of municipal governments and non-profit organisations, members of the NGO were mostly either county (thus, structurally national level) representatives or entrepreneurs. Their overall attitude to the meetings and to the whole programme appeared more efficiency-driven than that of the LPB; they also more often emphasised that they were doing voluntary work.

In what follows, I will concentrate on the activities of the NGO, the LPB and the EC as the combined effort of those structural units decided a project's fate. I will look at the process of evaluation of project applications from the rural communities, which is the stage where the general ideology of the programme was tested and translated into practice, and where the disjunctures within development efforts were most clearly revealed.

WORSHIPPING RULES?

Attesting an image

Although the LPB was the entity demonstrating the participatory ideology of the programme, it was the NGO, given an executive role, that actually made the final decisions on whether or not a project from the community would be financed, albeit in accordance with the suggestions of the EC, with the agreement of the LPB. In reality, the NGO controlled the flow of money and the legal aspects of projects, and was the body that signed or refused to sign the contracts for projects. Indeed, those involved in the system considered the NGO to be in a better position to judge the feasibility and sustainability of projects, given its role in the structure and the experience of its members. Accordingly, the members of the NGO put more weight on the technical quality of the application. At the meetings of the EC, the NGO managed to dominate the decision-making process, and the LPB was inclined to be steered to accept the preferences of the NGO members.

The members of the NGO also felt they had accepted a great responsibility: signing the contracts; monitoring compliance of the projects. The Ireland-based observer commented that the NGO 'does not just see its role as an intermediary funding agent, but also considers itself to provide a useful review function, to assist with problematic grants, to ensure compliance with necessary conditions ...' (Burns 2003). One of the members of the NGO worded this in the following way:

The goal of the Partnership Board is to help the villages but this has to happen according to the rules ... When a child asks for money from the parents, it is the parent who sets the rules. S/he[2] teaches who sets the rules, teaches and leads. Partnership Board sets the rules – it is our common agreement. The other side is technical: the resources given have to be observable, the funds have to go to the right hole; the result has to be measurable and the process must be transparent. The NGO has the obligation to observe whether the usage [of money] is in accordance with the goals stated, and that it is achieved in accordance with the laws of Estonian Republic, as well as the good manners [of accountancy].

The members of the NGO regularly compared themselves with the LPB in terms of such parental metaphors, the NGO being the strict parent who demands accurate following of the practicalities of rules, fussing around with contracts and mistakes the 'children' have made, while the other 'parent', the LPB, responsible for teaching high values and ideals rarely understands these difficulties and realities.

While this positioning of the NGO vis-à-vis the 'ideological unit' (LPB) helped smooth acceptance of the preferences of the executive branch of the system, it was the task of creating the right image of 'trustworthiness' that was even more significant in establishing the relationship between the NGO and the foreign funding bodies. The NGO's contractual relations with the DFID subcontractor meant that (in principle) it was liable and could even be sued by the subcontractor. Although nothing signalled any such possibility (mostly raised jokingly) an image of trustworthiness had nonetheless to be demonstrated.

While it has been common in the critical literature on development projects to describe the manipulation, if not outright corruption, of the rules among development actors and local elites in Eastern Europe – as described for instance by Sampson (1996, 2002) and Wedel (1998) – this Estonian case indicates the opposite, namely a rigorous procedural adherence to established rules. Demonstrating that formal rules were being strictly followed in relation to financial matters in the programme was considered very important. Possibly attempting to emphasise the high standards that the NGO required in their financial dealings, it even threatened to sue one of the project leaders who it suggested had violated the rules for financial reports.[3] As the Irish observer reported:

[the NGO's] view is that the breaking of contract was not due to low capacity or mismanagement, but rather it was quite deliberate. As such, they feel duty bound to pursue the course of action as allowed for in the contract. They also feel that this will demonstrate their professionalism, and dependability. (Burns 2003)

Indeed, even though the case was later dropped, and the members of the NGO agreed after all that the faults were simply mismanagement, it had been possible to create the required impression of a professional, trustworthy guardian of foreign funds.

This impression was ultimately directed at the foreign partners. It could be seen as an effort to maintain the ownership of the programme, along the same lines as Eyben and León (this volume). However, it also addressed important local experiences and concerns. For instance, members of the NGO stressed the difference between institutions and individuals that were still living in the Soviet mentality, where rules were set to be broken, and the new, efficient, law-abiding Estonians who were perfectly Western in their attitudes. By their strictness towards possible wrongdoers, they emphasised that they were part of this new trustworthy Western mentality. It is possible that this kind of image-creation within local development structures is specific to post-Soviet development encounters. At least in Estonia, being oriented towards the West is still an entirely unchallenged direction in the public and political realm. Protests related to development interventions are mostly expressions of indignation that locals are misjudged to be less developed, less Western or poorer than they consider themselves to be or would like to be seen (see also Annist 2000). Accordingly, local developers use every opportunity to refute this potential impression.

Rules to follow, rules to bend

Formal rules were the most obvious and visible showcase to use in proving an image of professionalism to foreign partners. However, it is also true that such pious respect for accuracy and rules can involve a rather interesting exercise in bending the rules in order to uphold the image of coherence, trustworthiness, and normativity. This is illustrated in the process of marking or evaluating projects by the Evaluation Committee (EC).

At the evaluation meeting I attended, the committee consisted of four members of the LPB, plus one representative from the NGO (Raivo), and the county secretary of the programme (Egle). There were no LPB representatives from the non-profit sector. Thus, the EC consisted of a male entrepreneur (Toomas), two female municipality government representatives (Astrid and Angelika) and a female county government representative (Inna). Even though outside observers were required to attend the meeting, only I could be considered as an observer, albeit a less potent one since I was in no position to report the process to the LPB.

The overall atmosphere of the meeting was mostly amiable and light-hearted: working in the same small county, most people knew one another fairly well before being brought together within the programme. Gathering in the afternoon of a working day, they clearly indicated from the start that they wished to complete matters fairly fast. However, as the day progressed, it was clear that they could not avoid disagreements and would not try to take matters lightly. Heated arguments developed, although never to the extent of embarrassing or insulting anybody. Together with a few short coffee breaks, the evaluation of 16 projects lasted for six hours.

The evaluation took place in a well-equipped, well-lit modern office. The evaluators had a whiteboard and a laptop computer at their service. In the corner, a coffee-machine and a water dispenser purred to provide the refreshments. By contrast, the scenes of villagers conjured by their project applications and in the comments about their conditions and situations, gave a picture of a lack of skills and supplies, albeit combined with a certain eagerness to act. Here lack of equipment met good provision, professionalism met helplessness; the position of project writers was hardly equal to that of the evaluators.

Each evaluator had one sheet for each project on which to record marks, in theory prior to coming to the meeting. However, some evaluators only started to fill some sheets during the meeting itself. To allocate marks for the projects, members of the EC were given a set of features as weighted criteria: the projects were to be evaluated in terms of (a) their ability to diminish poverty and social exclusion (max. points 25); (b) the level of partnership (20); (c) the level of involvement of the community (20); (d) novelty (14); (e) the quality of the application (11); (f) any additional value created (5); (g) their influence in the target area (depending on whether they fell into the target area or not, the points given could be either 0 or 5). The weighting clearly indicates an inclination towards the ideological aspects that the application should demonstrate that it would be able to fulfil, as opposed to technical quality. The evaluation system was a combination of the LPB's general agreement on which things are important and the basic set of rules provided by the ideologues from Northern Ireland. The projects were given marks that eventually formed a score, which placed them on a shortlist. Those with the smallest score would have to be left out. Aside from being marked the projects were also discussed generally, opinions being given about the overall sustainability and potential of the project.

One proposal in particular exemplified the difficulties that the EC had to face in order to reconcile the rules with the requirements of the programme ideology. The committee had rejected one project during general discussion, considering it weak and pointless. Once the scores from each individual member of the EC were calculated, however, this project turned out to have more marks than two other projects which, it was felt, should get the funding. Since people were unanimous that this project was indeed rather bad, but felt tied to the marks they had given, some suggested they could just change the marks each of them had given to this project. Some others, Inna in particular, felt that this would not be right. The following discussion developed:

Astrid: What will we violate if we change the marks [already given]?

Toomas: The commission does not have to make its internal results public anyway.

Egle: Well, you still have to justify your decision![4]

Raivo: I won't since [the marks are] not the only criteria.

Astrid: It is easier for us to agree [on changing the marks], easier for Egle, and for the Partnership Board. It is easier to prove the outcome in the end [to the LPB].

Egle: Because these rules have been made up by the Partnership Board itself.

Astrid: Let's change its marks, let's do it Inna ...

Raivo still held that there was no need to change the marks if they agreed that marks are not the only basis for making the decision.

Egle: Since the marks *are* the criteria, there is nothing to do. Give it different marks and then it won't be in conflict with the rules.

Inna: I will be in conflict with my conscience.

Inna, who opposed changing marks because she found it unethical, and Raivo, who opposed changing the marks because he did not consider marks the only basis for decision-making anyway, eventually agreed that changing marks was the best way to appear compliant with the rules. Thus, they reduced the marks for the quality of this project to '0':

Raivo (relieved): But we helped our colleague and good friend [Egle].

Egle: It is better for me to justify [the outcome] to the Partnership Board.

Thus the process where the rules obstructed the decision the committee considered ideologically right was made to look all right for the LPB, and the committee appeared to have followed the rules.

The discussion about the meaning of rules in evaluating a project has more to it than just protecting the coherence of the EC. To paraphrase Bourdieu, presenting the evaluation as in accordance with the rules is an ideological use of a model and a specific representation within the development industry, conveying the image of having conducted a virtuous or regular evaluation. The evaluators put themselves in the right by following the rules, 'to give apparent satisfaction to the demands of the official rule, and thus to compound the satisfactions of enlightened self-interest with the advantage of ethical impeccability' (Bourdieu 1977:22). While it seems to be a matter of conflict between ideologically correct and procedurally correct decisions, in practice, it is also a decision about what image to present and how.

Personal data and suspicious motives: community projects under scrutiny

Rules have a considerable role to play in establishing the credibility of this image. However, the potential conflict between the dual set of rules – official and practical – has to be resolved through arguments of necessity. Raivo declares that 'gut-feeling' or general knowledge in relation to a project is extremely important. He says that no system of marking is ideal, and the committee should strongly rely on the personal knowledge about the people behind the projects. Some other evaluators state that rules are rules, this cannot be changed and the form of evaluation cannot be rejected. Raivo points out that the committee is trusted by the LPB to make expert judgements, and thus, whatever they base their decisions on should be correct. When others are still not convinced, he uses his position as a representative of the NGO in the EC and states that this organisation would anyway not support, thus not sign the contract with a project that is:

... in conflict with my own principles and the good manners [of accountancy]. Evaluation based on marks can only be the basis, not the final reason. We can tell the Partnership Board that the formula is good but we cannot use it as the absolute truth.

Thus, according to this rather dominant personality who is in a powerful position to argue his views, the personal data any evaluator has about a project should be used in addition to the project applications themselves. Personal data are seen as a justified and valuable source for deciding about a project. In order to make the personality-based decisions acceptable, the rest of the marks should be checked against this personal background data.

Even though the rest of the committee did not appear to accept such a view when directly confronted by Raivo, the process of evaluation itself did actually indicate a heavy reliance on personality-related information. This became most obvious when the projects were scrutinised for their motivations.

Suspicions are raised in relation to various projects, but the common reason is the fear that a project is written for self-gratification only – for instance, by people who have seen the call for applications and have jumped at the opportunity of getting money without any prior accepted need from the communities. Ideally, project leaders are those springing up from within the communities, and evaluators were clearly concerned about projects where the proposal's author might be suspected of not having community support. Projects that could not show how they involved the rest of the community were dubious. Raivo:

> [this project is written] ... for getting a salary, [there is] no inner motivation and afterwards there will be such troubles with those projects. I would eliminate this, we do not have resources or power to control it.

In another case, according to Toomas, the author of the project could easily be hoping to gain directly from the project funds: 'Knowing the person, the whole village centre will be located at her home!' Despite the fact that the guidelines of project application allowed applications for material items, Raivo comments: 'How cheeky is that! To ask for a TV!' It is considered cheeky exactly because of the assumption that the person is hoping to get hold of the item for his or her own, rather than communal, use, and has the audacity to think the fund would fall into such a trap and give the money.

The evaluators feel that selfish and personal reasons are clearly visible from the applications. Raivo in particular praises himself for the ability to see through the projects that are 'fishing for money': 'I have this [skill] that I can see [when a project is written for its own sake] ...'

On the other hand, the evaluators themselves realise that their judgements are based on something else than the words written on the application forms. As Toomas says: 'You just dislike the personality and then want to bash the project!' But later, Toomas himself asks about another project: 'Who wrote this [project]?' Raivo tells him the name and Toomas responds: 'Aaaaa! No, I wouldn't give money to her!' In a rare contrast, a project considered remarkably good is praised by Raivo: 'I trust this project, there is a marvellous person leading it!'

The most dramatic example of personality-based decisions where the project leader was basically heavily mistrusted was the project, mentioned earlier, that originally received funding from the first round of applications. From the start, some members of the NGO expressed their conviction that the leader of this project, an experienced and active person, is a fraud – only that his shady dealings had never been proven. They claimed that they went ahead and accepted the project – which was in fact well-written – because they would finally prove that he is an unworthy applicant and could discredit him. After a few months of activity, the project leader was indeed considered not to be compliant enough with the rules and his reports to lack clarity and transparency. The NGO and the programme team had 'caught him in action': not following the rules as strictly as required, presenting incorrect financial documents and, finally, arguing his case rather than deferentially accepting the accusations. Finally, the NGO and the national team withheld the money not yet paid and threatened the project leader with legal action. The basis of such a drastic decision was the personal information that the evaluators had about the project leader, which put his project documentation under great scrutiny such that any error could be considered proof of prior personal suspicions.

For the rest of the projects, the most immediate results from the EC members' suspicions was that the budget specified in the application was diminished by excluding any item or event the committee considered dubious. When involved in this process of sifting out the right projects, the committee clearly stood as the guardian of the principles and ideals of the general ideology of social inclusion advocated by the programme. However, the principal basis for suspicion was not the information written on the application forms, but rather the personality of the project writer. Personality-based reasoning appeared a far easier way to decide whether a project was trustworthy than guessing whether it left the right impression regarding commitment to inclusion. When analysing the projects' wording to guess the reasons for applying, the evaluators would reach their final conclusion: 'Knowing him/her ...'. Personal knowledge about the specific people may appear more understandable than a score of marks based on the rules set up for the EC. But the marks and mysterious overall scores were at the same time something that gave the decisions an air of certainty, of being based on something beyond personal knowledge. Such a combination of data created sufficient confidence that what was achieved was not ambiguous or personality-based, but formal and well grounded. Numbers become ambiguous and arbitrary opinions turn into manageable and neutralised verdicts (see Anders, this volume).

When I asked the evaluators about the disadvantages or advantages of the projects whose authors were known to them, Raivo agreed it might appear unfair but felt that the end result is still democratic since it arose from discussions between all the evaluators. It is obvious that democracy of this sort takes the form of partially informed persons sharing partial information with one another. When the committee comes together, they adjust their original impressions in the course of sharing the data. Such a meeting makes the committee ultimately more potent in making personal judgements, since most project writers are known to at least one of the evaluators. Since only the personalised, singular writer (and not the community) can be accused of wrong motivations, the committee declares a project not to be communally produced or to be otherwise wrongfully motivated, based on judgements about personality. Through this process, the communities behind project applications are no longer heard. When the name of the person who has signed the project is foregrounded and the community pushed to the background, the core principles of the programme are effectively nullified.

Returning the mistrust

Describing the disenchantment of the East Europeans with the effects of aid money, Creed and Wedel (1997) refer to 'aid frustration'. People strongly believe the money has gone into the pockets of local political elites (see also Giordano and Kostova 2002). While in L county people's direct reactions to the evaluation results never became apparent, in the neighbouring county, which was going through exactly the same processes, a website allowing people to air their views about county matters received a number of anonymous comments after the evaluation meeting, expressing suspicions about why certain projects received funding. The commentators indicated that, out of nine funded projects, three were in some way related to members of the local Partnership Board. It was suggested that the British embassy should be informed, so that this innocent foreign supporter of such self-gratifying local endeavours could spring into action. The issues of trust and mistrust were most directly related to the question of whether the funding decisions of the EC were unselfish (for the common good) or selfish (for personal gain). So the evaluators were themselves subject to suspicion on the same basis as they judged project applicants.

Interestingly, however, the data from L county suggests that personal motives at the EC meeting were in use for a different purpose than personal gain. While the accusation that the evaluation decisions were based on personal knowledge is indeed correct, we cannot assume that the specific funding decisions were made because the members of the EC or their personal acquaintances would gain from them. On the contrary, when the project evaluators considered the background information of a person known to them, it was more likely to be done to exclude the 'wrong' (ideologically incorrect, selfish etc.) applications than to include the 'right' (personally profitable) ones. Mostly personal information is used in rejecting or reducing the applications, thus disfavouring rather than favouring the known applicants. In studies describing aid corruption in Eastern Europe, people with bargaining power within the development industry find ways of favouring their friends and relatives. Personal connections thus lie behind the approval of the projects. This appears not to be the case here – perhaps in the context of disrupted sociality that appears to characterise today's Estonia even outside the rural communities, that is, among the development workers. In this context, bending the rules for the benefit of kin groups or other personal social networks is less likely, while the need to prove neutrality and impartiality to the outsiders becomes paramount – paradoxically, such proofs also depend on the information acquired within personal social networks.

Ruling out weaknesses

Despite certain suspicions amongst some onlookers, the developers managed to maintain the image of the procedural correctness of evaluation decisions, and to establish themselves as a strict and incorruptible institution making tough but fair decisions. The demand for transparency and dutiful observance of regulations within the projects themselves was, in turn, seen as the best basis for the projects funded, enabling them to deliver good results for the programme.

However, the processes that were justified as a need to be strict with money and rules actually compromised the core principles of the programme. The programme aimed to strengthen weak communities, yet the NGO expected communities to present highly viable, clear projects with economically exact budgets. Raivo voiced this opinion more than once:

I wouldn't have given money to any of them ... The project applications have to be correct! All right, if you are a complete beginner – but those days are over when people scribbled their application on a piece of paper and could get funding. Let's not support helplessness!

The effects of such an approach become even more obvious in the process of rejecting certain projects. One young woman, Erika, was working on a project that was to involve youngsters in building a youth centre in an empty house in her village. Initially, the Partnership Board she applied to sent a positive response concerning her project. However, over the course of the following months, the NGO set additional requirements, fearing that the project might not be sustainable. She failed to satisfy those requirements, partly because of certain unexpected events in local politics. At a meeting, the NGO decided she should not get the funding and painted a picture that presented her as unworthy of the funds. As a result, the Partnership Board voted the project out of funding.

In some ways Erika's project was not exactly exemplary of the central ideals of the programme: her ability to involve the rest of the community was not great, and the task she had set for herself was larger than her application indicated. However, on paper her plan had no obvious flaws, which was also the reason for her application being accepted in the first place. As she was personally unknown to all the evaluators, there was no way of knowing that she lacked inclusive capacity. The reason for this rejection was her inability – because of an unexpected political change in her municipality – to satisfy the additional requirements. In an attempt to stabilise and strengthen the system (see Harper, this volume), the exceptional events encountered by Erika – were deemed to fall outside the tight rules proudly set by the 'professional handlers of foreign money'.

Through an interesting twist in the argument, the members of the NGO suggested this was a good result, not only in terms of saving the funding bodies from a (potentially) unsuccessful project, but also from the point of view of the individual not receiving the funds. The negative decision about a project would also teach the writer something:

The goal is to teach also through *not* receiving money. Even the dismissal teaches something, it forces you to learn. All right, they don't know how to do it – actually, [giving them money despite that] is deepening their helplessness! When you give discounts, s/he comes back with exactly the same [application].

However, it seems logical to assume that, for the negative result to teach anything to the (non-)recipient, it should be explained thoroughly. Instead, none of the issues leading to the rejection of the proposal were explained to its author. All that the standardised letter of rejection stated was:

The Partnership Board honours you for your ability to consider the socially excluded target groups and their problems and is pleased that the community is willing to find solutions to its problems.
  Decision of the Partnership Board: not to fund.

Thus, instead of the wisdom the refusal was considered to bring, the recipient of such a letter would be left with the feeling of inexplicable failure.

Erika was a particularly interesting case because she herself could be classified as belonging to the category of the socially excluded in her community. Her failure to involve the rest of the community was mostly due to her marginal status in the village. In the eyes of the village that had some glimpses of her plans to apply for the funds, her failure in this was a further proof that she was a fairly pathetic or possibly even suspicious character. While this makes the rejection of her proposal devastating for her efforts at social inclusion, it could also be seen as highly embarrassing to the programme, for which such a person could have been a token of their own participatory and inclusive approach. Considering the examples from some other villages, helping her to overcome her marginality and to involve other members of the village could have been seen as something the programme was set out to do. However, the members of the NGO and the Partnership Board never experienced it that way. When I reminded the NGO members that they should be supporting those who are socially most excluded or marginal, especially when they show readiness to help themselves along with other people, the answer I received from two representatives was:

When money is involved, no marginality argument applies. Give money to the homeless and s/he uses it for the vodka if s/he is not taught.

In a similar manner, the representative of the training institution felt that Erika was a 'strange character'.

Clearly, what we have here is a classical case of managing the 'undeserving poor' (see also Howe 1990; Coelho, this volume) – but the case of Erika becomes even more telling when we consider how exactly such a failure (in terms of stated programme objectives) was neutralised. Erika's village as a whole was meant to be the pilot site for activating a weak community. But the whole community was eventually labelled a failure within an otherwise 'exceptionally successful' programme – as the participants rather unanimously concluded when the programme was brought to a close. However, when explaining this one-off disappointment in one of the programme's Progress Reports (KEPP 2003), it is Erika who is named as the community leader who lacks trust from that community, leaving the impression that it was because of her that this community turned out to be a failure. The fact that she was never expected to become a community leader but was to work with local marginal youth, with whom she may have developed strong affinity due to her own background, and was never intended to take charge of the pilot project, becomes hidden. Through such a move, this marginal personality becomes the culprit for the failure that the programme has had to face. Undermining the core principles of the programme, this rhetoric is justification for the fact that marginal persons (as well as perhaps weak communities) will (or even should) always remain the recipients of the aid, and not become active participants fighting for and managing the funds.

CONCLUSION

The majority of East European development literature reveals outright corruption or at least manipulation of rules, especially among the local managers in the developmental hierarchy. Moreover as Creed and Wedel (1997) point out, aid relies on personalistic relations between well-placed individuals, and informal networking can also be seen as a welcome way of organising people, something at the heart of the 'new' civil society and partnership atmosphere in particular. However, this case in Estonia appears to indicate a great respect for accuracy and observance of legalisms. The competitive environment for aid funds with people not unknown to one another in the context of the civil society of a very small country easily leads to accusations of favouritism. When we add to this the shadow of the Soviet past and its informal networks and nepotism, it is logical that the local development partners do their best to convince foreign funders who might still have their suspicions about the ex-Soviets, that they are most scrupulously following the rules and formal regulations.

To do this, local developers cannot afford to be seen to deviate from normativised numbers, and they have to ensure the results of any other form of decision-making appear to have been in accordance with the rules. The strict requirements appear to curtail the ability of selfish applicants, at the level of village project managers, to find ways to abuse the system. In practice, however, such ability is identified through personal data, heavily relied on even where it is not acknowledged. In a move Bourdieu (1977) would identify as misrecognition, personal data is concealed in a rightful result that is presented as an efficient way to prevent unworthy projects getting the go-ahead. The evaluators are put in the right, and see – as well as present – themselves as efficient and trustworthy managers of foreign funds. Behind such efforts at presenting the processes as 'democratic', 'transparent' and normative are the new sets of rules that the local players feel obliged to comply with in order to appear adequate, capable and also successful in further applications and engagements with the external players supposed to champion such values.

What becomes apparent from this example of project evaluations, is that such – albeit partly manipulative – adherence to formulae does not necessarily guarantee the best results for the aid recipients. Even more importantly, it runs counter to the empowerment philosophy and the general objectives of the programme that has set the rules. Strict rules lead to an inability to consider the exceptional circumstances that locals applying for funds may face. The stringent demands of the evaluation system mean that the projects that are rejected or cut back are often exactly those projects that the programme ideology should support: those from very weak communities or marginal individuals. At the same time, personal background data relied on by the EC pushes the community out of the picture in the decision-making process, replacing it with individuals who are either not trusted or socially marginal and thus lacking in capacity. Such results are inconsistent with the participatory and inclusive ideology of the programme.

Local developers can thus be seen as agents obstructing the practical realisation of the participatory ideals of the foreign developers. However, when they manage to explain that the failures of the programme arise from the local communities or individuals rather than the aid hierarchy, the foreign funding bodies are, in turn, very satisfied. Instead of being regarded as obstructions by the aid hierarchy, the evaluators' ability to show that failures of the programme can be blamed on the unworthy hidden agendas of local applicants offers an explanatory discourse that satisfies both the foreign funders and local implementers, appearing consistent with their own ideology.

Indeed, Pottier (1997), Rahnema (1993) and Woost (1997) all argue that participatory development is a façade in that, in reality, developers remain in charge, while the locals respond with helplessness and passivity. Considering the data above, it appears that locals also respond with mistrust. East European development literature suggests that people with bargaining power within the development industry would find ways of favouring their friends and relatives. Personal connections would thus be behind approvals of the projects. Along the same lines, the response from the locals in Estonia is to suggest that the decision-makers have hidden, unworthy reasons behind their decisions. Suspicions of favouritism from the local communities, on the one hand returns the same mistrust that has been directed towards them; on the other hand, such suspicions actually reject the efforts of the local implementers in building an image of supposed Western trustworthiness and incorruptibility. They even undermine this image precisely in the eyes of its target: the foreign funders, that is, the British embassy. However, this information is not something the foreign funders would look for, or that the local developers would provide them with.

Nevertheless, community suspicions, while certainly remaining influential locally, turn out to be quite misplaced, at least in the light of the processes studied here. Personal knowledge is used for disfavouring rather than favouring the known applicants: excluding 'wrong' applications rather than including the 'right' ones, based on personally motivated preferences. It is interesting to consider how this could be related to the level of fragmentation of social networks and lack of mutual support in today's Estonian society, paradoxically reflected in the system that is meant to (also somewhat paradoxically) neutrally and impartially promote the recreation of communities and social networks.

NOTES

1. This chapter is based on data collected through fieldwork undertaken in south-eastern Estonia from June 2002 to January 2004. The fieldwork constitutes part of my PhD research programme in the Department of Anthropology at the University College London.
2. Estonian language does not have a gender-specific third-person pronoun. Thus 's/he' is used throughout the following extracts when gender is not specified.
3. I will describe this case further in a later section of the text.
4. The secretary for the EC has to present the result to the Partnership Board.

REFERENCES

Abrahams, R. (2002) *Out of the collective frying pan? Ideals and practicalities in the reformulation and restitution of political and property rights in post-Soviet rural Estonia*. Working paper no. 34 (Halle/Saale: Max Planck Institute for Social Anthropology).

Alanen, I. (1999) Agricultural policy and struggle over the destiny of collective farms in Estonia. *Sociologica Ruralis* 39(3): 431–58.

Alanen, I., J. Nikula, H. Põder and R. Ruutsoo (eds) (2001) *Decollectivisation, destruction and disillusionment: a community study in Southern Estonia* (Aldershot: Ashgate).

Annist, A. (2000) Progress without protest. Special Issue: The Baltics. *Central European Review* 2(27), <http://www.ce-review.org/00/27/annist27.html>, visited June 2005.

Annist, A. (2003) Võimu ja apaatia dialoog [Dialogue between apathy and power]. In VIII Avatud Ühiskonna Foorum, 'Konflikt ja kokkulepe' [8th Open Society Forum, 'Conflict and Contract'], Tallinn, 25 April/Avatud Eesti Fond [Open Estonia Foundation] (Tallinn: Kunst).

Burns, K. (2003) Report on a visit to Estonian Rural Partnerships Programme, 26–28 May. Internal document. Enniskillen: Irish Central Border Area Network.

Community Workers' Co-operative (1996) *Partnership in action: the role of community development and partnership in Ireland* (Galway: Community Workers' Cooperative).

Creed, G.W. (1999) Deconstructing socialism in Bulgaria. In M. Burawoy and K. Verdery (eds) *Uncertain transitions: ethnographies of change in the postsocialist world*, pp. 223–43 (Lanham, MD: Rowman and Littlefield Publishers).

Creed, G.W. and J.R. Wedel (1997) Second thoughts from the Second World: interpreting aid in post-communist Eastern Europe. *Human Organisation* 56(3): 253–64.

DFID (Department for International Development) (2000) *Inception report*, December. London: DFID, Baltic States Rural Partnerships Programme.

EIU (Economist Intelligence Unit) (1999/2000) *Country Profile: Estonia* (London: Economist Intelligence Unit).

Giordano, C. and D. Kostova (2002) Social production of mistrust. In C.M. Hann (ed.) *Postsocialism: ideals, ideologies and practices in Eurasia*, pp. 74–94 (London and New York: Routledge).

Humphrey, C. (1991) 'Icebergs', barter and the mafia in provincial Russia. *Anthropology Today* 7(2): 8–13.

Howe, L. (1990) *Being unemployed in Northern Ireland: an ethnographic study* (Cambridge: Cambridge University Press).

KEPP (Kagu-Eesti Partnerlusprogramm [South-eastern Estonian Partnership Programme]) (2003) Aruanne 1. jaanuar–31. märts [Report 1 January–31 March] (Otepää: Kagu-Eesti Partnerlusprogramm).

Pottier, J. (1997) Towards an ethnography of participatory appraisal and research. In R.D. Grillo and R.L. Stirrat (eds) *Discourses of development: anthropological perspectives*, pp. 203–27 (Oxford and New York: Berg).

Rahnema, M. (1993) Participation. In W. Sachs (ed.) *The development dictionary: a guide to knowledge as power* (London and New Jersey: Zed Books and Johannesburg: Witwatersrand University Press).

Sampson, S. (1996) The social life of projects: importing civil society to Albania. In C. Hann and E. Dunn (eds) *Civil society: challenging Western models*, pp. 121–42 (London and New York: Routledge).

Sampson, S. (2002) Beyond transition: rethinking elite configurations in the Balkans. In C.M. Hann (ed.) *Postsocialism: ideals, ideologies and practices in Eurasia*, pp. 297–316 (London and New York: Routledge).

Stark, D. and L. Bruszt (1998) *Postsocialist pathways: transforming politics and property in East Central Europe* (Cambridge: Cambridge University Press).

UNDP (1999) *Estonian human development report* (Tallinn: UNDP).

UNDP (2000) *Estonian human development report* (Tallinn: UNDP).

Unwin, T. (1999) Estonian agriculture in a European context: political agendas and the Common Agricultural Policy. In Ü. Ennuste and L. Wilder (eds) *Harmonisation with the Western economics: Estonian economic developments and related conceptual and methodological frameworks*, pp. 227–49 (Tallinn: Estonian Institute of Economics at Tallinn Technical University).

Verdery, K. (1996) *What was socialism and what comes next?* (Princeton, NJ: Princeton University Press).

Wedel, J. (1998) *Collision and collusion: the strange case of Western aid to Eastern Europe, 1989–1998* (Houndmills and London: Macmillan).

Woost, M.D. (1997) Alternative vocabularies of development? 'Community' and 'participation' in development discourse. In R.D. Grillo and R.L. Stirrat (eds) *Discourses of development: anthropological perspectives*, pp. 229–53 (Oxford and New York: Berg).

Zbierski-Salameh, S. (1999) Polish peasants in the 'valley of transition': responses to postsocialist reforms. In M. Burawoy and K. Verdery (eds) *Uncertain transitions: ethnographies of change in the postsocialist world*, pp. 182–222 (Lanham, MD: Rowman and Littlefield Publishers).

8 UNSTATING 'THE PUBLIC': AN ETHNOGRAPHY OF REFORM IN AN URBAN WATER UTILITY IN SOUTH INDIA

Karen Coelho

The public don't know how to use the drainage system. The public character, they spit on roads, throw litter everywhere!

In terms of public relations, if we go meet the people, half the problem is solved! Even this morning, with the problem of the sewer line going under the temple – we have no idea how to solve that problem, but I went and met the man and inspected the site and spoke to the slum people. The man already feels better.

We learn about public relations and we have already killed the public! There is nothing we can do about that. If you really want to serve, increase the labour force! You ask four people to do the job ten people used to do, you will never be able to serve the public! (Quotes from three field engineers of Chennai's water utility, July 2001–Dec. 2002)

The notion of 'the public' takes on new meanings as state bureaucracies attempt to become more businesslike. This chapter, based on an ethnographic study of a reforming water utility in the south Indian city of Chennai (formerly Madras), shows how neoliberal reforms, drawing both on direct aid conditionality laid out by the World Bank, and more indirectly on the global orthodoxies of the New Public Management movement, produce local subjectivities in which the 'common sense' (Gramsci 1971) of notions like the state, the public and service are configured and aligned in new ways.

Moments of reform are, ideally, moments of critical self-reflection. They produce official evaluations of past record, present state and future goals, furnishing manifestos of the state's continuing or changing character and purpose. Semantically an open-ended concept invoking a contingent local relationship of past to present, the term 'reform' has acquired a fixed and absolutist set of meanings in its circulation through the global spheres of macro-economic adjustment, international aid and governance debates. From welfare reform in First World countries, to economic and sectoral reforms in Third World countries, and governance reforms worldwide, the term denotes a convergence of agendas toward the orthodoxies of neoliberalism. It now indicates emphases on fiscal austerity, optimising rates of return on investments, a retreat from transfer-based and relief-oriented welfarism, commercialisation and/or privatisation of state-run operations, and an increasing reliance on managerial technologies such as quantification, output-orientation and audit.

A study of the discourses of reform also reveals shifts in the terms in which states perceive, categorise and value social groups. State rationalities are re-examined, categories of deserving and undeserving are reformulated, and modalities of service delivery are reoriented toward these new formulations.

This chapter argues that the local translations[1] of reform through which field-level functionaries – in my case the depot (or divisional) engineers of the water utility – are interpellated and formed as public servants, produces a retreat or disengagement of the state from a certain kind of public. This claim may appear perverse at first, for two reasons: first, the reforms emphasise better performance and greater responsiveness in public service delivery; and, second, the invocation of 'the public' as the referent of the service, the crux of daily relations at the depots, was part of the discursive framework in which the engineers presented their work.

However, my attention was drawn to the peculiar semantics of their use of the term 'public'. 'A public just came in to complain about a drainage block,' one engineer told me. Apart from the linguistic idiosyncrasy in this usage ('a public' referred here to a single person), it indexed, at first impression, a generic gloss for clients of the service, a vocabulary paradigmatic of the subjective encounter between the government servant and the objectified, faceless 'other' that entered off the street into the professionalised space of the bureau – this is the public that Habermas describes as 'the abstract counterpart of public authority' (1989: 23). On closer examination, however, this impression of generality or abstractness turned out to be misleading: the meaning of 'the public' in the depot engineers' daily field of engagement referred to a particular stratum of clientele – the urban poor or the slum-dwellers, apprehended as a disorderly mass of citizenry, corrupted by local political patronage and inimical to proper service by the state. This usage was based on what emerged as an informal sociology that the field engineers had constructed out of their everyday encounters: a sociology that was structured by systematic categories of differentiation, and inflected by waves of reforms that have continuously shaped and 're-engineered' the organisation over more than 25 years.

The public that is thus discursively constituted does not present itself as the 'civil society' that the reforming bureaucracy is encouraged to engage with. Located in slums, at the tail-end of the piped water system and the fringes of administrative order, and dependent on the commons (public fountains) that are being steadily edged out of the neoliberal order of things, the masses of urban poor pose complex technical and social challenges for engineers caught in the exigencies of reforms. The meanings of a 'good service' are determined by the frameworks of financial viability, responsiveness to consumer demand (these consumers, in turn, constituted by tariff reforms and the elimination of subsidies), and stringent rationalities of cost-effectiveness fostered by a disseminating culture of audit. In this scheme, the urban poor are framed, on the one hand, as the protégés of populist political regimes responsible for the 'institutional failures' of state-run utilities. On the other hand, they are invoked – under the rubric of 'willingness to pay' discourses – as the ultimate beneficiaries of reforms that purport to enhance capacity in the service. Translated via the practices of engineers at the service interface, these frameworks of reform locate the poor, who continue to rely on free water through public standpipes, as undeserving, unruly, demanding and inextricably caught in a realm of politics that is, in turn, marked as a sphere of impossibility.

Thus, the engineers' fissured notion of the public and its hidden sociologies of caste and other orders, and the ambivalent engagement of reforms and the engineers with this public, illustrate the contradictory relationship between modernity and mass politics in India. This contradiction is captured to some degree by Partha Chatterjee's concept of 'political society', which he defines as a domain of mediating institutions between state and civil society, where civil society refers to the bourgeois associational forms derived from Western modernity, embodying the principles – or rather, the discourses – of equality, autonomy, contract and deliberative procedures of decision-making (Chatterjee 2001). Chatterjee argues that in the postcolonial Indian polity, civil society is shallow and an 'exclusive domain of the elite'. As such, it marks the classic incompleteness of the project of modernisation and of the pedagogic mission of enlightened elites in relation to the rest of society. In its normative self-concept, it excludes the 'actual public [that] will not match up to the standards required by civil society' (2001: 174). Political society, on the other hand, rests on a notion of 'population' as an aggregation of discrete, classifiable units of society – a notion that was produced by the governmentalities of colonial and modern states and their far-reaching and intimate welfarism. Thus, concomitant with the gradual development of civil society in modern nation-states, 'the possibility of a different mediation between the population and the state was already being imagined' (2001: 175). In Chatterjee's analysis, political society, while appropriating the rhetoric of citizenship and rights launched by the strategies of nationalist mobilisation and girding itself with the framework of modern political institutions such as parties, remains animated by different principles of association – those of patronage, charismatic leadership and identity. Habermas (1989) defines the public sphere, in its early existence, as a paradigmatically bourgeois space in which private property-holders got together to critically debate and monitor the exercise of political power. This bourgeois public sphere, according to Habermas, was dissolved by electoral reforms that enfranchised the non-bourgeois masses, and by the rise of the interventionist welfare state in the nineteenth century.[2] My analysis here, however, points to how the urban public sphere in Chennai, as delineated by the discourses and practices of frontline service providers, is constituted precisely by non-bourgeois, politically organised strata that pose intractable challenges to the order envisioned by state reforms.

Yet, as this study also shows, the mediation of this political society with the developmental state is receiving further impetus with governance reforms. My ethnography exposes internal inconsistencies in the agendas that have come to be glossed under the universalising discourse of reform – tensions that are revealed in their local engagements. Governance reforms, despite some cross-country variations, generally seek to improve managerial capacity in the state sector while strategically reducing the role of the state and promoting democratic politics.[3] In India, 'increased engagement with local government institutions' is part of the manifesto of institutional reforms (WSP 1999). However, as this study shows, daily relations between engineers and local politicians at the frontline, within the context of sectoral reforms that carve out a space of autonomy from the political sphere, produce and reproduce antinomies of order and corruption, official and unofficial, service and patronage, us and them. These antinomies sustain a sterilised and instrumentalised view of local politics.[4]

INSTITUTIONAL REFORMS IN METROWATER: TOWARDS AN 'EFFICIENT AND VIRILE SERVICE'

How does municipal water supply, traditionally the domain of local self-government, a field of struggle between local bureaucracy, city councillors and their constituencies, come to be shaped and steered by a global regime of discipline? The process was set in motion 25 years ago, with the formation of the Metrowater[5] Board as an autonomous statutory body, removed from the jurisdiction of the municipal corporation and placed directly under a department of the state government. Thus, a divorce from local government was written into the constitution of the organisation. The board was created as the result of a major study sponsored by the World Health Organization (WHO) and the United Nations Development Program (UNDP) in 1976, and carried out by a consortium of multinational and British accountancy firms (Ferguson et al., 1978). Thus the birth of the organisation was engineered largely by foreign consultants, and was oriented from the start to international best practice. Fiscal imperatives were stressed from the start, and provided legitimation for all change. The autonomy to obtain, manage and invest funds was the primary motive for this institutional innovation. The proposal also envisaged high levels of professionalism, facilitated through expatriate training and consultancy, and 'excellence in management' as keys to revamping the water service (1978: 5.6). The gendered character of the reforms is captured in the study's vision of an 'efficient and virile service' (1978: 11.14). The document carries a celebratory tone: the creation of the Board is portrayed as no small achievement, a highly progressive step in the movement toward leadership in the water and drainage sector. From its inception, Metrowater was created to stand apart. In the document's emphasis on integrating all components of the hitherto scattered and fragmented water and drainage service into a coordinated, autonomous body, there are overtones of purifying the service, carving out its jurisdiction carefully, and removing its historical entanglements with its progenitors in the city corporation and other local bodies.

The immediate upshot of the formation of the Board was the interest of the World Bank. The Bank was already active in the wings before the organisation was set up, and was ready to fund large projects even before the institutional transformation was fully in place. As a retired senior engineer recalled, 'So, what was a pre-investment study turned into a set of proposals for funding – a milestone in the development of the Board, wherein it crossed two stages in one step: one, the move from the city corporation to a separate entity, and two, the move of attracting the interest of funding agencies.'

This moment of formation also brought the agency, directly and indirectly, into line with the orthodoxy of infrastructure sector reforms that had been emerging in World Bank-funded projects since the mid-1970s, culminating in the Bank's influential report entitled *Infrastructure for development* (World Bank 1994). The report outlines the failures of infrastructure utilities across the Third World under their hitherto predominantly state-run regimes, and shows how their typical features (such as a focus on capital investment at the expense of maintenance, chronically low capacity utilisation and overstaffing) derive from decisions being made on the basis of political expediency rather than sound utility-management principles. It identifies three core instruments for improving the efficiency of public sector infrastructure utilities: corporatisation, which 'establishes the quasi-independence of public entities and insulates infrastructure enterprises from non-commercial pressures and constraints', a pricing strategy 'designed to ensure cost recovery, which creates a desirable form of financial independence for public utilities ...', and contracts between governments and private entities if outright privatisation is not feasible (World Bank 1994: 37). Thus, in the Bank's view, financial and managerial autonomy, in effect autonomy from the political ('non-commercial') sphere, and an unwavering focus on commercial viability are the touchstones of a good service. While Metrowater was an early reformer within India, by the late 1990s these principles had become part of the national discourse of reform in the water sector.[6]

Another stream of emergent global orthodoxy influencing the character of the reforms in Metrowater and converging with the sectoral thrusts outlined above is that of the New Public Management (NPM), a movement that has gained worldwide ascendancy since the late 1980s as the dominant mode and format for public sector reform worldwide. NPM is closely implicated in the global agenda of trimming and privatising state roles. Originating in the Reagan–Thatcher political agendas of the New Right, it has, by now, found favour with many reforming Labour and social-democratic governments in the West (Hood 2001). According to Hood, NPM derives from a marriage of the New Institutional Economics, based on rational choice theory, and a recent strand in the long tradition of scientific management movements (of which Taylorism and Fordism were part) that offer a portable package of 'professional management' techniques to be applied across different types of organisations. Its core doctrines and programmes include: professional management in the public sector – the deployment of active 'free to manage' authority by executives, in contrast to the lumbering organisational labyrinths through which authority is diffused in 'old style' bureaucracies; management through quantification, requiring clear and measurable output-oriented goals, targets and indicators; the 'unbundling' of functions into 'manageable' corporatised units; the application of private-sector style incentive tools for staff, PR techniques in consumer relations, and contractual mechanisms for accountability to clients; and a focus on efficiency, defined as cost-effectiveness and achieved through austerity, fiscal discipline and the use of market tools such as competition and contracts (Hood 2001). Thus NPM represents a restatement of the public service ethic in the light of a competitive polity of multiple 'stakeholders'. It presents itself as an apolitical, instrumental framework, making possible the effective fulfilment of a wide range of policy and political goals.

Reforms in Metrowater, thus, reflect a convergence of globally defined economic, governance and sectoral agendas, coming together as projects of 'institutional strengthening'. This is defined as: commercialisation of operations, commodification of the resource (water) through tariff reforms and full cost recovery from users, and gradual privatisation of unbundled components of the service. As a senior government official in the water sector said, 'Commercialising the organisation has been very much on stream for more than ten years now: Metrowater has been functioning not like a government department but like a company for a while now!' By 2001, insider perspectives on the provenance of reforms varied substantially. Some officials in Metrowater insisted that they were internally generated in response to needs for expansion, processes of organisational reflection, or the efforts of dynamic and committed leaders. Others saw them as deriving directly from World Bank loan conditionalities, and a third group described a dialogic process between internal and external imperatives. Studies of aides-memoires of World Bank missions and of Metrowater's own project documents reveal a process of negotiation between the board and the Bank that produced the hegemonic agreement on Metrowater as a commercial entity. This process was at least partly textual, in which local ownership of the reforms was organised through a language of shared agreement embedded in the framework of conditionality. The aides-memoires of Bank missions, which find echoes in Metrowater's own policy documents, in turn reflect the Bank's *Infrastructure for development* report so closely that they seem to function as technology transfer manuals for institutional best practice.

Neither commodification of water nor commercialisation of the service were instantly accomplished. They involved sustained efforts over the 25 years since the organisation was formed – efforts that were discernible in policy documents and in the discourses of senior agency officials. They involved systematic changes at the levels of language, nomenclature and titling, producing new terminologies that defined new practices, revalued certain types of knowledge and realigned professional authority within the organisation. Among the key components of institutional strengthening was the expansion and centering of the audit function at all levels of operation. As an agency document claims, 'Various concepts such as transaction audit, compliance audit of government rules and procedures, systems audit, management audit, energy audit [etc.] have been ... used as tools to enhance productivity' (CMWSSB 2000–01: 83). The Management Audit wing, established in 2000, represents the only expansion in over eight years in an organisation that has been systematically shrinking its operations. The deployment of audit disciplines and the application of a rigorous cost–benefit calculus to all activities resulted in significant cost-cutting and a streamlining of agency expenditures. But auditors and financial managers also acquired larger roles in the 'public' sphere of the service: they were given a greater say in technical decisions, they routinely visited the field to check on water connections, and met with customers and contractors. This expansion of the audit function in Metrowater was part of the effort to discipline engineers into the new rationalities of commercial operations, but it was also part of a climate of increased vigilance in which engineers, especially at the frontline, were the primary objects of scrutiny. While agency administrators and reports described these changes as indexing a greater inclusiveness and interdisciplinarity in the interests of public accountability, engineers experienced the intensifying audit culture as a challenge to their traditional authority in the organisation, emblematic of a growing distrust and surveillance.[7]

These institutional changes, then, determine the conditions under which frontline engineers negotiate the calls to better public service articulated by the reforms. The next section explores the effects of these changes on frontline engineers' relations with the public.

THE FORMATION OF A PUBLIC SERVICE

This study frames the reforms in Metrowater as part of an ongoing project of state-formation in which discourses of transformation are deployed within structures of continuity. The more things change, the more the relations of rule that underpin ideas of the state are entrenched. The reforms mobilise new regimes of knowledge, planning and decision-making, a new 'culture of service' in which subjects of the state, both functionaries of the organisation and their clients, are disciplined. But they also produce a set of incomplete and unstable translations at the frontline, producing a fragile hegemony of 'the new bureaucracy.'

The Assistant Engineer (AE) or Junior Engineer (JE) in charge of a depot is a critical node of the organisation's public existence: the endpoint of technical line functions and the starting point of the public face of the state – the official who most directly 'represents' the service and answers to the public. Located near the bottom of the technical operational hierarchy, he or she is the immediate head of the depot, managing the depot's labour team and administration, including its revenue functions. S/he thus mediates several complex and intersecting relations – between the public and the depot labour, the public and the larger bureaucracy, the labour and the organisation, the local politician and the service. The depot engineers are the ultimate subjects of the reforms in that all the envisioned transformations take shape and substance through them; they are also the objects and the explicit targets of reforms, in that large components are designed to specifically discipline this cadre of officials. Acting at the intersection of agency and constraint, then, field engineers displace their conditions onto other aspects of their working environment – the labourers, politicians, senior officials or the public. Through a series of conflations and oppositions, engineers achieve a discursive space for themselves as purveyors of order, juxtaposed against the politicians and the public who constitute a realm of disorder, clientelism and patronage. In the translations of reform at the frontline, then, notions of the public, politics, order and service are constituted in peculiar ways.

There was nothing orderly and technical about Operations and Maintenance (O&M) at the depots. While technical functions, like repairs to hand-pumps, investigation into defective water supply and unblocking sewers were the core of daily activities, they formed only a small part of the substance of the service, the stuff that preoccupied and challenged the engineers all day every day. Or, rather, these technical functions were encrusted in a thick matrix of localised governmentality – the formation and exchange of social categories, recognitions and denials, a discourse embedded in and shaped by the practical exigencies of reform in the organisation. It became clear that 'the service' was formed in these sites and these relationships. The engineers are not civil servants in the classic sense of trained career bureaucrats, yet they are government servants in that their jobs carry all the accoutrements of state sector employment. Some cohorts had been inducted into the organisation from the municipal corporation or from other public sector engineering departments; others had entered via the employment exchange, straight from diploma or degree courses in engineering. Apart from a few *ad hoc* and occasional training sessions (of a few days apiece), the job was learned on the ground, through what a senior engineer described as 'a process of trial and error, a host of unwritten dos and don'ts'. Despite this casual formation, the 'state idea' (Abrams 1988) is a powerful organising concept in the self-definition of engineers as public servants – their subjectivity is located squarely in the ideology of government service, and they present their actions and motivations as arising from its special imperatives, in contrast to those of private sector engineers. The remainder of this section traces how the disciplines and administrative optics of reform through which these subjects negotiate their field of agency at the frontline, shape a notion of the public as a body that is increasingly difficult to handle.

The public: a category of field governmentality

The depot engineer's job is one of daily encounters with people fixed in place by their geographic, physical and sociological infrastructure, presenting themselves at the depots with chronic and repeated patterns of complaints about drainage and water. Seeing like state engineers (Scott 1998), the functionaries classify their clients on the basis of their location in the technical paradigms of service and on residential class, modes of self-presentation across the counter and amenability to being served. The categories get slowly elaborated and fleshed out through comparative perspectives, as the engineers are transferred across different depots through their careers. The city's divisions are thus endowed with distinctive characters and reputations, and the engineer's professional consciousness is finely tuned into this relativistic field of settings wherein conditions (and 'opportunities') vary significantly. The two poles of this sociological field, then, are: the people from the slums and the 'VIPs', people from upper-class residential neighbourhoods.

The patterns of categorisation were consistent enough to form a set of tropes, complete with ascriptions about attitudes and behaviour. People from the slums, in this scheme, not only have repeated problems with sewage blocks because of poor drainage systems, but also tend to *cause* them owing to their propensity to put solid wastes down the sewers.

The sociology of the engineer is shaped not only by the state of people's drainage systems, but also by how they respond to his/ her efforts (or inability) to solve their problems. I found a powerful sociolinguistic schema that unified engineers across the board. People from the slums were almost universally portrayed as 'rough' or even 'rogue'. They were 'illiterate people who do not understand, will not accept' the constraints of the service, and they are prone to be violent. They 'only demand, they don't want explanations'. One engineer told me there were only two slums in his division, but that the whole area was actually 'like a slum, according to how they behave'. Another said: 'Pudunagar is not even a slum, but the people are not decent.' These vocabularies are coded with the overtones of what Pandian (2002) refers to as 'caste by other means'. As bureaucrats, the engineers were guarded in their discussions of caste with me. The denial of caste, as Pandian points out, is embedded in the practices and discourses of modernity, which 'delegitimises the language of caste in the domain of politics by annexing it as part of the cultural' (2002: 10).

The engineers' vocabulary of strategic silences, then, had recourse to terms like 'suppressed category'. When I pushed for elaboration, officials sometimes used state-sanctioned caste- or class-based identifiers such as 'SC' (Scheduled Caste) or 'LIG' (Lower Income Group, a category used in government housing schemes), or occupational identifiers such as 'fishermen'. One engineer claimed that the depot he was working in was 'the worst area, not only because of the congestion, but because of the category of people'. When I asked what category that was, he hesitated, then turned to one of his labour team for help: 'What kind of people live here? Tell her.' The worker said: 'SC, ST [Scheduled Tribe], Andhra people [the Adi Andhra subgroup of the Scheduled Castes] and Muslims.' But the engineers were eloquent about the attributes of these suppressed categories. One engineer described his division as a 'polluted area' and explained that by saying 'their way of protesting anything is to block the roads. They are very urban – used to demanding and expecting services.' They were also referred to as the *'poromboke* people',[8] denoting, presumably, their status as squatters.

By contrast, people from Annanagar, an area of the city with upscale new developments, were portrayed not only as better off, but also as better educated and consequently understanding of the difficulties that engineers faced. 'Decent' was a common descriptor for people from higher-income neighbourhoods, a term systematically counterposed to the 'rough' and 'harsh' people of the slums. As one engineer put it, 'Area 5 is very decent – there are residential houses with compound walls. Here they are rough.' One engineer recalled that people 'were more *nagarik* (civilised)' in his previous division. In those areas, as another engineer put it, 'you could explain the problem to people and they would accept'. An engineer who was serving in one of the better-off divisions of the city described her clients as:

Mostly government employees! Ninety percent are educated, so it is easy for us to convince them. The less educated are harder to convince – they come out on the street and make *galata*, threaten and demand. But from another point of view, for this lower class of people we are like gods! What we say goes – they don't know how to go to our superiors. The higher classes, they are always going above our heads!

Thus, the elite category of people, glossed also as 'VIPs' and occasionally as 'Brahmins', are associated with the tendency to go straight to the top with their complaints – to the Managing Director or the Chief Engineer, often by email. One engineer commented that the 'posh' people were sometimes confused about whom to complain to. But they were also described as 'sophisticated', which seemed to refer to their ability to demand special services from government and pay for them.

That the better-off areas tended to receive better service was acknowledged by engineers at all levels. A senior field engineer introduced me to the Annanagar zone claiming that the Board's performance and service was particularly good in this area because it was a VIP area with a lot of IAS (Indian Administrative Service) officers:

Response [from depot staff] is higher because reaction [from the people] and interaction is good. So, people are being served well here – if 70 lpcd [litres per capita daily] is the amount of water to be supplied, they are getting 70 lpcd here.

If 70 lpcd is the standard, not everybody gets it. 'The slums may only get 20 or 30 lpcd', this official remarked. The standard explanation for this was that they were in a 'tail-end' pocket, which in turn is explained by the claim that most slums have grown out of unauthorised settlements. Slums, thus, presented a nightmare of technical as well as social difficulties for the engineers – unplanned and unauthorised, many of them were clustered in low-lying and marshy areas along river banks, with cattle sheds and public conveniences exacerbating their drainage problems. Yet they were also, in many ways, the centre of the service. As a senior field engineer told me, the slums were prioritised in the allocation of mobile water supplies:

First priority is always given to slum groups, because others – the higher income people – can hire wells or buy water, they are not completely reliant on us. Also, they don't complain to us so much – most of the pressure comes from slums. These are the sensitive areas.[9] If we do not concentrate on serving the slums, next minute they are on the streets, protesting. We have observed this frequently.

While serving the poor, then, was a defining feature of the service for engineers – their badge of identity, the thing that made their job more than just a job, the aspect that distinguished them from private sector engineers – it was also a persistent thorn in their side. For the majority, this was the pre-eminent factor that decided the attractiveness of a given posting. The proportion of slum in the division was what determined how hard they would work, how much money they would make and how soon they would start jockeying for a transfer.

Disciplining the public

For all their emphasis on serving the poor, the field engineers were also, overall, unimpressed by what many of them portrayed as the state's populist policies toward the poor. Even the more sympathetic and conscientious among them were cynical about expanding services to a population that did not pay. Of all the people in the corridors of reform who insisted that the poor should pay for water, the field engineers in my study were among the most vociferous. One engineer declared:

The goal should be: only if you pay your taxes and charges, you can give a complaint. But here people say 'You are the government, you have to give us service.' And the organisation gives in to this: if people block the roads, they get water. The department keeps crying about losses – why won't there be losses? Take Melnagar – it has 800-odd tenements, in which there are 65 air-conditioners, 180 phones, almost all houses have TV and cable, but they don't want to pay a single *paisa* to the Board because they are TNSCB [Tamil Nadu Slum Clearance Board tenements] – that is like a quality assurance stamp, you cannot question them!

Another engineer who worked in a division with a large section of TNSCB tenements said:

People here – even those who have [money] will say they don't have and demand free facilities. This is the mentality of these people – they will not pay on time, then when there is a penalty they will question. They never keep track of their own dues.

One engineer walked me around a neighbourhood he designated as an 'improved slum', and pointed out several bore-wells installed to draw groundwater. Many were privately owned, hence the public fountains installed by Metrowater were not used much. These people paid no taxes, he told me. And they take their own sewer connections illegally from the main. 'They are above the law – they have no respect for the law at all, no regard for the department.' This attitude was also accounted for within the socio-geographic categories fashioned by the engineers:

In Annanagar, if you don't pay taxes or charges it is humiliating, here if you pay it is. There, taking water from a public pump is humiliating, here, if you have a house connection it is hidden. Here they believe that by virtue of their vote they should get facilities, not by paying.

Engineers also claimed that the public had become more demanding. This was a recent and growing phenomenon: 'We have had to learn to negotiate with them.' Some officials completely disowned the role of the government as a trustee of public goods and the public interest:

The difference between public and private goods is that public things are not looked after. NGOs should take on these issues, educate people to take care of and maintain the assets. The government cannot motivate people – they look at us and say, oh, that man has come again. It is not something that we have been able to do ...

And among a couple of older incumbents, there was a more deep-seated cynicism about their role of serving the poor. One mid-level field engineer, a deputy area engineer asked me:

Why are you interested in this area? There are no slums here – this service is defined by what you do for the slums! If I improve the conditions for rich people, there is no appreciation, even some suspicion of what I am getting out of it, but if the same effort is put into the slum, there is a lot of appreciation.

The discourse of the poor as undeserving because they do not pay, reproduced across the depots, had evidently been constructed over time, but was also clearly sharpened by the reforms' strong emphasis on revenue collection. A recent organisational innovation was to put depot engineers in charge of revenue collections. One group of engineers, when I asked them what the reforms had meant to their work, replied almost in chorus, 'Engineers have become revenue collectors, that is the main change!' Achieving targets in revenue collection is now a major indicator of depot performance: annual depot awards are based on this criterion, and engineers are encouraged to show initiative in discovering hidden revenue sources such as illegal connections. Engineers are also encouraged to demand whether clients have paid taxes and charges before they engage with a complaint. Not all engineers approved of these measures. One said:

The organisation is going completely in a commercial direction – mainly interested in collections and charging. Even if we don't supply water we still have to collect – this does not help us in dealing with the public!

Public fountains (PFs), the principal regular source of water in the slums, represent another recurrent source of headaches for the engineers, partly because they are the locus of collusions and battles for control among local residents, politicians, party workers and other powerful interests in the slums. They have a tendency to be privatised – I came across several that had their handles locked, or removed and privately stored. In one community, women reported that the public fountain was kept deliberately out of order because the local party worker made money off the tanker supply. The 'tragedy of the commons' discourse was frequently invoked by the engineers – nobody maintains the PFs, so they should be dismantled.

Among the latest initiatives of the Board are measures designed to promote individual water connections in the slums. This move was already being anticipated at the service interface at the time of my study: when people from the slums came in to complain about public fountains running dry, engineers sometimes simply recommended they get private connections. When one client raised the issue of affordability, an engineer asked her: 'Don't you watch movies? Don't you pay for a cable line? How come you have no money for water?' Thus, the governmentality of reform seeks to reconstitute the public as consumers, as taxable holders of private property in water, under the discourse of users, stakeholders, and 'willingness to pay'.

'Government officers hate crowds'

This comment was made by a retired senior bureaucrat in a speech about anti-corruption: he was talking about the effectiveness of collective pressure in forcing a response from bureaucrats. My own observations at the depots bore out, with extraordinary consistency, the trope contained in the comment. The field engineers displayed a marked antipathy toward the collective presentation of complaints. Their image of the slums, for instance, was one in which 'People come in person in a huge crowd and stand in front of you.' This image was produced repeatedly: 'They come in big gangs and demand more hand-pumps if tanks are being shut down.' Yet another engineer told me: 'If people come one or two to the office it's okay – if they come in groups of 50 or so it can be a problem!'

This antipathy to crowds was often frankly communicated to the clients. One engineer lectured the group of young men who had come to present a complaint: 'One person is enough, you should not come like this in groups.' But the group strategy was also frankly exploited by the clients for its recognised leverage. A member of the rebuked group retorted: 'We would come individually but when complaints are not handled we have to come in a big group, we have no choice.'

The fear of the group is backed up by a fear of the *mariyal*, a public demonstration involving a road-block or sit-in. This is a popular form of protest particularly among women, who squat or stand behind a barricade of coloured plastic water pots placed across the road. Many of the engineers had faced such protests, sometimes organised by politicians (these drew more attention from senior officials, who arrived at the scene post-haste in their jeeps), and sometimes spontaneous and locally contained. For engineers, the occurrence of such a public protest during their watch represented a major strike against their individual records of performance, and was therefore something to be avoided at all costs.

Juxtaposing the engineers' reactions to these crowds against their response to organised 'civil society' bodies from middle and upper class neighbourhoods – like residents' and neighbourhood associations and consumer activist groups – was instructive. Reforms encourage a closer engagement with these bodies, through events like the Open Houses. While these interactions increased the pressure for accountability from the engineers, it was evident that many engineers enjoyed interacting with these middle- or upper-class civil activists to whom they could explain things. Associations interacted with engineers in the orderly representative modes of civil society, and were usually perceived by the latter as cooperative and helpful, in contrast to the demanding delegations from the slums.

The complaint

The formal concept through which the service relationship is structured is the 'complaint'. This is both the statistical unit used to measure and monitor the service, as well as the operational unit, the practical organising tool of the daily service. Each visit to the office by a client is, in principle, turned into a complaint, entered into a register and used as the basis for deploying labour. Thus, the 'complaint' as the key operational measure of the service represents a form of individuation – a technology of administrative control as well as, in its demands for order and specification, a way of perceiving.

The reforms, built on the results-orientation of the New Public Management, focus on formalising and codifying the complaint as an indicator of depot performance – a reduction in the number of complaints indicates a better service. Procedures for recording, collating, calculating and responding to complaints have been improved: complaints are coded by type, and elaborate charts tracking the occurrence of types of complaints by week, month, quarter and year are created and analysed. Separate officers at Head and Area Offices are charged with monitoring monthly complaints charts, studying patterns and forwarding them to senior officers. The Citizen's Charter lays out standards and commitments with regard to the number of days within which complaints can be expected to be addressed.

As a measure to empower consumers, reforms introduced the system of the 'complaint slip', which allowed consumers to directly fill out their complaints in triplicate, with copies automatically sent to the Head and Area Offices – in contrast to the earlier system in which complaints were entered into a register by the depot official. The new system allowed a direct surveillance of the service interface from multiple points in the organisational hierarchy.[10]

The ethnography, however, revealed these innovations as constituting one more typical tool in the well-worn bureaucratic arsenal used by lower rungs of bureaucracy to assert control in situations where they lacked it. The act of registering a complaint was routinely subverted by depot staff. Only in one area – the wealthier divisions of Annanagar – did I see clients fill complaint slips themselves. In other areas engineers dismissed this method on the grounds that people were illiterate. Innumerable complaints, apparently regarded as unreasonable, were not written down. A substantial proportion of the problems I witnessed presented at the depots defied the format of the 'complaint' – they involved local conflicts over the placement of water taps, the timing of supply, the routing of drainage pipes or the appropriation of common property such as hand-pump handles. Or they made demands that the engineers had no chance of fulfilling, given their resource constraints. Thus the instrument of the complaint, structured as a problem of the individual consumer that is amenable to being solved, denies or renders invisible the field of struggle implicit in the collective character of access to water and sanitation in the city.

Public relations

Clients present themselves before the techno-administrative lens of the depot engineer often in states of intense distress provoked by several days of blocked sewers or dry water pipes. Thus the engineers derive a sense of their service in part from the registers of desperation that they encounter, which transform them from overseers of operations and maintenance to providers of succour and relief, from engineers into servants of the public. This, and the putative monopoly status of large parts of the service, contribute to a simultaneous awareness of power and a discourse of compassion among frontline engineers. Meanwhile, the pressures they face for improved performance are offset by a deepening water crisis and the tightened manpower and financial resources resulting from reforms. Thus, the engineer's subject formation as a public servant is interrupted and frustrated by the constraints imposed on their resources and power as well as by the pressures and compulsions created by public expectations, official rules and local political actors. The engineers are active negotiators and players in these struggles, and their own interests and stakes are fashioned in these processes. Their excuses draw on 'conventions of explanation' (Herzfeld 1992) in which compassion is expressed yet shown to be constrained by the stereotypical indifference of 'the system' – a stereotype which their clients share, and which allows the engineers to pursue their personal agendas without being, or being seen as, indifferent. The rhetorics of service are thus as much a way of explaining their victimhood as their power.

Public service, in this situation, comes to be governed by the rubric of 'public relations.' The reforms place a conspicuous emphasis on public relations, explicitly linking it with the drive toward cost recovery from users. Given the situation, however, public relations come to be defined by depot engineers as getting the public to 'understand' their constraints, or communicating the limitations of what can be expected from a government service. With striking consistency, engineers represented their public relations function as one of appeasement, this in turn achieved largely through their personal presence at the scene:

If I rush to the spot, 50 per cent of the problem is solved, just by my presence there – then even if I cannot solve the problem, I can explain to the consumers and they are satisfied.

Public relations was often articulated as the need to cover up for the failures of the service:

We are engineers, supposed to supply water, but we can never adequately supply, so our main job is to convince people. How successful we are depends on the category of people – this category here is never willing to listen. People basically want security – to be sure of their supply, if not today, that they will at least get it soon. So you have to give them assurances, make them feel comforted, even if the government is not capable of fulfilling the promises.

It also involved insider strategies for containing demand:

We cannot satisfy people 100 per cent – we *should* not, because they will then want 200 per cent! For example, we are supposed to provide 70 lpcd water, but we provide about 60. If we give 70 or 80, they'll expect 120 lpcd!

This climate has given rise to a discourse about skills in 'handling the public' as the only real skills needed for depot work. Even labourers who demonstrate some capacity in this area are recognised, and installed in 'white collar' positions in the depot office. The discourse has gendered contours: female engineers claimed to have more talent for the task of appeasement, while male engineers claimed that dealing with the (rough and disorderly) public was particularly challenging for female engineers.

While the imperative of 'satisfying the public' was repeatedly invoked to explain departures from rules, in general this imperative is portrayed by engineers as simply one more burden. 'The public has become more aware' was a phrase I heard often, along with 'The public has become much more demanding!' One engineer claimed: 'Earlier they did not know so much: what the official said was taken as the final word!' Public awareness, public participation and public demand are thus conflated, generically perceived as on the rise, and usually deplored. Part of the problem was that complaints now went directly to the top: 'Even a rickshaw-man will phone the Chief Engineer to complain!' Another engineer said:

Five or ten years ago they hesitated a lot to come to the office, now they have been made so aware that even little children come to complain. Senior officers have announced that even small complaints can be brought to them.

Habermas (1989) analyses the 'practice of public relations' as one that coheres the private firm and the public bureaucracy in producing a consumer-oriented and mediatised public that is no longer critical. By invoking the classic notion of the public that puts its reason to use, but appropriating these connotations to conceal the agency's private (business) intentions, the practice engineers consent.[11] My analysis, however, shows how the meaning and character of the concept of public relations, when translated via the depots, reflect and sharpen the state's relations of distance from and resistance to the public.

POLITICAL LANDSCAPES OF THE PUBLIC

A final but critical dimension that compounded the depot engineers' difficulties in 'handling the public' was the political mobilisation in the slums. A major trope of the public in the discourse of depot engineers was that of a chaotic field in which politics dominated over civility. Since the municipal elections in 1996 which installed an elected mayor and 160 councillors in the city council, the local politician (the councillor) has become the constant referent, the everyday foil against which the engineers conduct their daily affairs, negotiate relationships with large sections of their clients, and define themselves and their service. Engineers are obliged to work closely with local politicians, partly because, as they themselves acknowledge, the councillors are the real channels for complaints: large sections of the public, especially from poorer areas, tend to take their complaints to the councillor rather than to the engineers. In addition, recent directives of the board, in line with the thrust of governance reforms, emphasise cooperation with councillors. In reality, few engineers risk alienating councillors, especially since many favours and privileges in the system, such as transfers, are controlled and distributed through political connections.

However, the overwhelming characterisation of this relationship in the discourse of depot engineers is one of a massive nuisance: a domain of disorder and a source of daily tension. The vast majority of engineers in this study claimed that dealing with local politicians was by far the most challenging aspect of their jobs:

Politicians come and dominate in the name of the public – in all depots they are the biggest problem. They present themselves as social workers, but they are just politicians. In many cases, when the councillor is a woman, you have her saying one thing and her husband saying the opposite. It's like having two councillors! Some depots are completely dominated by the councillor – these are where there are soft AEs or JEs. But I cut this out right at the start – this is a JE's office, and will remain a JE's office!

Political pressure on the local water service is by no means new. But pressures formerly exerted by local party functionaries could be more easily written off into the domain of the informal. In the present situation, councillors exert an authorised, if indirect pressure, backed by their power in the city council.[12] When they are also from the ruling party of the state, their local control can be compelling. Some engineers claimed that political interference sometimes forced them to compromise on engineering norms. Others described direct conflicts with politicians:

I left that area because I had clashes with the local councillor – he wanted the people to go only to him, or that I should work through him, but I directly provided services to the people, and they approached me directly. He threatened me a few times, but I continued to work. But after some time I applied for medical leave and then requested a transfer from that place.

The sociological scheme of the depot engineers is once more invoked to explain this field of relations. Political interference, apparently, while not a problem in the better-off divisions, is typical of the slum areas. Also, according to some engineers, it is the 'low-class' politicians who tend to be troublesome. Most engineers, however, agree that it is because of the politicians that people in the slums have become so demanding:

The public only expect subsidies, they don't want to pay anything! Only after the 1996 councillors' elections all this has happened. It has completely changed public attitudes.

The widespread perception is not only that the field of the public is over-politicised, but also that the character of the political field is corrupt and counter-productive. The discourse of 'politics as the problem' is clearly used by field engineers to cover up the lack of control that they experience over their work. In the organisation as a whole, the relationship with politicians is marked with ambivalence – while official policies promote partnership with politicians, bureaucrats at every level accuse other levels of complying with political pressures, and everybody claims that this trend is on the rise. And, as the association with the political domain is implicitly linked to 'unofficial' transactions, politics is counterposed with the law through the conflation of 'unofficial' with 'underhand', illegal and so on. Ultimately, political interference is invoked as a case for privatising O&M:

If the place is privatised, you cannot pull strings through MLAs and party officials and all kinds of people. But now, because this is a government organisation, everybody feels they can come in and demand things.

Another engineer urged me:

The only hope for Metrowater – and you should write this down – is if it is completely separated from politics! It should not have any mix at all with politics. No ministers, nothing!

Thus, the concept of the public that undergirds the service at its point of interface with its clients, largely refers to the poor, or more specifically to slum-dwellers, people who dump solid waste into the sewage system, speak roughly, do not understand the problems faced by engineers and are illiterate, demanding, politically organised and unwilling to pay. In short, the public in the everyday official discourse of the water service refers to the uncivil masses. The relationship between officials and this public verges on the adversarial when it is not patronising and pedagogic: field engineers claimed that their senior officials lacked the *dhairyam* (courage) to stand up to the public and to politicians. Thus, interpellated by the rhetoric and the demands of better service, yet simultaneously caught in the climate of increased vigilance, the engineers produce a discourse of political society as one of intimidation and threat. This is a discursive scheme that invokes Habermas's thesis that the entry of non-bourgeois masses into direct relations with the welfare state in the nineteenth century transformed the arena of the public from one of rational-critical debate to one of conflict and political mobilisation.

However, Chatterjee points to an inner dialectic within the ongoing processes of democratic state-formation: 'Just as there is a continuing attempt to order these institutions in the prescribed forms of liberal civil society, there is probably an even stronger tendency to strive for what are perceived to be democratic rights and entitlements by violating those institutional norms' (2001: 176). Political society's claims on the state are made not through the orderly associational citizenship of civil society, but in a different form of collectivity, the crowd, the mass that the engineers abhor and fear. The politicised masses deal confidently in the currency of rights, yet these are collective rights, collectively demanded. Chatterjee claims that 'the very collective form in which [these masses] appear before the state authorities implies that they are not proper citizens but rather population groups who survive by sidestepping the law' (2001: 177). My case, however, illustrates how 'the law' itself is a local construct, a shifting and contingent myth of order purveyed by local state functionaries in their translations of reformist visions. These visions invoke (and speak for) the urban poor as the grounds for the new disciplines and efficiencies of service, in the process refiguring these populations as consumers-in-the-making. But the subjects of these discourses articulate and enact a profound challenge to these agendas in their ongoing politicised demands for welfare as right. Chatterjee's model fails to account adequately for how local negotiations between the state and political society fashion notions of law and order. His category of 'political society' also overwrites alternative 'uncivil' formations, such as the collectivities of women from the slums who, in my study, often bypassed or sidestepped local political formations in demanding services from the state.

CONCLUSION

'Managing infrastructure like a business, not a bureaucracy' is a slogan of the World Bank's report, *Infrastructure for development* (1994: 2). Reconceptualising water services as an industry responsive to demand, reconstituting the client as a consumer, and focusing on revenue means addressing the individual. For a service in which up to a third of the daily quantum of water is supplied through public modes, such as trucks, tanks and public fountains, this shift in paradigm represents a significant disengagement of the state from large sections of its clientele – sections that are known to be much more critically dependent on the system than the revenue-paying private consumers, as most of the latter rely heavily on private groundwater resources.

All of the rhetoric of reform and its new instruments of public service notwithstanding, the ethnography revealed that effective accountability on the ground was not based on individual demand. It was only through the practices of collective citizenry that responses were obtained from the state agency. The vision of an efficient corporate body capable of providing reliable water and sanitation services to the city's population on the basis of a neutralised commercial relationship remains, even if feasible or desirable, unrealised. The current constraints on the successful commodification of water are too many to list here. Claims to a basic need, meanwhile, are negotiated through a sphere of political society that takes the state's role and claims to reformed performance seriously, that demands accountability *en masse*. Water remains an issue that can readily bring people out to claim their rights vis-à-vis the local state. Despite the decades of technological and engineering discourse that has sheathed it, the current local economy of water remains intensely political. Local political mobilisations, however, are occurring in ways that unsettle the teleological program of good governance by, among other things, redeploying caste-based, religious or other non-'modern' identities.

The reclamation of political agency by uncivil people located at the margins of urban amenities and subsisting off the commons is not something the reforming bureaucrats in public utilities are prepared or willing to deal with. The public legible to their administrative eye is a public to be served, and as such is unserveable. In contrast to the immature public that fulfilled the pedagogic imaginings of developmental state elites, the public that the engineers at the frontline encountered was demanding, strategic and far too mature – a public in which even a child knew how to complain.

NOTES

1. The concept of *translation*, pivotal to this study, focuses attention on the difference between the vision of a policy and the reality of its conditions of implementation, a field of discursive and political action that is very inadequately theorised. Bruno Latour outlines the concept of translation as follows: 'In its linguistic and material connotations, it refers to all the displacements through other actors whose mediation is indispensable for any action to occur' (1988: 311).
2. In Habermas's analysis, the public sphere was a radically gendered space defined by the separation of social reproduction from the realm of political action. The rise of the welfare state transferred public functions to private corporate bodies, resulting in a societalisation of the state and a

repoliticisation of the social sphere, a scheme in which the public/private distinction could no longer apply. In its place, a new kind of social labour, a 'world of work', began to assume an objective and public character, both in large industrial enterprises as well as in public bureaucracies. As the occupational sphere became a quasi-public realm, exemplified by the concept of the 'functionary', the great administrative bureaucracies of welfare capitalism lost their public character.

3. Several critics have commented on the 'democratisation' component of the governance reform package as being largely instrumental, serving the agenda of economic liberalisation (Guhan 1997). Rob Jenkins (2001) sees aid agencies' active assistance to the 'democracy and governance' sector as part of efforts to create a conducive environment for market-oriented policies and better economic performance.

4. Rob Jenkins (2001) outlines a similar problem in his discussion of how international aid agencies use the concept of civil society in supporting governance reforms. Misreading history, and overloading the concept with a range of instrumental meanings that contradict each other, the agencies have generated a sterile concept of civil society that is bound to fail. '(T)he main difficulty is that the definitions are not capable of producing, *in a co-ordinated way*, the three main outcomes that assistance to civil society is meant to produce' (2001: 253, emphasis in original). Jenkins's argument is that the kind of civil society that USAID is putting its weight behind is one that is completely benign and derives from the premise – either naive or cynical – that all opponents of authoritarian rule are supporters of democracy. 'The dynamics of political movements and the constantly shifting motives which characterise political life bear little resemblance to the sanitised vision of civil society which USAID and other agencies seek to promote' (2001: 262).

5. This is the short name by which the Chennai (earlier Madras) Metropolitan Water Supply and Sewerage Board (CMWSSB, earlier MMWSSB) is generally known.

6. The Eighth Five-year Plan (1992–97) of the Government of India outlined a key principle for the sector: water being managed as a commodity and not a free service. This thrust was carried over into the Ninth Plan (1997–2002). The report of a national conference on reform in the water sector in India in 1999, outlining the principles of financial viability of services and a shift in the role of government from provider to facilitator, stated: 'The(se) principles ... shape a new paradigm in the implementation of water projects and require commitment from political, bureaucratic and civil society sectors' (WSP 1999: 4).

7. See Strathern (1996) and Shore and Wright (1999) for excellent analyses of the audit culture as an emerging technology of coercive governmentality that employs the growing demands for accountability to taxpayers and the vocabularies of quality assurance and empowerment of users, to lay out a punitive regime of surveillance, especially targeted at core professionals in public agencies. See Porter (1995) for an analysis of the growing emphasis on quantitative approaches in public professional bureaucracies such as the US Army Corps of Engineers, as part of attempts to restrain the expert judgment and professional discretion through which engineers and other public professionals, in earlier times, made decisions.

8. The term comes from '*poromboke* land', which usually refers to the common lands on the edges of villages.

9. 'Sensitive areas' usually indexed slum populations, precisely because of their tendency to protest vociferously. But bureaucratic categories, I found, were labile: during the extreme drought of 2002, the term was used also to refer to neighbourhoods with high concentrations of religious minorities, reflecting the political climate of the time, or to political centres like the hostel for state legislators.

10. Complaints could also be sent directly to the area offices and head office, via a 24-hour complaints line established at the Head Office, the Information and Facilitation Offices established in every area, or by email. All this was designed to allow consumers direct recourse to higher authorities, bypassing, if necessary, the frontline engineers.

11. As the state borrows the practice of purposive publicity from the practice of big private enterprises, Habermas argues, the public sphere becomes, as in feudal times, the court before which public prestige can be displayed, rather than one in which public critical debate can be carried out.

12. It is worth noting here that the key domain of political action in our context – municipal government – is very much in formation: the councillors are recently elected, their authority over the services is still ill-defined and tenuous, and the institutional forms of this emergent relationship with state bureaucracies are still under construction.

REFERENCES

WHO (World Health Organization), UNDP (United Nations Development Program) and the Government of Tamil Nadu (1977) *Final report on organization, management and finance*, study conducted by A.F. Ferguson and Co., Bombay, in association with Peat, Marwick, Mitchell and Co., London (Chennai: Metrowater Resource and Training Center Library).

Abrams, P. (1988) Notes on the difficulty of studying the state. *Journal of Historical Sociology* 1: 58–89.

Chatterjee, P. (2001) On civil and political society in post-colonial democracies. In S. Kaviraj and S. Khilnani (eds) *Civil society: history and possibilities* (Cambridge: Cambridge University Press).

CMWSSB (Chennai Metropolitan Water Supply and Sewerage Board) (Multiple years)

Annual reports (Chennai: Metrowater).

Foucault, M. (1991) Governmentality. In G. Burchell, C. Gordon and P. Miller (eds) *The Foucault effect: studies in governmentality* (London: Harvester Wheatsheaf).

Gramsci, A. (1971) *Selections from the prison notebooks*, ed. Q. Hoare and G.N. Smith (New York: International Publishers).

Habermas, J. (1989) *The structural transformation of the public sphere: an inquiry into a category of bourgeois society* (Cambridge, MA: MIT Press).

Herzfeld, M. (1992) *The social production of indifference: exploring the symbolic roots of Western bureaucracy* (Chicago and London: University of Chicago Press).

Hood, C. (2001) A public management for all seasons. *Public Administration* 69: 3–19.

Jenkins, R. (2001) Mistaking 'governance' for 'politics': foreign aid, democracy and the construction of civil society. In S. Kaviraj and S. Khilnani (eds) *Civil society: history and possibilities* (Cambridge: Cambridge University Press).

Latour, B. (1988) *The pasteurization of France*, trans. A. Sheridan and J. Law (Cambridge, MA: Harvard University Press).

Pandian, M.S.S. (2002) *One step outside modernity: caste, identity politics and public sphere* (Amsterdam/Dakar: SEPHIS-CODESRIA).

Porter, T. (1995) *Trust in numbers: the pursuit of objectivity in science and public life*. Princeton, NJ: Princeton University Press.

Scott, J.C. (1998) *Seeing like a state: how certain schemes to improve the human condition have failed* (New Haven, CT and London: Yale University Press).

Shore, C. and S. Wright (1999) Audit culture and anthropology: neo-liberalism in British higher education. *Journal of the Royal Anthropological Institute* 5: 557–77.

Strathern, M. (1996) From improvement to enhancement: an anthropological comment on the audit culture. *Cambridge Anthropologist* 19: 1–21.

WSP (Water and Sanitation Program – South Asia) (1999) *Politicians for reform: proceedings of the State Water Ministers' workshop on rural water supply policy reforms in India*. Cochin, Kerala (India), December.

World Bank (1994) *World development report: infrastructure for development* (New York: Oxford).

9   DISJUNCTURE AND MARGINALITY – TOWARDS A NEW APPROACH TO DEVELOPMENT PRACTICE

Rob van den Berg and Philip Quarles van Ufford

In this chapter Quarles van Ufford recounts an occurrence at a birthday party of the official Dutch development monitoring and evaluation unit in 2003, and van den Berg responds to his remarks. They then add some notes concerning their discovery of the importance of acknowledging 'disjunction' in development practices for improving both academic understanding (Quarles van Ufford) and administrative practices (van den Berg). The two stories converge on some broader reflections on the relevance of various forms of disjunction. The conclusion is that notions of 'marginality' and of 'narrative' may well be indispensable for improving a critical understanding of development interventions as well as of the art of administrative development practice.

A SPEECH AT A BIRTHDAY PARTY (QUARLES VAN UFFORD)

In February 2003 a seminar on the past and future of evaluation in Dutch development cooperation was held on the occasion of the twenty-fifth anniversary of the Policy and Operations Evaluation Department of the Ministry of Foreign Affairs. This is an independent professional unit, formally part of the civil service and situated within the Ministry of Foreign Affairs in The Hague. It is ensured some independence through its reporting to parliament through the minister. Two ministers and top members of the development bureaucracy attended the seminar. Although the importance and the achievements of the department were lauded by many speakers, a note of criticism was introduced in the afternoon by one of us, as director of the department, when noting that so many of the evaluation findings had not been acted upon by the minister, administrators or practitioners. He indicated that while the department's staff took pride in their work and were grateful for the positive remarks made by various high authorities, more should be said. Some problematic issues should be given attention as well.

First of all, he raised the question whether the public, parliament and the ministers were not expecting too much from evaluation. In a world increasingly dominated by news stories about crises, about humanitarian disasters, about scandals in society and politics, what role should be allocated to critical reflection on what happened in the past? Second, he questioned whether evaluation would be able to fully disclose what happened and why. Most importantly for this chapter, he referred to the learning loop within the ministry as being in danger of becoming a tired old traditional dance – sending an evaluation on to parliament with an acknowledgement that some mistakes were made in the past, that they had meanwhile been corrected and that in future things would surely be better. In his speech the director of the Evaluation Department now asked the highest authorities, especially the Minister of Development Cooperation, if they could ensure that better use would be made of the lessons learned from the past.

The impact of the speech was, in my perception, great. It was the greater as a certain sweetness of tone made the message inescapable. How could we understand – he requested us to clarify – the marginality of learning, when everyone agreed that the food for thought prepared by the evaluation department tasted so good? I had received the speech a few days in advance. The director had asked me to open the debate once the full impact of the speech had come to be felt in the meeting. I accepted his request. But what to say? There was no point in reiterating his critical analysis of a policy process closing itself off from insight into policies' consequences. There was no point in rehashing his description of the consistent marginality of learning from the field at the policy level. I felt that there was no point in telling the minister to do a better job. Earlier on I had analysed the constitution of domains of ignorance in policy making. The often very limited impact of feedback into policy making was hardly new to me. To my distress, I had witnessed the decision of the board of a major Dutch NGO to actually fire the evaluators since they demanded that lessons should be learned on the basis of their evaluative reporting from the field. Ironically, accompanying this dismissal was an official proclamation of the board's loyalty to processes of learning from experience in the yearly report. Some of my friends and former colleagues on the board then explained to me that they had been confronted with a choice between upholding the idealism of the Dutch constituency and heeding a demand to critically reassess official Dutch views on the basis of processes of evaluation, the 'learning tools' of the NGO. When put to the test, it had become apparent to me that learning from outcomes came second. The agency's views were primarily expressive of the donor's

Dutch sources of identity, its Dutch constituency. The 'beneficiaries' came second. This was the 'natural' priority.

Would there be a point in criticising the director general of the ministry, supposedly the spider in the web? On his desk all the relations and problematic linkages came together: the Dutch political scene and the minister, the Dutch press, parliament, as well as the so-called beneficiaries of aid. Criticising the director general would be beside the point. He was not, it seemed to me, failing personally. I decided to make a jump, a big one if possible: move away from the notion that there actually was an institutional centre at the ministry that could choose to learn or not. Perhaps it would be a step forward to suggest that there are no such zones of centrality in which actors are free to learn when they choose to do so. Perhaps we should come to see that we are using metaphors of administration that are quite beside the point, illusory, serving only some interests and not others. I suggested to the director of the Evaluation Department that he had put forward the wrong questions. He was making some false assumptions. Had he not assumed – I asked – that there actually was a centre that could choose to learn? Was the position of the minister herself, for instance, not too full of contradictions to do just that? He had assumed that there was a coherent whole and a centre. Disjunctures were, however, 'normal'. There was no point in continuing to suppose that official administration could be conceived as a 'machinery', well tooled, integrated, oiled and serviced, purposefully directed. Rather, the relationships between the different parts should first of all be regarded as highly problematic. I suggested that the problem perhaps was that we lacked the conceptual tools for dealing with these disjunctures in a relevant way. By not recognising them as inevitable and thus failing to learn how to deal with them in a more mature way, we were bound to do less well than perhaps was possible.

While formally responsible, the minister is in fact rather marginal to the forces shaping the outcomes of aid. The contexts are beyond her control. This contradicted official views, however, that she is responsible for 'her policies' to the Dutch parliament. While this assumption is perhaps inevitable in the Dutch political system of a parliamentary democracy, does this very assumption not become futile when applied to the domain of 'outcomes' of development aid? How must we deal with this apparent contradiction? The minister is primarily a Dutch actor, formally operating in a Dutch context and, as it were, condemned to believe and uphold the ironclad Dutch myth of a well-oiled administrative machine. But while this myth is a cornerstone in the Dutch parliamentary democracy, it is an illusion as far as development work is concerned. In fact, from that perspective she cannot escape marginality. What lessons would then be possible and which not? One would have to become more precise about the nature of her marginality. The myth of full political responsibility for 'her' policies is perhaps a fateful illusion. We are faced with systemic flaws, inevitable disjunctures, contradictions and irrationalities inherent in the system. While we uphold the myth – important as it may be in the Dutch context – it is an illusion in the field of international relations.

I suggested that, in order to answer the director's questions about learning, we would have to devise new ways of conceptualising international aid relationships. We must first of all stop fooling ourselves and try to deal better with the inherent disjunctures in the webs of relationships. Perhaps the notion of marginality, rather than the centrality of the main actors in the policy process may constitute a starting point for this conceptual renewal. Perhaps this may provide an important contribution to a new practical as well as scientific understanding of development practices. The higher up agents are in administration, the more marginal they are as far as learning from the field is concerned. It may help us to see the limitations and contradictory demands with which the minister and the highest civil servants have to cope. We may as a result also learn better to discern the room to manoeuvre relative to issues such as lessons from the field.

Perhaps we could start reflecting on the fact that there are only marginal sections, or a multitude of different and competing clusters of actors. Maybe we should start exploring the implications of the core theme of this chapter and of the volume as a whole: we must acknowledge disjuncture first; second, stop assuming that there is a centre at all; and, third, try to deal with that situation in the best possible way. Continuing to cling to notions of order and the assumption of a centre may well be counterproductive. The current popularity of conceptualising development administration as well integrated machinery actually does great harm to the quality of its work.

THE POTENTIAL CONTRIBUTION OF EVALUATION (VAN DEN BERG)

Quarles van Ufford's suggestions on disjuncture and marginality at the Policy and Operations Evaluation Department meeting led me to reflect further on the limitations but also possible contributions of evaluations to improve our policies, administration and practices. Evaluation is generally considered to have three functions: accountability, learning and insight. A good evaluation accounts for what happened. It provides lessons from the past for future use. It shines a light on mechanisms that we hoped would work, and which are now revealed to work, work partly, or not at all. In this last function it adds to our knowledge of what works and why.

However, all three functions are overstated, or, from another perspective, limited in nature. It is well known in the evaluation profession that to fully account for what has happened is usually more expensive than undertaking the activity (or policy) that is being evaluated in the first place. To do something can be very direct; to account for what you are doing is by definition indirect. To account for what you are doing through evaluation research means that you are not satisfied with a simple story of what happened (which can be very short). What is officially required in Dutch development administration is an independent assessment of what happened, through the independent gathering of facts and independent analysis of these facts leading to an independent judgement on what happened. To establish facts in an independent way is costly and time consuming. To establish all the facts is impossible.

Accountants have learned to deal with this. They take a small 'representative' sample of activities, look at the files and decide on the basis of this small sample whether the book-keeping is in order and the reporting of the organisation sufficiently reflects reality. Evaluators tend to need bigger samples. Nevertheless, I have never seen an evaluation that managed to look at 100 per cent of activities of the subject that was being evaluated. One hundred per cent accountability is thus a dream that cannot be achieved and should not be expected.

The potential for learning is also always overstated. Experts on learning know that learning is 'subjective': it is the subject who learns – not the teacher, the guru, the manager or the evaluator. Thus learning is by definition something that takes a different form and starts from a different perspective for each individual. Organisational learning has the same characteristics: if one organisation learns in one way, this does not mean that another organisation learns in the same way, or starts from the same perspective or has the same level of expertise and knowledge. Evaluators are confronted with multiple actors, multiple organisations, multiple countries, multiple sectors and multiple policies. Yet they are expected to come up with a uniform feedback model that will ensure learning on all levels by everybody. The different audiences are often acknowledged only in ensuring that different products come out of the same evaluation: reports, key sheets, brochures, CD-ROMs, and so on. Yet these different wrappings of a qualified judgement do not make a different evaluation.

Furthermore, learning is problematic because the audiences for evaluations are not in any way students. They are not 'prepared to learn' and will not get a diploma after listening to an evaluation presentation. They have agendas of their own – they have interests which they will try to defend, and they are actors on a stage which is constantly being besieged by other actors, while the audience is clapping or booing. Expectations of the learning potential provided by evaluation findings should not be overstated, to say the least.

Third, evaluations can only provide 'insight' or illuminate practices on certain occasions, in certain cases. First of all, the tools of the evaluator are the accepted tools of science, as well as common sense. Any evaluator needs to use accepted scientific methodology if he or she expects the audience to be convinced of the new insight that the evaluation establishes. If not, scientists will blast the report. However, most scientific tools are monodisciplinary, whereas development problems and most interventions trying to change things for the better are multidisciplinary. If we achieve any insight, it is almost by definition partial. One main characteristic of scientific methodology is that, in line with Karl Popper's thinking, it tends to be better at unmasking theories than showing what is really happening. In other words: it is often easier to show that a suspected causal linkage between your money and the amount of happiness in the world does not exist, than that it in fact exists (all things remaining equal). Scientific methodology, which we need to rely on to establish insights, is in fact geared towards destroying insights. Creative scientists establish new insights, and use scientific methodology to prove that the previous theory is wrong. It may be one step too far to ask evaluators to become creative scientists.

Many evaluations have scored brilliantly with common-sense insights. However, a more prudent and fair judgement of these successes would no doubt establish that these insights were to some extent of the variety of 'the emperor has no clothes': that is, establishing a truth that everybody already perceived, but was afraid to voice because it was not considered politically correct to do so.

In light of these three functions and the limited way in which evaluations can fulfil them, evaluators need to be realistic and humble – and the audience for evaluations needs to be aware of their limitations. These disjunctures between the ideal and the actual should be taken seriously and as a starting point for our thinking about the role of evaluations.

DISCOVERING THE IMPORTANCE OF DISJUNCTURE FOR DEVELOPMENT PRACTICE (QUARLES VAN UFFORD)

While preparing the final version of the introductory text to the recent EIDOS volume, *A moral critique of development: towards global responsibilities* (2003), it suddenly occurred to me that various bits and pieces of the argument were all pointing in one direction: the notion of disjuncture had to come first.

Development practices emerge from a confrontation with various kinds of disjuncture, while at the same time keeping strangely silent about them. All practitioners of development, students, administrators and citizens alike, focus on notions of order. Order comes first, whether in the past or in the future. Disjunctures are there to be overcome, to be solved, to be wiped out. The insight that disjuncture comes first and order (or equilibrium) only after that was a shock, a break with deeply embedded past convictions of which I had not been fully aware. It became apparent that the assumption of order had to be overcome and that it was paramount to learn to distinguish between different kinds of disjuncture. The notion that disjuncture comes first and cannot be overcome seemed to have many advantages. It allowed for the insight that our modes of confronting disjuncture had been biased indeed, a flight from a serious acknowledgment of the broken nature of our societies by defining alluring dreams of a better world and behaving as if they are within our grasp.

In development studies we have been preoccupied with successive notions of order since 1945. Marxist and modernisation theories competed with different dreams of a better world. The preoccupation with order in the future was a critical feature of development studies. Every debate was about processes of ordering and overcoming structural obstacles. It was as if everyone was running away from the past. Historical awareness was substituted by projected mirror images, for example, if there was modernity out there then the past must have been traditional.

Development was a practice of dreaming, of hope on a global level because the present and recent past had been ghastly: modern nations had destroyed each other on a global scale since 1914. Holocaust, the destruction of civil society and the killing of young generations, and the already visible collapse of a colonial order, did not provide a pathway to moral and political reflection of future global relations. The concept of development that was already emerging during the Second World War had to relate to a view totally different from both present and past. Hence, acts of dreaming development, and a moral and political preoccupation with the future, became of the greatest importance. The ahistoricity of development was an asset not a liability. The priority was to move beyond global disaster, away from massive death and destruction. 'Never again!' How could the past provide a starting point? The empty concept of development was a container concept, allowing all agents to enter into it their specific dreams of a better future. Development was about dreaming.

In development these practices of dreaming could be embedded in political theories of historical rationality of various kinds, Marxist and Weberian. The promises of unfolding historical rationality fitted specific requirements and fitted the needs of dreaming. There were specific models of modernity, out there in the future, to be grasped. These theories were preoccupied with specific notions of order, promising to overcome, as it were, contingencies of the past. The need for a new order could be matched to specific views of a possible unfolding historical rationality. But still the acts of dreaming preceded other considerations.

This did not change in the 1980s and 1990s, when a rather politically empty and nihilistic focus on management techniques and modes of managing historical change took over from competing notions of political rationality. Now 'goals' of development turned into 'targets', a martial metaphor setting the stage for development policy as rather manageable, straightforward 'shooting exercises': accountable, measurable, unambiguous, filled with promises of effectiveness and efficiency, and learning – for a new generation of development 'soldiers'. The notion of logical frameworks steering the project and policy cycles took over the role of Marxist or Weberian rationality. But the price was great: development was shielded from a serious confrontation with the real world. We have now become, as it were, totally addicted to promises of order. Development practitioners of various inclinations are becoming 'junkies', almost aggressively dependent on a regular 'shot of order' and quite willing to pay a high price: out of touch with reality and living in a world which, in increasingly vicious and uncontrolled ways, is becoming virtual.

I discovered that I, too, had been an 'addict of order', telling myself that my critical studies had an important role to play. These could become a tool – I reasoned – for improving policy processes. Much like the development administrators I had long been studying, I clung to a dream of the possibility of historical rationality and progress, even while I was deconstructing this very belief in my studies of specific agencies, programmes and policies. Now it became clear to me: disjuncture comes first. How to deal with that? We must perhaps learn as Polish philosopher Kolakowski urges us to do – to become a 'liberal, socialist, conservative', that is, to allow ourselves to conceptualise historical process in new ways: as incompatible, contradictory, random, accidental as much as – sometimes – orderly. So we may begin to acknowledge the wisdom of the Polish bus driver who urged his passengers to 'please step forward to the rear' (Kolakowski 1978: 46). There is more to this than idle postmodern playfulness. These lines were written not long after Kolakowski had moved to England, escaping a communist regime in Poland which put severe ideological constraints on intellectual debate in the 1970s.

DISCOVERING THAT IN DEVELOPMENT DISJUNCTURE COMES
FIRST (VAN DEN BERG)

Reflection on disjuncture led me back to my youth. In Dutch high
school I read *The world of Null-A* by Canadian science fiction writer
Alfred E. van Vogt (1948). This novel was based on the Polish engineer
and philosopher Alfred Korzybski's *Science and sanity*, first published
in 1933. Korzybski proposes a non-Aristotelian logic, which does not
divide statements into categories of 'false' or 'true', but recognises
that statements may be neither true nor false, but 'null-A', or non-
Aristotelian.[1] This led to a new system of General Semantics which is
supposed to help people become sane, since it claims not to confuse
statements about reality with reality itself. This last insight – which
is of course not unique to Korzybski – is illustrated time and again in
van Vogt's novels. The actors in his 'Null-A' stories are shown to be
making mistakes if they take descriptions or models of the world as
'true' representations of the world. The Institute of General Semantics
in Texas, USA[2] has as its motto: 'It's not what you think.' But if that
is the case, what can we 'think' about reality?

Non-Aristotelian logic has, since Korzybski, appeared in many
guises, for example as 'fuzzy logic' in computer programming. The
disjuncture between words and reality is at the core of discussion in
the philosophy of science. This has in some cases led to disconnecting
the two, for example when Wittgenstein and his followers claim that
much of philosophy is an internal language phenomenon, which is
only weakly related to non-language reality. At the same time, society
is dominated by people who claim to think less but do more. This
leads to an increase in non-scientific 'doing'-knowledge: the 'how to'
publications in many areas, perhaps predominantly in management.
From a scientific perspective, most if not all of this literature is very
light on theory and heavy on practical prescriptions. In the wake
of the economic success of many of these pragmatic prescriptions
(nothing breeds success like success) the public policy domain has
adopted many of these approaches. Results-based management is
one of them. Another common feature of these approaches is that
they are actor based: if you as the primary actor in your world (or
company) start to act in a certain way, or to think about the 'results'
that need to be achieved in a certain way, success will follow.

The scientific approach, by contrast, tries to negate the actor. It
tries to achieve a disinterested, objective, or at least intersubjective
view of the problem, organisation or trend in society. This 'view
from nowhere', as it has been termed by American philosopher
Thomas Nagel (1989), leads to general ideas and general solutions,
but does not provide concrete advice for a physical actor in a physical
situation. Nagel argues that scientific models, by their very nature,

lead to a denial of the autonomy of human actors – all human actions are explained away as caused by other actions. Action is only possible if we adopt a particular, specific, subjective perspective.

Although the disjuncture between models of reality and reality itself, between theory and practice, between understanding and action, between our particular view versus a 'view from nowhere' seem to be undercurrents in many discussions, at the same time we need to recognise that most efforts on both sides of the disjuncture are geared towards resolving it. Science claims that it strives towards ever better models of reality, and many scientists hope that perhaps in future a 'theory of everything' will become available, which will no longer allow for disjuncture anywhere. Action-oriented management theories appear to claim to build up from actual practice a theory or model of how to act as a person, an organisation or a society in order to achieve results. Here the disjuncture will become obsolete from the other side: general knowledge (of the technical 'how to' kind) will be based on a true grasp of what happens 'on the ground'. Both sides tend to recognise the disjuncture as a temporary state of affairs, a 'mistake' rather than a fundamental starting point.

Fortunately, results-based management has not yet captured all areas of international (or national) activity. Many people and organisations still act out of a moral need to do so rather than out of an instrumentalist view that a certain result can be achieved if the right tools are applied to the job. A very good example is the organisation Anti-Slavery International,[3] which is the world's oldest human rights organisation. It was founded in 1787, when the first abolitionist society was formed in the United Kingdom. If the founders had adopted the logical framework approach, they would very quickly have decided that the goal was unachievable in the short run. They were ambitious: they wanted nothing more and nothing less than to abolish slavery in the world. They still have not succeeded in doing that, even though they have some very good results to look back on (abolishing the slave trade in 1807; abolition of slavery in the English colonies in 1833). The organisation is still active today, not because they believe that results can be guaranteed in the near future, but because they feel a moral obligation to act. It has been argued that they follow a 'logic of appropriateness' rather than a 'logic of consequences' (March and Olsen n.d.). It seems quite clear that in many areas of international policy we are in fact following logics of appropriateness rather than a logic of consequences, yet the debate about development issues is always in terms of 'results' and 'consequences'. Furthermore, it seems that the logic of appropriateness is more suitable for confronting a disjuncture than the logic of consequences, which tries to tie the world down to one interpretation of reality.

KINDS OF DISJUNCTURE IN DEVELOPMENT PRACTICE (QUARLES VAN UFFORD)

If indeed 'disjuncture comes first', then what does this mean? What kinds of 'brokenness' may we distinguish? What are the inherent flaws in our conventional concepts that we must reconsider? Let us mention three disjunctures.

Practices of hope, of politics and of critical understanding are indispensable for a viable view of development; yet these practices do not fit together. Efforts at linking these three kinds of practices without acknowledging the disjuncture or incommensurability between them have ended in disaster – the building of 'prisons'. This argument by Foucault was followed up in the domains of development by Escobar and others.

In development discourse, acknowledgement of this disjuncture is still largely absent. The recent formulations, for instance, of quite eschatological 'millennium goals' – projected futures as lightning rods for development planning and politics that allow critical measurement of actor performance from year to year – reflect the very flaws of unacknowledged disjuncture. We turn acts of hope into goals and targets, and fail. The practices of politics as administration – of an audit culture extracting policy processes from their contexts – has successfully marginalised practices of hope and of critical understanding. (Administrative) order is held thus to yield progress. As noted above, this is no more than a nihilistic form of developmental daydreaming. Monique Nuijten (e.g. 2004) has argued convincingly how hope is being commoditised, and as a result emptied and made harmless, by development administrations. Development turned into 'administered hope' signals a global attack on other forms of historical awareness, as wider social and historical wholes drop out of sight. The destruction of meaning is the outcome of a new, narrowly defined, global model of governance and administration. Current development ideology thus may become in the end a closed system, a new form of secular fundamentalism, a blinded eschatology. Instead of being a concept which helps open up outlooks, hope closes them down again. Any creative *hoping* relationship with a wider world beyond current confines and entrapments is smothered by development's hope-generating machines (Nuijten), as notions of administrative manageability become the baseline of development's discourse. These can only create 'beneficiaries', which again removes creative agency from individuals and communities.

The disjunctured nature of our moral views of development is the second kind of disjuncture we need to acknowledge. Hannah Arendt (1958) distinguishes between three fundamental human activities, each subject to a set of distinctive moral rules. These domains of human activity are *labour, work* and *action*. For our purposes work and action are most relevant. Work is the domain of *homo faber*, the designer and constructor. We build our house, that is, an artificial world to be distinguished from the natural environment. In this domain the considerations and rules are instrumental in kind.

Arendt's domain of the 'agent' as culturally and politically responsible actor is quite different from the instrumentality of the domain of *homo faber*. As agents, we are involved in a web of relationships in which our identity is distinctive and fluid; in which the question about our past, where we come from and to whom we belong, is dealt with. As agents, our present and future moral and political responsibility finds its form and space in distinctive narratives. These narratives make it possible for us to learn to act and find our place in a basically plural situation in which the narratives differ and can be exchanged, where narratives make life possible because they may give space to all human experiences and the changing historical contingencies are confronted. Both in our speech, that is, our narratives, and in our acts, we may enact our moral responsibility in a twofold condition: that of 'equality and distinction' (Arendt 1958: 175).

The relevance of Arendt's distinction for our discussion of the changing conceptions of development is obvious. Today we witness the immanent sacralisation of morality, the dominance of *homo faber*, in the domains of development. Development's moral universe now makes almost universal use of the abstracted models of replicable management techniques. Abstracted from the specific contexts in which they originated, these models of unbound instrumentality are now thought to be applicable on a global scale. This moral universe almost totally dominates the agenda of development and so leads to a worldwide proliferation of new forms of forceful applications by multilateral agencies, governments and larger NGOs caught in the financial webs of the providers of funds.

The view of human beings as creators of a plurality of 'stories', the narratives and the struggles to give meaning to all this, is now quickly vanishing. Development debates are distanced from the historical realities and thus from specific webs of human relationships and efforts to cope with the need for meaning. The distinct stories are gradually being destroyed. The logics of appropriateness – born in the struggle to give direction to one's responsibilities in concrete relations and political responsibilities – are almost totally sidelined by the logic of instrumentality. This costly reification and application of a very restricted experience must be regarded with great suspicion.

The disjuncture in development administration is the third kind we need to deal with. The work of professionals is no longer perceived as emanating from specific forms of global responsibility embedded in shared, negotiated narratives about development. Rather, the concept of development is, as it were, lifted away from the arena of global political debate. It is professionalised and politically and morally 'neutralised'. Development is transformed into a 'mental commodity' – a product. Enter *homo faber*.

We now witness a deep contradiction between two processes: (a) a quite forceful imposition of increasingly hierarchical models of organisation (accompanied by an aggressive closing of mental boundaries, isolating development from its specific contexts); (b) a rather frantic crumbling of the linkages between the various agents in collaboration (cf. Quarles van Ufford 2004). The fabric of relationships between the different agents and levels of organisation are torn apart. The specific and mechanical nature of the demands put on development work lead to paradoxical consequences. Meaningful relationships between official instrumental discourse and the concrete transformations actually taking place are evaporating. Insights into the actual relations in the domains of development practice are being obscured in aggressive ways by the demands of a mechanical official discourse. This leads to the construction of virtual realities, which have serious negative impacts on real-life learning processes. Chaos and profound dislocation are the direct result of the application of mechanical modes of organisation (Mintzberg 1979: 335ff). The negative consequences can be discerned in the West as well as in developing countries. Destruction of the quest for authentic and meaningful development narrative takes place both upstream and downstream of development practice. Such is the insidious effect of the new instrumental morality – little noticed and hidden behind a façade of empty idealism – the oil that operates the machinery of development.

The image of a closed logical system of effectiveness, and all that comes with it, is defended and upheld at great cost. In the whole range of deconstructive studies, development anthropologists have analysed the dynamics of development work, showing the great gaps between intentions and outcomes (for a recent overview of these academic debates, see Roth 2003). These carefully argued insights indicate the emergence of development practices that are in contradiction with the data generated by the highly mechanical operating machinery of development itself.

We conclude that an effort must be made to bring history back into our notions of development. We must break with the conceptual constraints set by increasingly far-fetched, abstract and artificial images of a world order. Restoring the historicity of development means giving space to various distinctive narratives. The remarks of Hannah Arendt are very much 'to the point'. In development, a moral vision of a plurality of narratives has been lost. History has been destroyed in aggressive ways. The instrumental morality of *homo faber*, important as it may be, must be framed in wider moral and political narratives. We must regain insight into notions of moral and political appropriateness. These may take a different shape, linked as they are to various notions of historic authenticity in the different parts of the world. We are in danger of losing meaning both upstream and downstream.

Our engagement in development as administration and intervention has become increasingly narrow. Administration has become segmented from wider contexts. Artificial and abstract models of orderly social engineering have become highly problematic. Urgently needed, therefore, is a close look at the managing of development 'upstream'. In this chapter we have tried to show how the actors within development administration are confronted with the destruction and loss of meaning in their work; how they are confronted with totally unrealistic assumptions. Often despair pervades administrations. The mechanisms of unrealistic assumptions of order, then, come at great cost. Acknowledging disjuncture and marginality, on the other hand, may constitute a creative opportunity at various levels.

We may start to perceive the mechanisms by which current myths and assumptions legitimating the operations of development agencies become counterproductive. 'Things just do not fit'. The administering of development cannot be made to fit in a mechanistic way. We may thus start to discern the core issue in the administering of development which Buijs (2004: 105) described so well: 'The desire to work on a universal alleviation of suffering has resulted in a claim to universality regarding the specifically western means of how to achieve this.'

At the actor level – agencies as well as individuals – the notion of *prudentia* must be restored. Virtue ethics may be an answer to the serious shortcomings of universalising moral discourses. This virtue of *prudentia* reflects a keen awareness of disjuncture; an awareness of the absence of absolute certainties. *Prudentia* urges us to be reasonable as the discourses of reason so clearly are failing. We must try to make the best of it as the quest for a universal good policy or good governance becomes futile. We must start to provide room for manoeuvre to the various actors, and debate what kinds of coping with disjuncture require what kinds of *prudentia*, that is, emerging insights allowing for some sort of moderation. Such awareness of 'zones of administrative insecurity, of indeterminacy' (Buijs 2004) may well be a precondition for improvement. This may open our minds to the importance of debating the various modes of coping with uncertainties. These may require that we start to open ourselves to the importance of development conceived as a meeting point of different and distinctive narratives.

The virtue of *prudentia* may acquire a different substance in varying situations. It may become a tool for dealing with diversity. It means that, in development administration, the willingness and capacity to provide different narratives is nurtured rather than killed from the outset. We have argued that the process of evaluation, in which judgements are commoditised, does not lead to a 'good' policy process in which lessons are learned in a systematic way. On the contrary.

Nurturing prudential and other key virtues may help us to break with unrealistic assumptions of centrality in our views of interventions in development. We indicated above how these assumptions may lead to virtual and mechanistic practices of administration. These are harmful, leading to feelings of helplessness and despair among the actors. Acknowledging the fact that development knows many centres urges us to explore zones of uncertainty and to debate the best possible ways to deal with these.

This renewal may also benefit from the concept of 'marginality' in development administration. Awareness of marginality makes us sensitive to the nature of various limitations and disjunctures in the process of administering development. All actors, upstream as well as downstream, share this characteristic. We must stop running away from this insight. The concept of marginality may provide an important new angle of approach to the dynamics of development administration and may well have many useful practical consequences.

A CODA

We wish now to come back to the beginning of the chapter: the birthday party. In the chapter we set out to experiment a bit, telling two stories, each different to be sure. But we have been sharing some key insights as well, right from the start. Our inputs into the chapter build on a shared effort to acknowledge as well as we could disjunctures in our own work, whether of a scientific or an administrative nature. In the first story, Quarles van Ufford intended to infuse his story with a critical view of academic traditions that had been too confrontational and orderly in their analyses. Any notion of a 'pure' anthropology of development as opposed to the dirty and applied tradition is nonsensical. Critical development studies has – we feel – been paying too a high price for an exaggerated preoccupation with notions of order emerging from a frontal attack on development's practices of intervention. The relatively recent post-structuralist traditions are a case in point. Criticism has rightly been made, time and again, of the branches of a development anthropology that were preoccupied with advising and with consultancy work. Anthropological analysis, to its harm, became too preoccupied with administrative agendas (e.g. Mosse 2004). Prices were paid. But criticism must be extended too to the so-called 'purely' academic traditions which emerged in the last two decades. Various students paid the price of a flawed understanding of development interventions as a result of their tendency to 'round up' and systematise their analyses of agencies and interventions in too orderly a way. These lost sight of the basics of development's messiness.

We must allow new linkages between academia and development agencies, experiment with new zones of uncertainty both in administrative and scientific practices. This may give rise to new and fruitful forms of cooperation, and to new scientific as well as practical insights. In this chapter we have made an effort in experimenting a bit with this agenda. Perhaps the effort was of some use. New practices of collaboration along these lines may well help us find new insights not only in practical terms, but also in our critical academic understanding of what is going on in the domains of development.

NOTES

1. In mathematics this idea was introduced by Brouwer in the same decade.
2. <www.general-semantics.org>.
3. <www.antislavery.org>.

REFERENCES

Arendt, H. (1958) *The human condition* (Chicago: University of Chicago Press).

Buijs, G. (2004) Religion and development. In O. Salemink, A. van Harskamp and A.K. Giri (eds) *The development of religion and the religion of development*, pp. 101–09 (Delft: Eburon).

Kolakowski, L. (1978) How to be a conservative-liberal-socialist. *Encounter* 51(4).

Korzybski, A. (1933) *Science and sanity: an introduction to non-Aristotelian systems and general semantics* (New York: Institute of General Semantics).

March, J.P. and J.P. Olsen (n.d.) *The logic of appropriateness*, Arena Centre for European Studies, Working Paper P 04/09 (Oslo: University of Oslo).

Mintzberg, H. (1979) *The Structuring of Organizations* (Englewood Cliffs, NJ: Prentice Hall).

Mosse, D. (2004) Social analysis as product development. In O. Salemink, A. van Harskamp and A.K. Giri (eds) *The development of religion and the religion of development*, pp. 77–89 (Delft: Eburon).

Nagel, T. (1989) *The view from nowhere* (New York: Oxford University Press).

Nuijten, M. (2004) The 'hope-generating machine' and the positionality of the anthropologist'. In O. Salemink, A. van Harskamp and A.K. Giri (eds) *The development of religion and the religion of development*, pp. 51–59 (Delft: Eburon).

Quarles van Ufford, P. (2004) Can we still save the charisma of development from its applications? In *FAU conference: new perspectives on poverty reduction – towards a new poverty agenda*, pp. 10–27 (Copenhagen: Danish Association of Development Research [FAU]).

Quarles van Ufford, P. and A.K. Giri (eds) (2003) *An Anthropological Critique of Development: In Search of Global Responsibilities* (London: Routledge).

Quarles van Ufford, P. and D. Roth (2003) The Icarus effect: the rise and fall of developmental optimism in a regional development project in Luwu district, South Sulawesi, Indonesia. In P. Quarles van Ufford and A.K. Giri (eds) *A moral critique of development: in search of global responsibilities*, pp 76–101 (London: Routledge).

Vogt, A.E. van (1948) *The world of Null-A*. New York: Simon and Schuster.

NOTES ON CONTRIBUTORS

Gerhard Anders is assistant professor at the Institute of Social Anthropology in Zurich. His research interests are the anthropology of development, the anthropology of law and the transnationalisation of law.

Aet Annist is a doctoral student in the Department of Anthropology, University College London, working on the intersections of theories and practices of development and post-socialist change. As a researcher and lecturer at the University of Tartu, Estonia, she is working on crime and media, and protest and globalisation.

Rob van den Berg is the Director of Monitoring and Evaluation of the Global Environment Facility in Washington, DC. Previously, he was the Director of Evaluation of the Dutch Ministry of Foreign Affairs. He studied contemporary history at the University of Groningen in the Netherlands and has worked in various positions in development co-operation and foreign affairs, in Paramaribo, Brussels and The Hague.

Karen Coelho has a PhD in anthropology from the University of Arizona in Tucson, AZ, and an MPhil in development studies from the Institute of Development Studies, Sussex. Her current research focuses on the changing state, cultures of neoliberalism and urban governance. She is currently an independent researcher affiliated with the Madras Institute of Development Studies and the Department of Anthropology at the University of Arizona.

Rosalind Eyben is at the Institute of Development Studies in Susssex. She has spent most of her professional life working inside large development organisations and is now trying to make sense of this experience and explore how the international aid system can be more effective at supporting progressive social change.

Jilles van Gastel worked at the Dutch Ministry of Foreign Affairs between 2002 and 2004 first as a policy assistant in the working group planning, monitoring and evaluation, and later as a research assistant for the evaluation of research and development cooperation at the policy operations and evaluation department. She is currently a PhD candidate at Wageningen University.

Jeremy Gould is a Fellow of the Finnish Academy based at the Institute of Development Studies of the University of Helsinki. He is currently involved in an ethnographic study of the legal profession in Zambia.

Ian Harper is Lecturer in Social Anthropology at the School of Social and Political Studies, University of Edinburgh. He worked for a number of years in public and community health programmes in Nepal and India, before retraining in anthropology. He is currently researching issues around human resources in the health sector in relation to neoliberal reform and conflict in Nepal.

Rosario León, from CERES, Bolivia's leading independent social research institute has always been interested in the workings of power. She was in the vanguard of participatory approaches that sprang from local action to making global connections and from there she has come back home to battle against everyday practices of exclusion.

David Lewis is Reader in Social Policy at the London School of Economics and has published mainly on development policy issues in South Asia. He is author of *The Management of Non-Governmental Organisations* (2001) and co-author with Katy Gardner of *Anthropology, Development and the Postmodern Challenge* (1996).

David Mosse is Reader in Social Anthropology at the School of Oriental and African Studies, University of London. He is author of *The Rule of Water: Statecraft, Ecology and Collective Action in South India* (2003) and *Cultivating Development: An Ethnography of Aid Policy and Practice* (2005).

Monique Nuijten is senior research fellow of the Royal Netherlands Academy of Arts and Sciences at Wageningen University in the Netherlands. She is currently working on a research project on community organisations and forms of local–global governance in Mexico, Peru and Brazil. She has published on land reform and the law, organisation in development and the different dimensions of state power. Her latest book is *Power, Community and the State: The Political Anthropology of Organization in Mexico* (2003).

Philip Quarles van Ufford is affiliated, as emeritus, to the Department of Anthropology of the Vrije Universiteit Amsterdam, and is advisor to the research institute Percik in Salatiga, Indonesia. He is preparing a volume on relationships between different religious communities in Central Java and writing a book on the dynamics of development policy practices.

INDEX

Compiled by Sue Carlton